Charles Henry Mockridge

The Bishops of the Church of England in Canada and Newfoundland

Being an illustrated historical Sketch of the Church of England in Canada, as traced through her Episcopate

Charles Henry Mockridge

The Bishops of the Church of England in Canada and Newfoundland
Being an illustrated historical Sketch of the Church of England in Canada, as traced through her Episcopate

ISBN/EAN: 9783743336469

Manufactured in Europe, USA, Canada, Australia, Japa

Cover: Foto ©Lupo / pixelio.de

Manufactured and distributed by brebook publishing software
(www.brebook.com)

Charles Henry Mockridge

The Bishops of the Church of England in Canada and Newfoundland

TABLE OF CONTENTS

DIOCESE OF ALGOMA :   PAGE.
    First Bishop—Dr. F. D. FAUQUIER...................... 267
    Second Bishop—Dr. E. SULLIVAN....................... 328

DIOCESE OF ATHABASCA :
    First Bishop—Dr. W. C. BOMPAS...................... 283
    Second Bishop—Dr. R. YOUNG........................ 341

DIOCESE OF CALEDONIA :
    First Bishop—Dr. W. RIDLEY 316

DIOCESE OF COLUMBIA :
    First Bishop—Dr. G. HILLS.......................... 163
    Second Bishop—Dr. PERRIN. 373

DIOCESE OF FREDERICTON :
    First Bishop—Dr. J. MEDLEY 112
    Second Bishop—Dr. H. KINGDON 326

DIOCESE OF HURON :
    First Bishop—Dr. B. CRONYN........................ 150
    Second Bishop—Dr. I. HELLMUTH.................... 250
    Third Bishop—Dr. M. S. BALDWIN................... 334

DIOCESE OF MACKENZIE RIVER :
    First Bishop—Dr. W. C. BOMPAS..................... 283
    Second Bishop—Dr. W. D. REEVE 362

Diocese of Montreal:

	PAGE.
First Bishop—Dr. J. Fulford	133
Second Bishop—Dr. A. Oxenden	244
Third Bishop—Dr. W. B. Bond	302

Diocese of Moosonee:

First Bishop—Dr. J. Horden	256
Second Bishop—Dr. J. A. Newnham	375

Diocese of Newfoundland:

First Bishop—Dr. A. G. Spencer	96
Second Bishop—Dr. E. Feild	101
Third Bishop—Dr. J. B. Kelly	239
Fourth Bishop—Dr. Ll. Jones	297

Diocese of New Westminster:

First Bishop—Dr. A. W. Sillitoe	322
Second Bishop—Dr. John Dart	377

Diocese of Niagara:

First Bishop—Dr. T. B. Fuller	291
Second Bishop—Dr. C. Hamilton	351
Third Bishop—Dr. J. P. DuMoulin	379

Diocese of Nova Scotia:

First Bishop—Dr. C. Inglis	1
Second Bishop—Dr. R. Stanser	37
Third Bishop—Dr. J. Inglis	43
Fourth Bishop—Dr. H. Binney	141
Fifth Bishop—Dr. F. Courtney	360

Diocese of Ontario:

First Bishop—Dr. J. T. Lewis	175

Diocese of Ottawa:

First Bishop—Dr. C. Hamilton	351

Diocese of Qu'Appelle:

	PAGE
First Bishop—Dr. A. J. R. Anson	339
Second Bishop—Dr. W. J. Burn	371

Diocese of Quebec:

First Bishop—Dr. J. Mountain	26
Second Bishop—Dr. C. J. Stewart	50
Third Bishop—Dr. G. J. Mountain	58
Fourth Bishop—Dr. J. W. Williams	196
Fifth Bishop—Dr. A. Hunter Dunn	369

Diocese of Rupert's Land:

First Bishop—Dr. D. Anderson	123
Second Bishop—Dr. R. Machray	209

Diocese of Saskatchewan:

First Bishop—Dr. J. McLean	275
Second Bishop—Dr. W. C. Pinkham	356

Diocese of Selkirk:

First Bishop—Dr. W. C. Bompas	283

Diocese of Toronto:

First Bishop—Dr. J. Strachan	78
Second Bishop—Dr. A. N. Bethune	231
Third Bishop—Dr. A. Sweatman	309

THE RT. REV. CHARLES INGLIS, D.D.
First Bishop of Nova Scotia.
Born, 1734. Consecrated, 1787 Died, 1816.

THE BISHOPS OF THE CHURCH OF ENGLAND IN CANADA AND NEWFOUNDLAND.

1. THE RIGHT REV. CHARLES INGLIS, D.D., FIRST BISHOP OF NOVA SCOTIA, AND FIRST COLONIAL BISHOP.

CHARLES INGLIS was by birth an Irishman. He came of a clerical race, his father, grandfather, and great grandfather having been clergymen of the Church of England. He was born in the year 1734, when his father, the Rev. Archibald Inglis, was living in Glen and Kilcarr, Ireland. The thirteen colonies of the new world were then British territory, and many a young man left the old land with high hopes for the future as he went forth to seek his fortune. Of these was young Inglis. We find him as a very young man teaching in the free school at Lancaster, Pennsylvania. This was a school established by a society in England for the purpose of educating the children of German colonists. It was a Church school, the Archbishop of Canterbury being its head.

The heart of the young Briton, however, seems to have been set upon the sacred ministry, but to obtain Holy Orders in those days was a difficult matter for those living in the colonies. It meant a journey across the Atlantic—in days when navigation was perilous and slow. Mr. Inglis went, and in the year 1758, at the hands of the Rt. Rev. Thomas Hayter, Bishop of London, was admitted to the diaconate, and also to the priesthood. Armed with the Bishop's license, with an appreciation of Holy Orders which such an effort to obtain them alone could give, he returned to his home in the colonies, where we find him in the year 1759 ministering to a scattered people at Dover, in the State of Delaware, a narrow strip of land lying between Maryland and the Atlantic Ocean, and touching at its northern extremity the State of Pennsylvania.

His mission comprised a whole county, the County of Kent. It was thirty-three miles long and thirteen broad, and had a population estimated at seven thousand. Here, in an unhealthy climate, he laboured with unflagging zeal. Two churches enlarged, one rebuilt, and a fourth erected were visible fruits of his labour. In 1763 the Society for the Propagation of the Gospel in Foreign Parts (which in future we shall designate by its well-known initials, "S.P.G."—a society formed in England in the year 1701 for the purpose indicated by its name—a society without which the Church could scarcely have existed in early days in the colonies) received a letter from him, in which he said that his mission was in "a flourishing state, if building and repairing churches, if crowds attending the public worship of God and other religious ordinances, if some of other denominations joining, and a revival of a spirit of piety in many, can denominate it such"; though there were still "left lukewarmness, ignorance, and vice enough to humble him sufficiently, and exercise, if he had it, an apostolic zeal."*

The unenlightened condition of the Indians—Mohawks, Oneidas, and Tuscaroras—gave Mr. Inglis much concern, and through his efforts the S.P.G., that ever-ready society, sent missionaries and teachers to Schenectady, Fort Hunter, and Johnstown. He himself also worked vigorously amongst them.

After a missionary career of six years in this district, Mr. Inglis, having lost his wife, and suffered considerably in his own health, accepted, in 1765, the position of assistant minister of Trinity Church, New York, then described as "a small square edifice," but having a wealthy and aristocratic congregation. Two years after his appointment, Mr. Inglis received the honorary degree of M.A. from King's College, New York, and three years later became a governor of the college. A few years after he received the same degree from Oxford.†

The rector of the church was Dr. Samuel Auchmuty, who soon found Mr. Inglis to be a worthy and valuable assistant. But dark and dreary days set in for both, and for all Church people throughout the colonies, as they struggled with the mother land for their independence. Though Washington was himself a member of the Church, the great bulk of Church people were Loyalists, and, as such, suffered greatly as

*See Digest of S.P.G. Records, p. 36.
†" The Church in Nova Scotia." By Rev. A. W. Eaton, p. 127.

the struggle continued. In 1774, Mr. Inglis, in a letter which he wrote to the S.P.G.,* gives a most harrowing description of the sufferings that the Loyalist clergy were called upon to endure. What wonder if many of them fled, as we know they did, to places of safety?

In the spring of 1776, Washington entered New York. Dr. Auchmuty, Rector of Trinity Church, felt unable, through failing health, to face the troubles that threatened, and withdrew to Brunswick, in New Jersey. Mr. Inglis remained at his post. On one Sunday he received a message that Washington intended to be present at the church service, and desired the omission of the State prayers. To this, however, no attention was paid. On another occasion a band of soldiers marched to the church with fixed bayonets and to the sound of fife and drum, as Mr. Inglis was officiating. Women fainted and children cried. Every one felt that if Mr. Inglis should venture to say the prayers for the King, he would be shot. The intrepid parson, however, faltered not, but did what he felt to be his duty. No harm came to him, though he had very good reason to believe afterwards that harm was intended. God had more work for His valiant servant to do.†

In July, 1776, the Declaration of Independence was made. Clearly, then, there could be no permanent place in New York for a man like Mr. Inglis. After con-

---

*Anderson's "History of the Church of England in the Colonies," iii., p. 464.

†This circumstance has its counterpart in an incident in the English Civil War, related by Rev. H. G. Youard, Vicar of Whitegate, Northwich, in *The Clergyman's Magazine*, No. 61. One of Cromwell's soldiers levelled his musket at the Vicar of Preston, during divine service, and threatened him with death if he dared to read the prayers for the king. The Vicar, turning to the man, simply said:—"Soldier, you do your duty, and I will do mine"—and continued calmly reading the prayers for the king.

ference with his vestry, the churches, Trinity and St. Paul's, were closed. Mr. Inglis himself withdrew to Long Island. He had married as his second wife Margaret, daughter of John Crooke, Esq., of Ulster County, New York, and he now sends her and their "three helpless babes" seventy miles up the North River. In September, British troops marched into New York. The hopes of Loyalists revived. Mr. Inglis returned, found his house pillaged and most of his property destroyed. He held service on Wednesday, but before the week ended a fire broke out in the city, by which over one thousand buildings were destroyed, and among them Trinity Church, with its library and schools. Whether this was an accident or the work of an incendiary is not known. St. Paul's Chapel and King's College were saved, it is said, through the exertions of Mr. Inglis himself.

Dr. Auchmuty dragged himself to New York to witness the wreck of his property and work. Nothing was left to him. Even his wife and daughters were in the hands of the enemy. Still he resumed his work, occupying St. Paul's Chapel. Melancholy work must this have been for both rector and assistant. It soon proved too much for the older man. In March, 1777, he died. The vestry met and elected Charles Inglis Rector of Trinity parish. The church was in ruins, and property to the extent of £22,000 sterling had been lost. Mr. Inglis was inducted in the presence of a few people, by placing his hand upon the blackened ruins of the church that had been burnt. In the following year, 1778, the University of Oxford conferred upon the new rector the honorary degree of Doctor of Divinity.

During the War of Independence the Church of England in the colonies suffered terribly. Congregations were dispersed, and clergymen fled to England or elsewhere. As the war drew to a close, it was but a shattered remnant of its former self. In Virginia alone, where, at the beginning of the war, there were one hundred and sixty-four churches and ninety-one clergymen, most of the churches at its close were in ruins, and twenty-eight clergymen only remained.

But out of this gloom sprang a fresh light. When it was seen that Independence was inevitable, some of the clergy met in March, 1783, to select one of their number to be their bishop. Dr. Seabury was chosen to be Bishop of Connecticut, as soon as consecration could be obtained from the Old Country. At this meeting a letter was drawn up and addressed to "His Excellency, Sir Guy Carleton," who was then in chief command of the British forces in the American colonies.* The subject of this letter was the great need that existed for appointing a Bishop for Nova Scotia. Amongst other reasons given the following is worth recording, as showing the mind of the leading colonial Churchmen of the day:

"While orders are only to be had in England, the danger of the sea, the expense of the voyage, and the difficulties of transacting business among strangers will ever, as it ever has done, discourage the greater part of those gentlemen who would go into orders if the danger, expense, and difficulty attending a voyage to England could be avoided. We do know that many, nearly a fourth part of those who have encountered

*See "The Irishman in Canada." By Nicholas Flood Davin.

this danger, have lost their lives in the attempt. We also know that many have been obliged to incur debts on this occasion, which the scanty subsistence they were obliged to return to has scarcely enabled them to discharge in many years. To this also it has, in a great measure, been owing that while dissenters have had ministers enough to satisfy every demand, and even to crowd into every place where they could possibly support themselves, the Church has never had clergymen enough to supply the larger towns, and when any vacancy has happened it has been so long before another incumbent could be procured that the congregation has, in a manner, been dispersed, and the labours of his predecessor nearly lost."

There is something truly pathetic in this appeal, especially when it is added: "We beg leave to observe that the clergy of most of the colonies have been soliciting the appointment of American bishops at different times for many years past, and the answer ever has been that the present time was not a proper one, but a more favourable opportunity must be waited for."*

Such was the touching complaint of early days; and if Churchmen are ever inclined to wonder why the Anglican Church is not as strong in America and the colonies as they may think it ought to be, the wonder really is that it is as strong as it is, and that it did not become extinct when forced to be so long without the episcopate.

The letter above mentioned was dated New York, March 21st, 1783, and is signed by Charles Inglis,

*See Archives, Nova Scotia Historical Society.

Samuel Seabury, and sixteen others. A second letter, dated the 26th of March, briefly recommends the Reverend Dr. Thomas Bradbury Chandler, "now in London," as "the gentleman to be appointed the Bishop for Nova Scotia." The second letter is signed by the same names as the first, except that it is wanting in that of Thomas Moore, and that Jeremiah Learning in the first is written Jeremiah Leaming in the second, and John O'Dell becomes Jonathan O'Dell, and Isaac Browne, Isaac Brown without the *e*. Probably clergymen and others were not as particular about their names in those days as they are now; but so, with these variations, the names are published.

In July, by a final treaty with Great Britain, the United States of America became a separate and independent nation. Then followed the persecution of those who had been loyal to the British crown, the confiscation of their property, resulting in their hasty flight from everything that had been dear to them at home. Dr. Inglis lingered after thousands and thousands had gone, and then at length departed to begin life over again on British soil. About this time also his second wife died, leaving three motherless children, one son—his firstborn son having died when nine years old—and two daughters, to the unfortunate refugee as all that remained of his old and once happy home.

Dr. Seabury, after many vexatious delays and complications, was consecrated by the non-juring bishops of Scotland on the 14th of November, 1784, and returned to Connecticut, the first bishop to occupy a diocese anywhere on earth (outside of Great Britain and Ireland) in connection with the Anglican communion; the first bishop on the honoured roll of the American episcopate, which to-day has attained to the number of about eighty prelates.

Bishop Seabury.

The great bulk of refugees who came to be known as United Empire Loyalists fled to Nova Scotia, some to New Brunswick, and other parts of what is now called Canada. Dr. Inglis seems to have gone to Nova Scotia, and from there to England, where he was as early as May, 1785.* He took with him to the motherland a letter from Sir Guy Carleton to Lord North, recommending him to his Lordship's favourable notice as being " the rector of the principal church in New York, a zealous Loyalist, who, on that account, had lost a considerable landed estate by confiscation, and was at length obliged to relinquish a valuable living in the Church."

Here Dr. Inglis met his friend, Dr. Chandler, whom he had recommended for the proposed bishopric of Nova Scotia. He found that England had treated him well, Oxford having conferred upon him her highest degree, and the Government having increased his stipend from £50 to £200 a year.†

* " The Church in Nova Scotia," etc. Eaton, p. 124.
† Anderson's " History of the Colonial Church," vol. iii, p. 469.

Early in 1787 two clergymen arrived in England from the United States seeking apostolic consecration at the hands of the Archbishop of Canterbury. These were Dr. William White, Bishop-elect of Pennsylvania, and Samuel Provost, Bishop-elect of New York. They were consecrated on the 4th of February at Lambeth Palace by Dr. John Moore, Archbishop of Canterbury, assisted by Dr. Charles Moss, Bishop of Bath and Wells, and Dr. John Hinchcliffe, Bishop of Peterborough. It was a very quiet service, the congregation consisting chiefly of the Archbishop's family and household, together with the officiating clergy.* Whether Dr. Inglis was present at this service or not, he must have taken a lively interest in it, as it was an important step in setting the infant Church of the United States (with which in colonial days he had been so closely connected) on its feet.†

Before the year closed, the arrangements for establishing the bishopric of Nova Scotia were completed. Dr. Inglis did all he could, while in England, towards the accomplishment of this much-desired work. The S.P.G. had started, in 1711, an "American Colonial Bishops' Fund," the interest on which was now available for the support of a bishop as soon as one could be obtained. This has been paid regularly ever since to each occupant of the see of Nova Scotia.‡ Dr. Inglis and the English authorities tried

---

*"American Church History," vol. vii. (Tiffany), p. 363.

†Dr. James Madison was consecrated in England Bishop of Virginia in 1790, and Dr. T. J. Claggett was consecrated Bishop of Maryland in 1792 by the four American bishops. Thus commenced the absolute independence of the Church in the United States.

‡The income from this fund is now £203 10s., but is to cease at the next avoidance of the see. Besides this, however, there is an income of £384 ($1,920) from a fund belonging to the see in the hands of the S.P.G.

to induce Dr. Chandler, who had been recommended by the American clergy for the post, to accept the position; but, through failing health, he declined. The bishopric was then offered to Dr. Inglis, who accepted it.

Thus a devoted Loyalist, who had lost his all through unswerving attachment to his king and country, was rewarded by being placed first on the list of colonial bishops. It is an honoured list, embracing the names of noble missionaries who are world-renowned for apostolic zeal and self-denying work. These bishoprics now number close upon one hundred (to say nothing of the seventy dioceses in the United States), marking the growth of a little over a century, and at their head stands the honoured name of Dr. Charles Inglis.

He was consecrated at Lambeth on the 12th of August, 1787, by Dr. John Moore, Archbishop of Canterbury, assisted by Bishop John Thomas, of Rochester, and Bishop Beilby Porteous, of Chester.

It now becomes necessary to go back a little in the course of time in order to get some knowledge of the diocese over which Dr. Inglis was called upon to preside. The ownership of Acadia, or L'Acadie, as the French called it, the territory now embraced by Nova Scotia and New Brunswick, was, in early days, in constant dispute between England and France. It was definitely settled by the "Peace of Utrecht," which was made in 1713, that the disputed territory, along with Newfoundland and "Hudson's Bay" (then a trackless wilderness, with here and there a trading post), should belong to England, while Quebec (then known as "Canada"), Prince Edward Island (then called Isle St. Jean), and Cape Breton Island should be the property of the French.

England thus found herself possessed of a large territory inhabited almost exclusively by French,—an alien people, differing from themselves in forms of religion and in language, and rebellious at heart. To induce English settlers to come in and occupy the land a proclamation was issued in 1749, calling upon English people to emigrate to Nova Scotia. As a result, a number of people left the motherland in thirteen transports and a sloop of war, all under the command of Colonel the Hon. Edward Cornwallis, fifth son of Baron Cornwallis. They sailed into Chebucto, the finest harbour in the world, moored their vessels, cut down trees, and erected a primitive town, to which they gave the name of Halifax, in honour of George Montague, Earl of Halifax, then President of the Board of Trade and Plantations. These were, in the main, Churchmen; they had with them a "Mr. Anwell, clergyman," the Rev. Wm. Tutty, and Mr. Moreau, a schoolmaster. The surveyors, in laying out the town, were instructed to set apart a square or block of land for the site of a church. On this was afterwards built a church, the frame of which had to be brought from Boston, then a thriving colonial town. It was dedicated to St. Paul, and, though altered somewhat in form from its original shape by some additions made to it at different times, stands still on the same site, the oldest church in the whole of British North America.

Mr. Tutty, supported by the S.P.G., was the first incumbent of Halifax. Mr. Moreau was placed over the French Protestants. Mr. Anwell, not proving satisfactory, was recalled. The Rev. John Breynton was appointed assistant to Mr. Tutty in 1752, and soon afterwards succeeded him as second "missionary at Halifax."

St. Paul's Church, Halifax, N.S.

By degrees other posts throughout Nova Scotia were occupied, the earliest being Lunenburg, Annapolis, and the wide missions of Hants and King's and Cumberland counties. There seemed but little chance for the Church, because the inhabitants in the very best parts of the province were almost entirely French

Acadians, who, of course, were Roman Catholics. But two events happened in the course of a few years which gave the Church an unlooked-for impetus. One was the expulsion of the Acadians in 1755—the French inhabitants of the lovely Annapolis valley having been

Rev. Dr. Breynton, first Rector of St. Paul's, Halifax, 1752.

forcibly ejected from their homes; and the other was the capture of Quebec by General Wolfe in 1759, by which the whole of Canada passed into the possession of the British crown. Thus when the United Empire Loyalists were obliged to leave the United

States in 1783, there was British territory on their own continent ready to receive them. Then came to Nova Scotia thousands and thousands of United Empire Loyalists, many of them clergymen, who began spiritual ministrations among the refugees as they formed for themselves new homes.* In the following year, 1784, New Brunswick (which had been known simply as the County of Sunbury) was separated from Nova Scotia, and formed into a new province—made ready, as it were, to receive the refugees as they still kept arriving from the United States.

Such, then, was a portion of the diocese over which the first colonial bishop was called upon to preside. To it was added, as if a mere trifle, Newfoundland, Prince Edward Island, and Upper and Lower Canada! Halifax, the first see city, commanded then, as she does now, a magnificent view of her peerless harbour, where the great warships of the Empire may ever find security and rest. On the crown of the hill was built the first block house, and the wooden dwelling places clustered round it. Here lived the governors of Nova Scotia from the days of Lord Cornwallis till 1786, when Lord Dorchester (formerly Sir Guy Carleton) was appointed Governor-General over all the British provinces in America. Then there lived at Halifax a Lieutenant-Governor, the first of whom was Captain General John Parr. St. Paul's Church was then surrounded by ample grounds, where British forces from time to time were wont to parade.

To this pioneer city came, in the year 1787, the Right Reverend Charles Inglis, D.D., to be bishop of the

---

*About 18,000 arrived in Nova Scotia, 11,000 in New Brunswick, and 10,000 in the valley of the St. Lawrence. H. Y. Hind, "The University of King's College."

Church of England "as by law established." No doubt he was welcomed with firing of guns and much parade, as was fitting in those days when a bishop was an officer alike of Church and State.

The following is the list of parishes and clergy as the new Bishop found them :*

NOVA SCOTIA.

Annapolis,	Rev. Jacob Bailey.
Cornwallis and Horton,	Rev. John Wiswell.
Cumberland,	Rev. J. Eagleson.
Digby,	Rev. Roger Viets.
Guysboro,	Rev. P. De la Roche.
Halifax, St. Paul's,	Rev. J. W. Weeks.†
" Garrison Chapel,	Rev. Dr. Mather Byles.
" St. George's,‡	Rev. B. H. Howseal.
Lunenburg,	Rev. R. Money.
Parrsboro,	Rev. T. Shreve.
Shelburne,	Rev. William Walter.
Sydney (Cape Breton),	Rev. Rana Cossitt.
Windsor,	Rev. W. Ellis.
" (unattached),	Rev. Isaac Brown.

NEW BRUNSWICK.

Fredericton,	Rev. S. Cooke.
Gagetown,	Rev. R. Clarke.
Kingston,	Rev. J. Scovil.
Maugerville,	Rev. John Beardsley.
St. Andrews,	Rev. S. Andrews.
St. John,	Rev. George Bissett.

*For a very interesting account of the clergy of Nova Scotia and New Brunswick mentioned in this list see "The Church in Nova Scotia," etc., by Rev. A. W. Eaton ; and for an equally interesting account of those in Canada see "The Church of England in Canada, 1759-1793," by Rev. H. C. Stewart. The Newfoundland list is gathered from the S.P.G. Digest.

†Mr. Weeks was curate-in-charge. The Rector, Rev. Dr. Breynton, was in England at the time, and never returned to Halifax.

‡This is not the present St. George's, but a little wooden Lutheran chapel that was built for the Germans. They afterwards, however, connected themselves with the Church of England. This quaint little building still stands in Halifax, and is attached to St. George's Parish.

LOWER CANADA (QUEBEC).

Montreal,	Rev. David C. de Lisle.
" (assistant),	Rev. James Tunstall.
Quebec,	Rev. David F. De Montmollin.
" (unattached),	Rev. Philip Toosey.
Sorel,	Rev. John Doty.
Three Rivers,	Rev. L. J. B. N. Veyssière.

UPPER CANADA (ONTARIO).

Cataraqui (Kingston),	Rev. John Stuart.
Ernestown (Bath),	Rev. John Langhorne.

NEWFOUNDLAND.

Harbour Grace and Carboneer,	Rev. J. Balfour.
Placentia,	Rev. John Harris.
St. John's,	Rev. Walter Price.
Trinity Bay,	Rev. J. Clinch.

Besides these, there were five livings in Bermuda (where the Church was and is "Established"), and probably as many clergymen.

We have taken the trouble to compile this list (chiefly from the S.P.G. Digest) because it shows the condition of the Church when the episcopate started on its way in Canada (with Newfoundland). All told, Bishop Inglis could not have had more than forty clergymen throughout the vast extent of country that composed his diocese.

One of the first concerns of the Bishop was with regard to the establishment of a Public Grammar School and College for the education of the youths of the country, chiefly with a view to procuring men properly qualified for the sacred ministry of the Church. The Assembly of Nova Scotia met towards the end of October, 1787, and voted the sum of £400 towards the establishment of an academy, as requested by the Bishop, who had great influence with the Government at Halifax. The headmaster was to be a " clergyman of the Established Church, with a salary of £200 sterling, and to have under him a professor of mathematics and natural philosophy, to receive £100." The governing body was to consist of the Lieutenant-Governor, the Bishop, the Chief Justice, the President of the Council, and the Speaker of the House of Assembly.

One would have supposed that a school of this kind would have been established at Halifax, the see city and the capital of the province, but for some reason this was not done. The place chosen was Windsor, which then must have been but a very small village. It is situated on the banks of a tidal river or arm of the sea which sweeps in and out from the Bay of Fundy with the rise and fall of the tide. Here was once a flourishing Acadian village with two (Roman Catholic) churches. Its French name was Pizèquid, the name also that was given to the river. But when the French were ejected, and their houses and churches destroyed, the French names were changed to English ones, the river being called the Avon, and the town Windsor. It is about forty miles from Halifax.

Here the new academy was established. It was opened in a private house (rented for the occasion) on November the 1st, 1788, with Mr. Archibald Peane Inglis, a nephew of the Bishop's, as the first headmaster. It opened with seventeen pupils, of whom John Inglis, the Bishop's son, was one.

The Bishop's first visitation was made in 1788, when he paid a visit to New Brunswick. In the absence of railways and steamboats and public conveyances, except of the slowest and most cumbersome kind—if, indeed, there were these—at a time when good roads were unknown in Nova Scotia, and when forests were thick and parishes or missions very few and far between, the journeys of Bishop Inglis must have been tedious and laborious. But how glad must have been the exiled clergy to see him!

In the following year the Bishop paid a visit to Quebec and Montreal. He reached Quebec on the 11th of June "on His Majesty's frigate Dido." He was received by a salute of eleven guns, and welcomed by the Rev. Mr. De Montmollin, rector, and Rev. Mr. Toosey, minister of the church in Quebec. From Quebec he went to Three Rivers. Here he preached in the church of the Recollet Fathers, loaned for the occasion, and presented a hundred loaves of bread to be distributed to the poor. Reaching Montreal on the 9th of July, he was warmly received by the rector (Rev. D. C. de Lisle) and churchwardens, who saw in this visit the "smiling prospect that the Protestant Church in Canada would emerge from obscurity, and acquire under the auspices of a bishop a full enjoyment of her rights."

At this time there was no Anglican church in Montreal, but the Bishop procured for them from the Government the use of the chapel of the Jesuits, and gave them an "English assistant minister," the Rev. Mr. Tunstall. This was the commencement of Christ Church (now the Cathedral), Montreal. On returning to Quebec the Bishop seems to have visited Sorel, where there was a church. At Quebec the Bishop delivered his injunctions to the clergy. They were fourteen in number, and indicated the mind of a kind, wise, and pious ruler. It was about this time that the Bishop appointed Rev. John Stuart his commissary for Upper Canada. The number of candidates confirmed at Quebec was 130, and at Montreal 170.* The clergy, eight in number, whose names we have already given, presented the Bishop with an affectionate address, to which he gave a suitable reply. He preached his farewell sermon in the Recollet church at Quebec, and then embarked on a sloop of war, where he was received with a salute of eleven guns, and immediately started for Halifax with a fair wind.

An Act was passed in this year, much to the gratification of the Bishop, by the Nova Scotia Legislature, for founding, establishing, and maintaining a college in the province. This was the beginning of King's College, which was established at Windsor, close to the Academy. The Rev. William Cochran, an Irishman, and a graduate of Trinity, Dublin, having laboured for a while in the United States as a teacher and professor, and having been ordained by Bishop Inglis, was appointed Principal of the Academy in succession to Mr. A. P. Inglis, and was also appointed in the following year temporary principal of the college.

Bishop Inglis visited Shelburne in this year. This was a village in the woods, hastily built by refugees from the United States. Here the Bishop met many old friends, with whom, no doubt, he conversed freely

*See " Annals of the Colonial Church (Quebec)." Hawkins.

over the miseries of civil war. The devout people had built a wooden church, and this the Bishop consecrated. When Lieutenant-Governor Parr died in 1791, Bishop Inglis officiated at his funeral with all the pomp of State ceremonial. John (afterwards Sir John) Wentworth succeeded him.

In 1793 Bishop Inglis had the extreme happiness of seeing Quebec set apart as a separate diocese, and this relieved him of all responsibility as to Canada and the distant west. Up to this time five parishes or missions had been added to the roll in Nova Scotia (viz., Preston, Falmouth, Wilmot and Aylesford, Granville, and Yarmouth), and four in New Brunswick (Nashwack, Sussex, Woodstock, and Belle Isle).*

In 1794 the building of King's College at Windsor was completed. It is built in the old-fashioned German style, of stone; but, being sheathed with wood, has the appearance of a frame building. It stands on a fine commanding site, with beautiful scenery around it, both far and near.

It was about this time that the Bishop began to fail in health. The winds fresh from the ocean were too strong for him in Halifax. He purchased a farm in the township of Aylesford, about ninety miles from Halifax, in the valley of the Annapolis River, and built a house there, which he called "Clermont." Here he found rest from the worries of his public life in Halifax. "I have leisure," he wrote, "for those literary pursuits which my station requires, and which from inclination and habit are now become my greatest amusement and

---

* See "Clerical Guide," by Rev. Forster Bliss, second edition, p. 263, for a list of the clergy of Nova Scotia at this period.

gratification." "Clermont" still stands, a remnant of the earliest colonial days in Nova Scotia. Close to it is St. Mary's Church, built of wood—nearly all the

King's College, Windsor, Nova Scotia.

churches of Nova Scotia to this day are built of wood —of a stout frame, which so far has defied the ravages of time. Though built in 1790, it is still substantially the same church as when Bishop Charles Inglis used to worship within its walls. The shingles which cover it are said to be the same as those included in the original bill of costs. The cost of the building, it may be mentioned, was £475 1s. 5d., of which £222 4s. 6d. was given by Governor Parr.

Clermont, Aylesford, Residence of Bishop Inglis.

This enforced retirement from active work on the part of the Bishop had a bad effect upon the diocese, and especially upon King's College, the management of which was left to the governors without the supervision and firm hand of the head of the diocese, which, in its infant days, was sorely needed. In drawing up the new statutes, Judge Croke, a man of stubborn will and strong prejudices, insisted that a clause should be introduced requiring all matriculants to sign the Thirty-nine Articles. Bishop Inglis held this to be a great mistake, especially in an infant colony, which could hope to have but one university. The effect would be not only to prevent all dissenters from attending King's College, but also to shut off many even of those who were members of the Church. He wanted to have King's College the general university for the province, and was quite satisfied that it should be under the control of the Church of England. Events showed that the Bishop's policy was the true one. In defiance of him the statutes were published with the objectionable clause inserted. In fact, he seems scarcely to have been consulted in the affairs of King's College. Dr. Cochran was not eligible under the statutes to be principal, and one Dr. Cox, in 1804, was sent out from England to occupy the post, but he died in the following year. Then followed much wrangling and disputing. Dr. Cochran put in a claim for the principalship, and was supported by the Bishop. The governors, however, without the knowledge of the Bishop, appointed a Mr. Porter, of "Brazennose" College, Oxford. The Bishop's letters to Dr. Cochran on the subject show a kind disposition, and a desire to accept the inevitable, rather than contend with men who determined to pay but little deference to his authority. King's College has never recovered from this unfortunate dispute, for though the objectionable statutes were modified in after years the estrangement had taken place, and the worst fears of the Bishop were realized. The immediate result was that the attendance at the college, which, from 1790, had averaged eighteen, fell, in 1803, when the statutes were published, to 3.5, and would have ceased entirely but for the grammar school.*

* "The University of King's College," by Henry Youle Hind, p. 46.

It is to be noticed in the correspondence of this period that Bishop Charles Inglis is always addressed as "Right Reverend Sir," not as "My Lord," a title which, it is said, he never assumed.

In 1815 we find that the parishes and missions of the dioceses were, in Nova Scotia, fifteen (Chester, Sackville, and Rawdon having been added); New Brunswick, eight; Newfoundland, three; or twenty-six in all, exclusive of the five or six "fixed quantities" in Bermuda.

In the year 1816 Bishop Charles Inglis died at the age of eighty-two. He had had many troubles, but had met them all with quiet, Christian fortitude, and in a manner which left behind him a revered memory.

Of his children, John became the third Bishop of Nova Scotia; Margaret was married, September 19th, 1799, to Sir Brenton Halliburton, Chief Justice of Nova Scotia; and Anne was married to the Reverend George Pidgeon, for many years rector of Fredericton, New Brunswick, and afterwards of St. John. Mrs. Pidgeon died at Halifax in 1827, aged fifty-one. Sir Brenton Halliburton describes his father-in-law as a gentleman of the old school, dignified, but not formal, with a slight figure, and an open, intelligent countenance. In preaching he had great energy and earnestness, he says, and in conversation was cheerful and communicative. He was of studious habits, and was well read, but was free from pedantry.*

* "The Church in Nova Scotia," by Rev. A. W. Eaton, p. 128.

2. The Right Rev. Jacob Mountain, D.D., First Bishop of Quebec.

THE original name of the Mountain family, we are told, was De Montaigne.* They were refugees from France, who, to escape the persecutions to which the "Revocation of the Edict of Nantes" by Louis XIV. subjected them and all Huguenots or French Protestants, fled to England. The representative of the family at that time was Monsieur Jacob de Montaigne, who was glad to settle down to the quietude of rural life in the county of Norfolk. He purchased a small estate, which was known as Thwaite Hall, near the city of Norwich.

A son of this M. de Montaigne married in England, and, dying young, left a widow with two sons, the younger of whom bore the family name of Jacob. He was born in 1751. He graduated at Caius College, Cambridge, and was admitted to holy orders. In 1781 he married a Miss Kentish, co-heiress with two sisters, of Little Bardfield Hall, in the county of Essex, and was presented to the living of St. Andrew's, Norwich. The Bishop of Lincoln (Dr. Pretyman) subsequently appointed him examining chaplain, and presented him with the living of Buckden, in Huntingdonshire.

* See "The Last Three Bishops Appointed by the Crown for the Anglican Church in Canada," by Fennings Taylor, p. 140.

THE RT. REV. JACOB MOUNTAIN, D.D.
First Bishop of Quebec.
Born, 1751.   Consecrated, 1793.   Died, 1825.

Here he was when the call came to him to go forth beyond the seas to be Bishop of Quebec.

Quebec was then but a little primitive town, situated on a rocky promontory in the broad St. Lawrence River—a town filled with French and Indians, kept in place by the ubiquitous British soldier.

Lower Canada, from "time immemorial," has been largely connected with the French; but, in 1759, on the capture of Quebec by General Wolfe, it was ceded to Great Britain. Still the French element was allowed to remain, possessed of rights which one would hardly have supposed would have been granted to a conquered people.

With the British troops came Rev. Michael Houdin, of New Jersey (then a British colony), and Rev. John Ogilvie, of Albany, New York, both S.P.G. missionaries. Mr. Houdin remained a couple of years in Quebec, and Mr. Ogilvie was stationed at Montreal till 1764, when he went to be assistant minister of New York.[*]

We next read of Rev. John Brooke and a Rev. Mr. Bennet, army chaplain, as ministering in Lower Canada,[†] but their positions were not permanent. With a view to affording spiritual ministrations to the French, the S.P.G. sent, in 1764, three French-speaking clergymen in English orders. Of these, two were Swiss, Rev. M. de Montmollin, who was stationed at Quebec, and Rev. D. C. de Lisle, who was placed at Montreal. The third, who rejoiced in the name of Le-

---

[*] His associate in this work, under the rector, Dr. Auchmuty, was Rev. Charles Inglis, afterwards first Bishop of Nova Scotia.

[†] See S.P.G. Digest, p. 137.

gere Jean Baptist Noel Veyssières, was a "discredited Recollet friar," but was accepted for English orders, and stationed at Three Rivers. This gentleman does not seem to have been much more credit to his Anglican than he had been to his Roman orders. This movement was not attended with success, for these foreign clergy did little or nothing among the French, and were despised by the English-speaking people for their broken English.* In 1774 one Rev. Lewis Guerry was sent from England to take charge of the "fourth parish" in Canada, which was Sorel. He found the country, however, in such a disturbed state that after a year's residence in Quebec he returned to England, where he resided for ten years, receiving from the Government regularly £200 a year as the "holder of a Canadian benefice"! In 1777 the Rev. John Doty, S.P.G. missionary at Schenectady, New York, took refuge in Canada from the troublesome times that set in with the War of Independence. With him also came a number of people, like himself, refugees. He was allowed to minister to some Mohawk Indians who had established themselves near Montreal. In 1784 he was appointed to Sorel, Mr. Guerry having "exchanged his benefice" with a Rev. Philip Toosey, who came to Canada, but does not seem to have been attached to any parish.

These clergy, with a Mr. Tunstall, who had been appointed assistant (English) minister at Montreal, six in number, were the only clerical staff in Lower Canada when Bishop Charles Inglis visited it in 1789.

*For an interesting account of these clergymen, see "The Church of England in Canada, 1759-1793." By Rev. H. C. Stuart.

At that visitation the Bishop appointed Rev. Mr. Toosey as his commissary in Canada.

When, therefore, in 1793, it was determined in England, by a more rapid movement than the British Government was wont to make in such matters, to establish a bishopric at Quebec, Mr. Toosey naturally expected to be appointed bishop, and sailed to the motherland with that object in view; but his expectations were doomed to disappointment. The younger Pitt, on the advice of Dr. Pretyman, Bishop of Lincoln, appointed the Rev. Jacob Mountain to that position.

After being duly consecrated (on the 7th of July, 1793), he set sail on the 13th of August for Quebec. To leave England for Quebec was regarded in those days as practical expatriation, an exile from hearth and home. Dr. Mountain, therefore, took his hearth and home with him. His being made Bishop was a great family event, for his own household and immediate relations accompanied him to the new land. The inventory was as follows: The Bishop, his wife, four children, two sisters, one brother, one sister-in-law, one nephew, and two nieces—in all, thirteen. After a voyage of thirteen weeks these thirteen Mountains arrived in Quebec.* The brother that came with him was Rev. Dr. Jehoshaphat Mountain, who resigned the rectory of Peldon, in Essex, to share the Bishop's fortunes in Quebec. He was accompanied by his wife, son, and two daughters.

It is said that the Roman Catholic Bishop of Quebec saluted his Anglican brother with a kiss on

*So it is quaintly stated by Rev. A. W. Mountain in his "Memoir of G. J. Mountain, D.D."

both cheeks, and said that "it was time he should come to keep his people in order."

The scenery in and about Quebec is surpassingly lovely, and in a beautiful spot, amidst trees, where were

> "Firs, and venerable oaks and shades,
> And purling rivulets and deep cascades,"

the Bishop took up his residence. It was called Woodfield, and was situated about three miles from Quebec. Here Bishop Mountain spent many happy years, as his family grew up around him. His son George, who afterwards became the third Bishop of Quebec, always used to speak in terms of deep affection of this old home. The children all had a loving veneration for their father, who seemed to them " like some superior being moving in and out amongst them."

The first Bishop of Quebec occupied the see for thirty-two years, during which time his labours were abundant, and his journeys long and tedious. He appointed his brother assistant minister to M. Veyssière at Three Rivers, and he seems to have taken complete charge of the parish, for M. Veyssière's name does not appear any more in the register. On his death in 1800 Dr. Mountain became rector of Three Rivers.

The Rev. Mr. Toosey, who had expected the bishopric of Quebec, received from the English Government £150 in compensation for his disappointment. He returned to Canada as bishop's commissary, and ministered to the congregation at Quebec. On his death in 1797 the Bishop appointed his nephew, Rev. Salter Jehoshaphat Mountain, to succeed him.

At this time the Bishop called the attention of King George III. to the fact that there was no Anglican church in Quebec. The congregation had been using the Jesuit chapel. We are told that the king, at his own expense, proceeded to build a church in 1799,

The Anglican Cathedral, Quebec.

on the site of the Recollet property, of which the Government had taken possession. The corner stone was laid by His Excellency R. S. Milnes, Lieutenant-Governor of Quebec, assisted by "the Right Rev. Jacob, Lord Bishop of the Diocese," on the 11th of August, 1800. The necessary funds were provided by the Commissariat Department in sums of £300 at a time. The cost of its erection was about $80,000.* It was consecrated on the 28th of August, 1804. The organ, imported from England, was the first ever heard in Canada.† This church, a plain but substantial rectangular edifice, still stands, and serves as the cathedral church of the diocese. It was built first to be a "Metropolitan Church," the Government evidently intending that Quebec should be the metropolitical see of Canada. When the cathedral was opened it was provided with a surpliced choir; but this continued only for about twenty years after the Bishop's death, when it was discontinued.

The work in Lower Canada proved to be discouraging. Little or no addition was made to the clerical staff till the year 1800, when the S.P.G. opened two fresh missions, one at Quebec, under Rev. J. S. Rudd, and the other at St. Armand and Dunham, under Rev. R. Q. Short. As yet there were only three parishes, viz., Quebec, Montreal, and Three Rivers, that were able to maintain themselves; the rest had to be supported entirely from England by the S.P.G.

By the Act of Parliament, 31 George III., one-seventh of all lands, known as "Clergy Reserves," was

---

* See "The English Cathedral of Quebec," a valuable pamphlet by Fred C. Wurtele.

† S.P.G. Digest, p. 144.

to be set apart for the maintenance of " a Protestant clergy," but this seems to have been but of little use to the clergy of Lower Canada. The Roman Catholics had great privileges, which enabled them to build churches and establish parishes, while the Anglican missions were languishing. For this there seemed to be no redress. The liberal terms granted to the French at the time of the conquest now began to tell for their benefit. Hence the work of the Anglican Church never was of an encouraging nature in Lower Canada (Quebec).

But the diocese of the first Bishop of Quebec stretched far into the west, and was bounded only by the Pacific Ocean. To the west, then, as far as the track of man could be followed, the Bishop would occasionally go. Journeys of this kind he took, as a rule, every three years. An attempted trip from Quebec to Montreal, in 1813, is worth mentioning.

The Bishop, with two sons and a daughter, and two servants, embarked at Quebec in a bateau. This vessel was provided by the Government. In the middle of it, under a neat awning, sat the Bishop in a great old armchair. The crew consisted of a pilot and four rowers, for whom fifty pounds of pork and thirty loaves were provided by agreement, in addition to which the pilot was to receive £4, and the men nine dollars each.

Owing to the sudden illness of the Bishop's daughter the company had to return to Quebec after having spent three days in going only fifteen miles ! On the 22nd of July the Bishop left Quebec for a second and more successful attempt with his own horses. He reached Montreal on the 27th. At Lachine the party embarked in a bateau for "Upper Canada." The first point reached was Cornwall, where Rev. W. Devereux Baldwin, D.D. (or Baldwyn), was stationed. The next was Williamsburgh, in charge of Rev. J. G. Weagant (or Weageant), who officiated alternately in German and English. He had been a Lutheran minister, but the Bishop ordained him, and his congregation joined the Anglican Church with him.* Kingston was reached on the 8th of September, where the Bishop was entertained by Rev. Mr. Stuart. From Kingston he went up the Bay of Quinte in a canoe, with ten Indians and an interpreter, provided by the Governor, Sir G. Prevost.

Journeys of this kind were very expensive. The cost of a canoe trip from Montreal to Detroit is set down by the Bishop at £150, or about $750. He spent money freely on these occasions, on the grounds that his salary was given him, not for his private benefit, but as the means of usefulness, and also to maintain the dignity of the episcopal office. Though his salary was large, he did not save any of it for himself. Sometimes, of course, he travelled by land, "in waggons," as he himself described it, "over high mountains and through deep valleys and woods, on roads composed of rocks and roots, only exchanged occasionally for short, but deep black swampy soil." Yet the Bishop never suffered from fatigue. "I never took cold," he says, "though wet through on the water, and sleeping on the shores of the lakes in tents and often in strange houses." Wherever he went he preached, and made arrangements for the establishing of future churches.

* At this place we are told that the collections were taken up in a little bag at the end of a long stick, and in the bag was a bell, which was intended to wake any person who might happen to be nodding when the collector made his circuit!

Bishop Jacob Mountain gives now and then quaint descriptions of things he saw on his visitations. He describes the old church at Barton (near Hamilton, Ontario) as "the property of the public, and accessible to teachers of all persuasions"; and of the Methodists he says: "There are a few Methodists of the worst description wandering about the country, but much discouraged by the discerning part of the people, and in no great credit with the rest."

In his son George, afterwards to be more fully spoken of, the Bishop had an unfailing comfort. Ordained by himself, as he had been previously baptized and confirmed by him, he was appointed, after a brief residence in Fredericton, to the incumbency of Quebec Cathedral. This was in 1816, when Rev. S. J. Mountain moved to Cornwall, in Upper Canada. In 1821 the cathedral parish was made a rectory, with the Bishop's son as first rector. At the same time he was made Archdeacon of Lower Canada, and was always of great assistance and comfort to his father.

In 1815 the S.P.G. placed at the Bishop's disposal £200 a year for the support of students in divinity while studying with clergymen of experience and learning. This, in the absence of a theological college, was a great boon to a young country. Several young men educated in this way proved themselves afterwards to be very excellent clergymen.

In a colony of such early date there were but few facilities of education, but the first Bishop of Quebec lost no opportunity in urging upon the Government the necessity of establishing grammar schools throughout the whole country, and also of setting up a university.

The Bishop did not see much result from this, but it bore fruit in due time. The foundation of McGill College, Montreal, is directly due to him.

Eight times the Bishop went over his enormous diocese, making the journey, which amounted to about 3,000 miles, every three years.

Early in 1825 the Bishop, feeling the infirmities of age, sent his son, the Archdeacon, to England to make what arrangements he could for granting him some relief in his onerous duties; but before the date of the letter which the Archdeacon addressed to his father announcing the success of his mission, the good Bishop had gone to his rest. He died unexpectedly on the 18th of June, 1825, at the age of seventy-four, having been thirty-two years a bishop.

He left sixty-one clergymen (including three Archdeacons) in the whole diocese, where, at his arrival thirty-two years before, he had found but nine. This increase, however, was mainly in the west, eleven only being in that territory now known as the Diocese of Quebec. When appointed, there was a church only at Sorel, and the foundations of one at Niagara. He left sixty churches, either built or in progress of building.

He is spoken of as an excellent preacher, indeed, one of the greatest preachers of the age, a man of unsullied piety and unflagging zeal. Through modesty on his part very few of his charges or sermons were published, enough only, it has been said, to make us wish that he had given to the world a great deal more.

THE RT. REV. ROBERT STANSER, D.D.
Second Bishop of Nova Scotia.
Consecrated, 1816.   Resigned, 1824.   Died, 1829.

3. The Right Rev. Robert Stanser, D.D., Second Bishop of Nova Scotia.

THE early history of the Church of England in Nova Scotia is closely connected with that of St. Paul's Church, to which reference has been already made. The aged and revered Dr. John Breynton, the first rector, after years of hard toil, retired to England, apparently with the intention of returning to his work; but this he did not do. He resigned in 1790, and in the following year Rev. Robert Stanser, M.A., of Jesus College, Cambridge (son of Dr. Stanser, Rector of Bulwell), was sent out as a "candidate for the rectory" of St. Paul's, the actual appointment of a rector in Nova Scotia being in the hands of the congregation.

The date of Mr. Stanser's birth we have been unable to ascertain. Nor of himself have we been able to glean many particulars. He was not sent out, however, till "his character in learning, morals, and ability had been thoroughly investigated," with the result that he was found to possess "a truly Christian spirit, as well as the other qualifications of a minister of the Gospel." The congregation unanimously elected him as second Rector of St. Paul's. He appears to have discharged his duties at St. Paul's with great diligence and assiduity, in doing which he was much assisted by

his amiable and accomplished wife.* In 1798 the
S.P.G., on the recommendation of Bishop Charles
Inglis, increased his salary to £70 a year as " a mark of
their approbation of his diligent conduct in the duties
of his mission," and, at the same time, he was allowed
an assistant. In 1800 (after a return from a visit to
England) a new rectory was built, and completely
furnished by the parishioners. In 1812 he was voted
an additional £300 a year, and no less than three hundred persons joined his congregation.

He had a congregation which included the Lieutenant-Governor, officers of the army, ministers of
State, and even (as in the case of the Duke of Kent,
Queen Victoria's father, who for a time was commander-
in-chief of the forces in Halifax) royalty. He had as
well some of the poorest of the poor, and a few Indians,
yet to all he was the true pastor, and took his place
easily amongst all sorts and conditions of men.

When Bishop C. Inglis died in 1816, his son, Rev.
John Inglis, who had been his father's mainstay and
ready co-worker, naturally expected to be offered the
bishopric, and with a view to that sailed for England.
But in the meantime a number of the influential men
of Halifax secured a petition from the Provincial Legislature requesting the appointment of the Rector of
St. Paul's, who was also chaplain to the House of
Assembly, to the bishopric. The petition went over in
the same ship which conveyed the Rev. John Inglis,
who, shortly after his arrival, was not a little surprised
to find that his expectations regarding himself were not

* See article by Rev. Dr. Partridge (now Dean of Fredericton) in *The
Canadian Church Magazine and Mission News* for May, 1888.

to be realized. The bishopric was given to Dr. Stanser; but because of this advancement the Crown claimed the privilege of appointing the next Rector of St. Paul's, and gladly bestowed it upon Mr. Inglis, in consideration of his important services in the active superintendence of the diocese during the long illness of the late Bishop, giving him at the same time £200 a year additional salary, and £100 for an assistant.

In 1815 Dr. Stanser lost his wife, and, overwhelmed with grief, went to England for rest. He was, therefore, in England at the time of his appointment, and was consecrated on May 16th, 1816, at Lambeth.

But this whole action proved to be a great mistake. Dr. Stanser's working days were over. He had received, a short time before his wife's death, injuries in helping to extinguish a fire in Halifax,* and the two events together, coupled with approaching age, rendered him unfit for the work of a diocese like Nova Scotia. Having met his clergy, and with the utmost difficulty performed the offices of visitation, confirmation, and ordination, he returned to England in the spring of 1817 in broken health, and did not see his diocese again.†

The need of a bishop at this time was sorely felt in King's College, Nova Scotia. Bishop Stanser seems to have attended four meetings of the Board of Governors, two in 1816 and two in 1817. An earnest effort was made to remove from the statutes the stringent clauses against dissenters by an appeal to the Arch-

*S.P.G. Digest, p. 863.

†S.P.G. Digest, p. 119. But in the "Historical Sketch of Newfoundland," published in pamphlet form by the S.P.G., it is said that Bishop Stanser visited Newfoundland in 1816, etc. This must be an error.

bishop of Canterbury. The effort was unsuccessful. The secret of the dislike of the Government at home to dissenters lies in the suspicion entertained regarding their loyalty. The Imperial Government was spending $30,777.00 towards the maintenance of the Church in the Diocese of Nova Scotia, feeling sure that this would best promote attachment to the British Crown. At this time Lieutenant-General George Ramsay, ninth Earl of Dalhousie, was Lieutenant-Governor at Halifax, and was much opposed to the exclusiveness of King's College. Through his influence another college was built in Halifax—a college that should be open to all. It was called after him, Dalhousie College. Thus a golden opportunity, never to recur, was lost by the Church people of Nova Scotia.

In 1821 the Rev. John Inglis, D.D., commissary of the diocese, was elected a member of the Board of King's College, and a substantial stone building, at a cost of $25,526, was erected in the college grounds for the Academy, or school for boys. The money was obtained from duties collected at Castine, which was captured by the British in the war of 1812. In the following years an agitation took place in favour of removing the college from Windsor to Halifax, uniting it with Dalhousie College, but Chief Justice Blowers entered such a strong legal protest against it in 1824 that the project was abandoned.

And during all these years Nova Scotia was without a bishop. Earl Bathurst, in the House of Lords, explained that he had asked Bishop Stanser to resign, but that the Bishop, who had " very little private fortune," declared he could not do so. "What could I do, my Lords?" he further said, "could I have said to him, 'Go back to Halifax and die, or stay in this country and starve'? [Loud cheers.] If there be blame for having acted thus I am alone responsible; the society (S.P.G.) are exonerated."*

Earl Bathurst, however, procured for him an allowance of £350 per annum from the Government at Nova Scotia, £250 from New Brunswick, and £200 from the S.P.G., and on this annuity, about $3,500 a year, which the noble Earl thought was not an "extravagant sum," Bishop Stanser resigned.

He resigned in 1824, and died in London in 1829. Thus through the infirmities of the first Bishop and ill-health of the second, Nova Scotia had been either practically or actually without an episcopal head for seventeen years—a disaster which must have told heavily upon her early work. About this time it was estimated that only about one-fourth of the population of the Diocese of Nova Scotia belonged to the Church of England.

While in England Bishop Stanser was addressed always as "My Lord," a title which has been extended to colonial bishops ever since, though the first colonial bishop had never assumed it. It came about, we are told, in this way. When consecrated, a question arose as to whether he should be designated or addressed the same way as the English bishops. The point was settled by the Prince Regent emphatically saying to him, when introduced at a levee, "How do you do, my Lord Bishop? I am glad to see your Lordship."

*See "The University of King's College," etc., by Henry Youle Hind.

The Bishop had three sons and five daughters. His sons died unmarried, so that his name has died out. The daughters all married, and we were able to get, about five years ago, the silhouette likeness of the Bishop which accompanies this sketch (the only portrait of him, we believe, that exists) from his granddaughter, Mrs. Ingles, of Radcliffe-on-Trent, Notts, England.

St. Mary's Church, Aylesford, N.S.

THE RT. REV. JOHN INGLIS, D.D.
Third Bishop of Nova Scotia.
Born, 1777. Consecrated, 1825. Died, 1850.

4. THE RIGHT REV. JOHN INGLIS, D.D., THIRD BISHOP OF NOVA SCOTIA.

JOHN INGLIS, the only surviving son of the first Bishop of Nova Scotia, was born in New York in 1777, the year when his father was inducted Rector of Trinity Church by placing his hand upon its blackened ruins.* He was therefore a boy of ten years of age when his father arrived in Halifax as Bishop of Nova Scotia. He was the first boy who entered the Academy at Windsor. He received also his higher education at King's, of which University he was one of the earliest graduates. His father intended to send him to Oxford, but he does not seem to have done so. He was in England, however, in the year 1800, for Sir John Wentworth sent a despatch through him to the Under Secretary of State. "This will be presented to you," he says, "by Mr. Inglis, only son of our Bishop. He is a sensible, discreet gentleman." He was ordained to the sacred ministry by his father in 1801, and was appointed the second missionary at Aylesford, where also he had been made a justice of the peace. He thus lived with his father at "Clermont," and proved to be a valuable assistant to him, not only in Aylesford parish, but also throughout the diocese as his commissary.

*See page 5.

Recovering from his disappointment at not receiving the bishopric at his father's death (an account of which has already been given in the life of Bishop Stanser), he found ample occupation in his duties as Rector of St. Paul's, Halifax, and as the ecclesiastical commissary of the diocese. Dr. Inglis went to England in 1824 to solicit subscriptions for King's College. In the same year Bishop Stanser resigned the bishopric, and Dr. Inglis was appointed in his place. The result of his visit was an accession to the funds of King's College to the extent of £3,823. He procured also donations of books to the library. On the 25th of March, 1825, he was consecrated in England third Bishop of Nova Scotia. On his return to Halifax he was welcomed by a salute of twenty-six guns from the frigate *Tweed* and from Fort Charlotte, and by the ringing of the church bells. Proceeding at once to the work of his extensive diocese, he divided it into four archdeaconries: (1) Nova Scotia, under Venerable Robert Willis, who succeeded him as Rector of St. Paul's, Halifax; (2) New Brunswick, under Venerable George Best, Rector of Fredericton; (3) Bermuda, under the Venerable Aubrey G. Spencer, who was also made Rector of Paget and Warwick; (4) Newfoundland, under Venerable George Coster, visiting missionary.

During the first year of his episcopate he consecrated forty-four churches, and confirmed 4,367 persons. In 1826, in a man-of-war, he visited Bermuda, and was probably the first bishop who had ever been there. Divided into nine parishes, each having church and glebe, it could muster but four resident clergy. Here the Bishop confirmed 1,200 people, of whom 100 were negroes.

He also made arrangements for the establishment of schools among the poor, and also for the higher class of pupils.

During the summer of 1827, having the Government brig, "Chebucto," and sometimes a frigate, at his command, he visited the different parishes and missions in Nova Scotia and New Brunswick, and also the out harbours of Newfoundland. He found that there were twenty-three schoolmasters in the island, each receiving from the S.P.G. £20 a year over and above the pupils' fees. He visited also Cape Breton, where he placed a missionary, Rev. James A. Shaw, who could speak French, and thus reach the settlers from the Channel Islands. Up to this time Rev. Charles Ingles, Rector of Sydney, had been the only clergyman in Cape Breton.

In 1828 the Bishop reports 3,500 communicants in the diocese, with twenty missions marked "no returns." In this year a charter was obtained for King's College, Fredericton, which, as then constituted, was open to all denominations, but was under the management of the Church of England. In time all religious tests were abolished in this institution, which therefore ceased to be in any sense a Church university.

Bishop J. Inglis speaks at this time in the highest terms of his clergy, whom he found, as a general rule, "laboriously engaged." But he evidently felt, at the same time, that there was sore need for many more missionaries in almost every part of his enormous diocese.

In 1829 the parishes and missions supplied with clergy are reported as follows:* Nova Scotia, 30; Fredericton, 23; Newfoundland, 9; Bermuda, 6—in

*See Rev. C. Forster Bliss' "Clerical Guide."

all, 68. The new places added since 1787† are as follows:

Nova Scotia: Amherst, Antigonishe, Aylesford, La Have, Dartmouth, Horton, Liverpool, Newport, Truro, Weymouth. *Cape Breton:* Sydney, Arichat. *Prince Edward Island:* Charlottetown, St. Eleanor's.

New Brunswick: Bathurst, Carleton, Douglas, Grand Lake, Hampton, Miramichi, Prince William, Sackville, St. George's, St. Stephen, Shediac, Westfield.

Newfoundland: Bonavista, Ferryland, Green's Pond, Port des Grave, Twillingate.

Bermuda: Paget and Warwick, Somerset, Smith and Hamilton, Pembroke and Devonshire.

Bishop John Inglis proved himself a stout champion for the welfare and rights of King's College. Largely through his influence the objectionable tests of Churchmanship—tests which debarred all dissenters from entering its walls—were removed. Professors and fellows, however, out of deference to the wish of the Archbishop of Canterbury (Dr. William Howley), were still required to sign the Thirty-nine Articles. The internal discipline of the college also was rigorously scrutinized, and found so defective that strenuous efforts had to be made to bring recalcitrant students into subjection to lawful authority.

Bishop John Inglis lived at a time when many reform questions were disturbing the minds of men both in the old land and abroad. They all pointed in the direction of curtailing the power and emoluments of the Church and all her institutions. Church "tests"

†See pages 16 and 17.

everywhere were being removed, and State aid for Church purposes withdrawn. They were the troubles which led to the rebellion in Upper Canada, and, of course, they touched Nova Scotia. After due notice all grants to King's College from the English Government were withdrawn. This the Bishop and other governors of King's were unable to prevent, but when a demand was made that the college should surrender its charter it was met with a respectful, but firm refusal. Sir Peregrine Maitland (who had been Governor in Upper Canada) was Lieutenant-Governor at the time in Nova Scotia. In 1830 he brought before the Provincial Assembly the desirability of uniting King's College at Windsor with Dalhousie College at Halifax. From this action the Home authorities seem to have inferred that this was a burning question in the colony. When it was found out that this was not the case the matter subsided, and King's was allowed to remain at Windsor, and in possession of its royal charter. Bishop John Inglis was the chief mover in this matter, and secured the valuable interference of the Archbishop of Canterbury on behalf of the rights of the college, his Grace being by statute its patron. The number of students, however, at King's College, it is only right to remark, has never been very large, and during the unhappy discussions regarding it there were two years, 1834 and 1835, when only two entries were made each year.* Rev. Dr. Porter resigned the principalship in April, 1836. He was succeeded by Rev. Dr. McCawley, Professor of Hebrew and Mathematics in King's College, New Brunswick. He received a salary of

*"The University of King's College," etc., by Dr. Hind, p. 82.

£400 sterling, besides a stipend from the S.P.G. for doing clerical duty at Falmouth.

It was not the fashion in those days for the clergy and laity of the Church to meet together in synods; but Bishop John Inglis laid the foundation for it in Nova Scotia by forming the Diocesan Church Society. It was formed to supply books, and tracts, and missionary visits to destitute settlements, sustaining King's College, aiding students in theology, and assisting in the erection and enlargement of churches. In 1846 he formed the "Alumni Association of King's College," which has proved to be ever since a valuable support to the institution.

It is unnecessary to speak in any further detail of the continued visitations and labours of this indefatigable Bishop. Suffice it to say that they were numerous and systematic. In 1846 he held a visitation of clergymen in Halifax. Thirty were present, and of these twenty-six were King's College men, and, with few exceptions, had been ordained by himself. He lived to see undoubted signs of progress and development in the Church he loved. In 1839 he saw the formation of two dioceses, one for Upper Canada (Toronto), and the other for Newfoundland and Bermuda. In 1845 he had the extreme happiness of seeing New Brunswick formed into the separate Diocese of Fredericton. Since then no further diminution of the Diocese of Nova Scotia has been made. He lived also to see a diocese formed (in 1849) in Rupert's Land, among the Indians and fur traders of the far Northwest, and still another (in 1850) at Montreal. But this he saw and little more. The first Bishop of Montreal was consecrated in England in August, 1850, and in the following October the third Bishop of Nova Scotia, who had gone to England with the hopes of recruiting his failing health, departed to his long rest. He died in London on October 27th, 1850, and was buried in the churchyard of Battersea. Though buried in England, a tablet to his memory was placed, as was fitting, in St. Paul's Church, Halifax.

Bishop John Inglis was in possession, it is said, of a princely income, amounting in all to about $12,000 per annum,* but owing to expensive journeys, generous hospitality, and unstinting charity, he died possessed of very little. "Clermont," his paternal estate at Aylesford, he bequeathed to King's College.

His wife was the daughter of the Hon. Thomas Cochran, Speaker of the House of Assembly, to whom were born three sons and three daughters. The second son is well known in history as Sir John Eardly Wilmot Inglis, who distinguished himself in the Indian Mutiny of 1857.

Bishop John Inglis was noted for his genial and pleasant disposition. He was called the Chesterfield of the episcopal bench, and, "next to George IV., the most polished gentleman of his time." His memory still lingers in Nova Scotia, where, for twenty-five years, he was known as the "good Bishop," or, towards the last, "the dear old Bishop."

*Of this £2,000 per annum was paid by the Imperial Government, but ceased at Bishop Inglis' death. See "The Church in Nova Scotia," by A. W. Eaton, p. 235.

5. Hon. and Right Rev. Charles James Stewart, D.D., Second Bishop of Quebec.

THE progress of the Church in Lower Canada at first was very slow. In 1815, after twenty-two years of the Quebec episcopate, there seems to have been only two missions added to those in existence when it was established. These two were South Armand and Dunham. At the former was stationed the Hon. and Rev. C. J. Stewart, at the latter Rev. Charles C. Cotton. The story of the career of the Hon. Charles J. Stewart is in a high degree creditable to himself and the holy religion which he professed. He was the fifth son of the Earl of Galloway, and was born on the 13th of April, 1775. His education was begun at home under a private tutor, and completed at Corpus Christi, Oxford. His mind from the first was naturally drawn to the alleviation of suffering humanity. His sympathies were strongly with those who were trying to abolish slavery. As a student he would not take sugar in his tea, because sugar was a product of slave labour. This showed an element of consistency rare in humanity. After Mr. Stewart had graduated M.A., his cousin, the Earl of Aboyne, presented him with the united rectories of Orton, Longueville, and Botolph Bridge, which he held for eight years, at which time a desire to perform missionary work began to stir within him. While considering to what field he should

THE HON. AND RT. REV. CHARLES JAMES STEWART, D.D.
Second Bishop of Quebec.
Born, 1775. Consecrated, 1826. Died, 1837.

go, being himself first inclined to go to India, he fell in with an appeal from Bishop Jacob Mountain, who at the time was in England, and who was greatly in need of missionaries in Canada. This determined him. He gave himself for missionary work in Canada.

It was at a time when the missionary spirit was at a very low ebb in England, and men wondered that the son of a British nobleman should give up comfort and ease at home to live a lonely and sequestered life abroad. Had he gone to increase his fortune by work in some distant gold mine they would have understood it, but when he went to spend it for the spiritual welfare of man the so-called Christian world of the day looked on in wonder.

Mr. Stewart arrived at Quebec on the 27th of September, 1807, where he remained for a few weeks. Though a most excellent man he was not prepossessing in appearance. Miss Mountain thus wrote of him on his first arrival in Canada:

"We have had a most wonderful young man here who has charmed us all, and, indeed, even those who were prejudiced against him. I mean Mr. Stewart, who, you doubtless know, has come to act here as a missionary, and so unusual an undertaking in a man of family independence could not by the world in general be attributed to any but an enthusiast and a Methodist. The papers mentioned his coming to convert the Indians. You see the effect of such conduct as his. With no advantages of person or address, with real disadvantages of voice and manner in the pulpit, before he left Quebec he gained general respect, and certainly did make converts of those who were disposed at first to call the real goodness of his designs in question. He met with every discouragement here, except from a very few persons, yet he continued steadfast in his perseverance." He reached St. Armand, a seigniory situated about seventy miles southeast from Montreal, on Saturday, the 21st of October. Some one there endeavoured to discourage him from attempting to hold services, assuring him that some clergyman had tried it before, but was obliged to leave because of the great wickedness of the people. "Then," he replied, "this is the very place for me; here I am needed, and, by God's grace, here I will remain."

And here he did remain until the place became a flourishing mission. Here he built two churches, one at Frelighsburg, and the other at Philipsburg. The great cost of the building of these churches was met by Mr. Stewart himself. "Devotion to God's service

Frelighsburg Church.

made me a missionary" was his motto. It is doubtful whether any devotee of wealth, or agnosticism, or profligacy, ever had as great a joy as that of Mr.

Stewart when the Frelighsburg church—"the first place of worship in this whole region of country"—was finished. It was opened and consecrated by Bishop Jacob Mountain on the 20th of January, 1809, in the presence of a large number of people, some of whom had come hundreds of miles to see what, to many of them, was a curiosity—a church in the wilderness. A picture of this church has been preserved. It formed the model for many others which were afterwards erected by the energy and liberality of this apostle of the woods.

In Frelighsburg there still stands, in a dilapidated condition, the small frame building which was occupied by Mr. Stewart and his servant man.* Here the missionary lived in the simplest manner possible.

Rev. Mr. Stewart's Residence at Frelighsburg.

In 1815, Mr. Stewart left his mission for a visit to England. Great grief was felt by his people at his departure. But he remembered them when away, for in England he collected £2,000 to help him in further missionary work. After taking the degree of Doctor of Divinity he returned to Canada in 1817. Finding St.

* So we are informed by the present esteemed Incumbent of Frelighsburg, Rev. Canon Davidson, D.D. It is a pity that some steps could not be taken to preserve this building, or save it at least from dilapidation.

Armand in a flourishing condition under Rev. J. Reid, who had been his co-worker as schoolmaster, he would not disturb it, but, giving it up to him entirely, he took up work in a neglected district named Hatley. Here Dr. G. J. Mountain (the Bishop's son) found him occupying a small garret in a wooden house, reached by something more like a ladder than a staircase; here he had one room, in which were his little open bed, his books, and his writing table—everything of the plainest possible kind. The farmer's family, who lived below, boarded him and his servant. "And here," says Dr. Mountain, " buried in the woods and looking out upon the dreary landscape of snow, some thousands of miles away from all his connections, many of whom were of the highest nobility of Britain, this simple and single-hearted man, very far from strong in bodily health, was labouring to build up the Church of God among a people who were utter strangers to the Church of England"*—or, indeed, it might be added, to religion of any kind.

Here he lived on the simplest fare: on Fridays he subsisted upon potatoes and salt only, his practice being to spend every Friday in "fasting, meditation, and prayer."

He considered himself a "missionary on a large scale," and, therefore, remained single, although " to do so," he said himself, "involved a great sacrifice. But to the Church it is a great advantage. I am always ready to go or to stay anywhere for a long or a short time, and no place and every place is my home." He computed his personal expenses—for himself and

* See " Lives of Missionaries, North America," S.P.C.K., p. 184.

servant—as amounting to about £250 a year. "This leaves me," he remarks, "of my income £400 a year for public and private beneficial purposes."

In his missionary work Dr. Stewart is said to have built or commenced twenty-four churches, nearly all on the model of the Frelighsburg Church.

About this time large numbers of emigrants from the Old World began to pour into Canada. In the year 1819, we are told that as many as 12,000 arrived. Dr. Stewart, therefore, thought it best to give himself up to the work of a travelling missionary. With this end in view he resigned Hatley in 1819. In the first six months of 1820 he travelled through a circuit of 1880 miles. We hear of him in the far west of "Upper Canada" (Ontario), and in every direction. Greeted everywhere by the sound of the woodman's axe, this modern apostle went from place to place, over roads that beggar description, and suffering discomforts that would scarcely be believed.

In 1821 he was in England; in 1822 he was travelling again through the woods of Canada; in 1823 he returned to England as the Bishop's commissioner to defend the claim of the Church to her rights under "Act 31, George III.," which set apart one-seventh of the land for ecclesiastical revenue. This Act the Canadian House of Assembly had begun to attack. It was the first onslaught upon the "Clergy Reserves."*
Returning in November, 1824, he continued his unwearied missionary labours, and on the death of Bishop Jacob Mountain, in June, 1825, Dr. Stewart was appointed by the Crown authorities in England

* See p. 32.

the second Bishop of Quebec. He was consecrated in England on the 21st of January, 1826, by Archbishop Sutton (of Canterbury), assisted by Bishops Howley, Van Mildert, and Blomfield. Returning to America, he preached, at the request of Bishop Hobart, in Trinity Church, New York. On June 4th, 1826, he was installed in Quebec Cathedral.

The details of ten succeeding years of watchful, steady, and severe labour need not be given here. It was the repetition, at regular intervals, of the long journeys he had already taken as a travelling missionary. His journeys, as a rule, were made on horseback. He soon found that his enormous diocese, the western portion of which was rapidly increasing in population, was entirely beyond his strength.* He therefore urged upon " His Majesty's Government " to appoint a coadjutor bishop. This was granted, and Archdeacon George J. Mountain was selected for that post, and consecrated in England on February 14th, 1836, with the title of Bishop of Montreal.

Weak and enfeebled in body, Bishop Stewart left the care of his diocese to this younger and stronger bishop, and sought rest in the land that had given him birth. He was only sixty-one years old, but his hair was very white, and his face pallid; his limbs were weak, and supported him but feebly. He lived a short time with his brother, the Hon. Edward Stewart, at Brighton. Here the Rev. J. S. M. Anderson, incumbent of St. George's Chapel, visited him, and at the Bishop's request read for him the Order for the Visita-

---

*The population of Upper Canada in 1826 was 164,000. During Bishop Stewart's ten years' episcopate it had more than doubled.

tion of the Sick. All the responses, even to the alternate verses of the seventy-first psalm, he repeated accurately from memory. At the conclusion he asked Mr. Anderson to say over him *the prayer for a sick child*, making necessary alterations in a few of the words. "But read it all," he said; "weak and aged as I am, I desire to draw near, with the guileless spirit of a child, unto my God and Saviour."

He took up his residence in London with his nephew, the Earl of Galloway, where, accompanied by two faithful servants, whom he had brought with him from Canada, he lingered till the thirteenth of July, 1837, when he quietly passed away. He was buried in the family vault at Kensal Green, near London, by the side of his brother and sister.

Though not handsome in face, and somewhat ungainly in build, without any pulpit gifts whatever, his utterance and delivery being against him, this missionary of the western world was a man of noble mind and sterling worth. Canada has been the gainer to an extent not generally known by his self-denying devotion to the cause of God.

6. The Right Rev. George Jehoshaphat Mountain, D.D., D.C.L., Third Bishop of Quebec.

WHEN Dr. Jacob Mountain, first Bishop of Quebec, arrived in his diocese, he had with him four children. The second o these was born in Norwich, England, on July 27th, 1789, and named George Jehoshaphat. Amid the lovely scenery and rural quietude of Woodfield (his father's residence), about three miles from Quebec, he was brought up. His father had a private tutor for him. It is recorded in the Bishop's journal, March 28th, 1796, "This day George began his Latin grammar," before he was seven years old.

At sixteen he was sent to England, and entered at Trinity College, Cambridge, where he graduated in 1810. His regret at leaving his father's roof was most marked. It drew from him a poem which, considering his youth, is one of decided merit. It is entitled, " O, Must I Leave Thee, Woodfield ? "* and reminds one of Eve's lamentation, "Must I Leave Thee, Paradise?"

Returning to Canada in 1811, he had the happiness of preparing for Holy Orders under the direction of his father, and of assisting him in his duties as his private secretary. His father, who had already baptized and confirmed him, also ordained him. He

* The poem is given *in extenso* in " Memoir of G. J. Mountain," by his son, Rev. Armine W. Mountain.

THE RT. REV. GEORGE JEHOSHAPHAT MOUNTAIN, D.D., D.C.L.
Third Bishop of Quebec.
Born, 1789.   Consecrated, 1836.   Died, 1863.

was made a deacon on August 2nd, 1812, and priest on January 16th, 1814. He assisted his cousin in the parish duties of Quebec. Exactly two years after his admission to the diaconate (August 2nd, 1814), his father married him in the cathedral of Quebec to Mary Hume, daughter of Deputy Commissary General Thomson, and immediately afterwards the young couple left for Fredericton, New Brunswick, which for a short time was to be their home. By water on transports, by land on horseback or on foot, by penetrating forests and crossing rivers, they arrived on the 27th of September.

After two years' work as Rector of Fredericton, he was called back again to Quebec to be the incumbent or "officiating clergyman" of Quebec, his cousin, Rev. Salter J. Mountain, having gone to Cornwall (Upper Canada). He was then made "official" of the diocese, and assisted his father continually in his duties.

In 1819 he received the degree of D.D. from the Archbishop of Canterbury, and accompanied his father in his last visitation to Upper Canada. In 1821 he was made Archdeacon of Lower Canada, in which capacity he made long and extensive journeys from Montreal on the west to distant Gaspé on the east. In May, 1825, his father sent him to England to procure, if possible, assistance for him in his episcopal duties; but when the Archdeacon had completed satisfactory arrangements he heard of his father's death, which took place suddenly on the 18th of June.

With a heavy heart he returned and resumed his archidiaconal duties, which he was to continue under the saintly and apostolic Bishop Stewart. The greatest affection and confidence subsisted between them. They were co-workers for the Church which they both deeply loved.

In 1826 the Archdeacon visited Gaspé for the second time, and then journeyed to York (Toronto), in the distant west of Upper Canada, visited the Eastern Townships (about Montreal), and the districts contiguous to Quebec—long and tedious journeys, taxing greatly the strength of man. His own account of his journeys, sent to the S.P.G., are most interesting. He was a keen lover of nature, a close observer, and this enabled him to use his fine descriptive powers to the best possible advantage. The roads may have been rough and tedious, but the forests and rivers were grand, and while the birds sang in the branches, and the waters murmured in current and cascade, there was poetry amidst the hardships of life.

In 1832 Quebec was visited with cholera. In little more than two months one-tenth of the population of Quebec, which then numbered 28,000, was carried off. In two consecutive days the Archdeacon himself buried more than seventy bodies. He never left his post for a day, but gave himself up entirely to ministering to the sick and dying. These sad duties extended even into the country. A horse was kept saddled in his stable night and day to enable him and his curate to meet the calls from a distance. Their rule was to take night calls alternately, but on many nights they were both out, and for whole days together unable to return home.

Bishop Stewart soon began to grow feeble, and by the year 1835 he felt that he must have a coadjutor.

Dr. Stewart, at the time, as Bishop of Quebec, was in the receipt of £3,000, or $15,000 a year. This he received from the Imperial Government. One-third of this (nearly $5,000) he was willing to devote to the support of an assistant. But this was considered in those days an exceedingly small income for a bishop. Dr. Mountain, therefore, went to England in August, 1835, to try to find some clergyman of "ample private means" who would accept the position. But being unable to do this, he was induced to accept it himself. He was therefore consecrated at Lambeth on Sunday, February 14th, 1836, by the Archbishop of Canterbury (Dr. William Howley), assisted by the Bishops of London (Dr. C. J. Blomfield), Winchester (Dr. Charles R. Sumner), and Gloucester (Dr. J. H. Monk). He was consecrated under the title of Bishop of Montreal.

Shortly after his arrival in Quebec, in September, 1836, Bishop Stewart was obliged to seek rest in England, where, in the following year, he died. Thus Dr. Mountain assumed the duties of the whole diocese almost at once. Yet it was not for many years that he consented to be called Bishop of Quebec. Montreal was rapidly becoming a place of size and importance, and Dr. Mountain longed to see a bishopric established there, and the retention of the title would have a tendency, he hoped, to bring the wished-for consummation into nearer view.

On the death of Bishop Stewart, the income voted by the Imperial Parliament to the Bishop of Quebec ceased, but a vote of £1,000 a year was granted to Dr. Mountain for life. Besides this, he received another £1,000 as Archdeacon and Rector of Quebec, which he was allowed to retain. A portion of the income as rector, however, he surrendered to the assistant clergy of Quebec."*

The number of clergy in the diocese in 1836 was as follows:

    In District of Quebec............................17†
    "   "   Montreal......................17
    " Upper Canada 51
                                              ——
    In all..85

There now follows an active career of journeying about from place to place, in and about Quebec, Montreal, and Gaspé in the far east, followed by a visit to Upper Canada, which in itself occupied a period of upwards of three months. This was in 1838. His spirit was stirred within him because of these sheep in the wilderness, that had no chief pastor. The wilderness was fast giving way to the industry of man, and flourishing towns, villages, and settlements were springing up everywhere. It was already vastly superior to Lower Canada in the number of clergy and in Church population, yet had no bishop. He saw also that the prospects of support for the Church from Government, either at home or abroad, were very dark indeed. He pointed this out to the clergy and laity of Upper Canada, at a visitation held at York (Toronto), and urged the immediate adoption of some plan whereby the Church might be supported by *voluntary contribu-*

* See " Memoir of G. J. Mountain," by Rev. Armine W. Mountain.

† The parishes and mission stations of this district were Quebec, Three Rivers, Leeds, Drummondville, Melbourne, Lennoxville, Eaton, Hatley, Gaspé Basin, and Carlisle.

tions. Had this principle been more widely depended upon, it would have been far better for the Church of the present day than the reliance upon Government or societies in England. At the close of this visitation the Bishop made a full report upon the state of the Church in Upper Canada to Lord Durham, Governor-General. This report gives the number of clergy in Upper Canada as seventy-three, the number of churches as ninety, and the number of adherents of the Church of England 150,000.

In the following year, 1839, to the Bishop's great satisfaction and relief, Upper Canada was taken off his hands by the formation of the Diocese of Toronto. In the same year the far east also received a new diocese in the separation of Newfoundland from Nova Scotia.

The "Bishop of Montreal" could now address himself more closely to his duties in Lower Canada. During the years 1839 and 1840 he visited assiduously and particularly in the neighbourhood of Montreal, with the hope of seeing a bishopric established there. Through the liberality of the S.P.G., the Bishop was able to establish a Divinity School at Three Rivers, under the charge of Rev. S. S. Wood, in the autumn of 1840. But the Rev. Lucius Doolittle, Rector of Sherbrooke and Lennoxville, offered through himself and his parishioners a large sum of money if a school and college should be set up in their midst. This led to the establishment of Bishop's College at Lennoxville. A preparatory school was opened there in 1842 under Mr. Edward Chapman. After the interruption of a severe illness, we find the Bishop in Montreal again, where in July, 1842, he was instrumental in forming the Church Society of the Diocese of Quebec—a wise measure designed to bring out the self-supporting powers of the people.

Soon after the formation of this society there was established (in 1842) a fund for the support of the widows and orphans of the clergy. This fund became very popular, and increased rapidly.

Bishop G. J. Mountain was a man in whom the missionary spirit burned with a fire that was strong and pure. Indeed the missionary spirit was beginning to assert itself with some show of vigour in many parts of the British Empire. Already, the colonial episcopate was beginning to diffuse itself throughout the world. Already besides the four dioceses of British North America, there were three in India, four in the West Indies (with Guiana), two in Australia, one in Gibraltar, and one in New Zealand, whither, in 1841, went the missionary apostle of the age, George Augustus Selwyn.

In keeping with this spirit Bishop Mountain now looked far off to the distant west, with a longing desire that a bishopric should be established there.

In 1799, some enthusiastic Churchmen of the Evangelical school formed, in England, a Church Missionary Society, which was to be for the heathen what the S.P.G. had been for the colonists. This C.M.S., as we shall in future designate it, established a mission in 1822 at the "Red River Settlement," in Rupert's Land, which was then an indefinite term by which the vast territory of British North America was designated. The mission was established for the purpose of ministering to the Indians, who were living in a most degraded condition of heathenism.

After some years of correspondence, the "Bishop of Montreal" made up his mind to visit this country, with a view to establishing, if possible, a bishopric there. This proved to be one of the most famous missionary journeys ever taken. It was arranged for under the auspices of the C.M.S. The Bishop could not, as the Bishop of Quebec is able to do to-day, get into a palatial C.P.R. "coach" and, in the midst of every comfort, reach Winnipeg in a few days. The journey involved a trip of about 1,800 miles by canoe, and was taken along the lonely route of the

Bishop G. J. Mountain on the way to Red River.

lakes and rivers, which then had very little but the sounds of nature as heard in the wilderness to awake their echoes. The canoe journey began at Montreal, which place the Bishop and his party reached from Quebec by steamer. The craft itself was of colossal proportions for a birch bark canoe, and was known as a " canot de maitre." It was thirty-six feet long, and was manned by fourteen voyageurs, each of whom was armed with a paddle. Six were French-Canadians and eight were Iroquois Indians. The Bishop had with him his chaplain (Rev. J. P. Maning), and his servant, who sat together in the centre of the canoe. Embarking at Lachine on the 16th of May, 1844, they proceeded up the Ottawa river. After about a week's travel they entered the river Mattawa, passed through several small lakes and other rivers till they reached Lake Huron, along the northern shore of which they coasted for 190 miles, when they arrived at Sault Ste. Marie, at the lower extremity of Lake Superior. Along the northern shore of this great lake (in itself a large inland sea) they coasted until they reached Fort William, where there was a station of the Hudson's Bay Company. "Here," the Bishop wrote himself in 1844, "is the boundary between Canada and the Hudson's Bay Company; and here you reach a height from which the waters fall either way."* At Fort William the large canoe was abandoned, and two smaller ones taken, they being more suitable for the difficulties they would have to encounter through the solitary regions of Rupert's Land. By the Rainy Lake and the Lake of the Woods, with here and there a river,

---

* The " Bishop of Montreal's " Journal, etc. (now a very rare book).

they reached Lake Winnipeg. In this part of their journey they met with many obstructions which obliged them to unload the canoes, divide all the "luggage" among the men, except those who had to carry the canoe, and walk past the barrier to where the water was again navigable. Of these *portages*, as they are called, there were many.

On this journey the ordinary rules of canoe travelling were observed. The party rose at three o'clock in the morning and journeyed till eight, then landed for breakfast and a halt of one hour. Then on again till two o'clock, when there is a halt of half an hour for a cold dinner, the journey being resumed till sunset. Then a tent is erected for the Bishop and his chaplain. Fires are lit, kettles are boiled, and a "supper" cooked. The men sleep on the ground in blankets or under the canoe, which is always pulled ashore and turned bottom upwards. If there is a good, fair wind, they sometimes do not land at all in the evening, but push on all night by means of a sail.

By extra exertion towards the last of the journey the Bishop was able to arrive at his destination at nine o'clock on Sunday morning, June 23rd, 1844, after a canoe journey of five weeks and two days. He found the Christianized Indians assembling in their little wooden church for divine service, and they, to their great satisfaction, heard the voice of a Bishop, and gave him a right royal welcome to the wilderness.

His stay was brief, for the navigation season was very short. On their way up they encountered thin coatings of ice, through which they had to paddle, and on their way back they must escape the high winds of

September, which make all canoeing on the big lakes very dangerous.

Red River Settlement Mission Station in 1844.

The Bishop, therefore, departed on the home journey on the 10th of July, and arrived at Lachine on the 14th of August; but the few weeks of his residence at Red River were a bright spot for the missionaries and their Indian converts in and among whom he went preaching and confirming, and imparting the episcopal benediction.

Shortly after his return from Red River, the Bishop had the satisfaction of laying the corner stone of Bishop's College, Lennoxville. The ceremony took place on the 18th of September, 1844.

The year 1845 was a year of importance for the Diocese of Quebec. In that year a very modest beginning was made in the way of instruction at Lennoxville. Owing to a munificent donation of £6,000 from an old friend of his, Bishop G. J. Mountain was enabled to engage a principal for the infant institution. Such was found in Rev. Jasper Hume Nicolls, a nephew of the Bishop's, a young man whom he induced to leave England for the purpose at a salary of £100 per year. He began his duties in a little old wooden house in the village, part of which was used as a store, the number of students in his charge being eight. The house was miserably cold, the rooms low and small, the discomforts many; yet the genial young Englishman made time for all concerned pass pleasantly and happily away.*

In that year, also, the Church Society was incorporated by Act of Parliament. It thus became a properly legalized body. From it the Bishop hoped great things, but his expectations were greater than the realization. He wanted it to be the means of forming an endowment for the work of the Church. Some subscriptions were given, and some land, but they were mainly gifts made by the Bishop himself and members of his family. The people of Canada little realized how much the Church owes, in property and prosperity, to the Mountain family.†

This Church Society was the foundation of those funds, which in every diocese are essential to its efficiency, such as Diocesan Mission Fund, Widows and Orphans' Fund, Superannuation Fund, etc. It was a useful provision, formed only just in time, to enable the infant Church to subsist when it should have to walk alone.

* Memoir of late Dr. Nicolls in "The Mission Field," 1879. S.P.G.

† See Archdeacon Roe's "Jubilee Memoirs of the Church Society of the Diocese of Quebec."

In 1845, also, the Bishop had the satisfaction of hearing that New Brunswick had been set off from Nova Scotia as a separate diocese, with Fredericton as its see city—where he, at the beginning of his ministerial life, had been a pioneer rector.

It is not necessary here to give in detail the unwearied journeys of this indefatigable Bishop, as he went now to Lennoxville, now to Montreal, and now to distant parts of his own districts, in performance of his laborious duties. Enough to say that he knew nothing but work.

Mention, however, must be made of the terrible visitation of ship fever which afflicted Quebec in 1847. In the midst of poor creatures dying by the hundreds of a loathsome and virulent disease, the Bishop and his clergy, many of whom came from their quiet, healthy country parishes for the purpose, moved incessantly night and day, ministering to the dying as best they could. Of the fifteen who devoted themselves in this way, five caught the plague and died, to their own lasting glory, but to the great loss of the diocese. The Bishop, though himself in the thickest of the fight, was amongst those who escaped.

In 1849 his exertions on behalf of Rupert's Land received their reward in the establishment of the new diocese, which bore its name, and in 1850 his golden dream for Montreal, too, was realized, for in that year the great, growing, commercial city received its first bishop. Then, and only then, the title of "Bishop of Montreal," which he had purposely held all this time, belonged to him no more. Henceforth he took his proper title of Bishop of Quebec.

Thus, in 1850, the Diocese of Quebec, in its present size and form, started on its new career. It commenced with a clerical staff of thirty-eight.

In 1851 the Bishop, after several years of correspondence, brought about a meeting of the Bishops of British North America. Bishop Fulford (Montreal), Bishop Strachan (Toronto), Bishop Medley (Fredericton), and Bishop Feild (Newfoundland) attended. Bishop Anderson (Rupert's Land) and Bishop Binney (Nova Scotia) were unable to be present. This was the first meeting of bishops in Canada, and it was held with a view to the establishment of synods and to the unification of the Church, at as early a date as possible. The Bishop of Quebec was the moving spirit in this conference, which lasted for a period of ten days, and resulted in a very able manifesto, which was issued and published abroad amongst the different dioceses of the country.*

This document was submitted to the Archbishop of Canterbury, with the hopes that the authority of the Imperial Parliament might be obtained for the holding of synods in the colonies. The reply of the Archbishop was unfavourable. Bishop G. J. Mountain, therefore, went to England in 1852. Here he met Bishop Feild (Newfoundland), Bishop Binney (Nova Scotia), Bishop Broughton (Sydney), Bishop Gray (Capetown), and Bishop Davis (Antigua), all of whom were interested in the question of self-government for the Church in the colonies. Conferences of these Bishops took place in England. Here were voices

---

* This document is printed in full in "A Memoir of G. J. Mountain, D.D., D.C.L.," by Armine W. Mountain, p. 292, *seq*.

not only from British North America, but from Australia, Africa, and the West Indies. In these conferences the Bishop of Quebec presided. A joint conference was also held of these colonial bishops and eighteen English bishops, presided over by Archbishop Sumner of Canterbury.* The result was that a bill was introduced into Parliament by the Archbishop, and taken in hand by Mr. Gladstone in the House of Commons.

Lennoxville University in Olden Days.

But the bill did not pass, and the colonial bishops were as they were. But this was all for the best in the end. They returned to their distant dioceses resolved to take the matter into their own hands, and establish diocesan synods as soon as circumstances

* This gathering might be regarded as a prelude to the Lambeth Conferences, not many years afterwards to be inaugurated.

would permit of it. At this conference it was arranged that Quebec was to be the metropolitical see of British North America.

In 1853 a royal charter was granted by the Queen to Bishop's College, Lennoxville, by which it became a university.

At this time Bishop G. J. Mountain was sixty-one years old, but his work was by no means done. He had now a comparatively compact diocese, and there remained yet much to be done to set it in order. Besides a spiritual father, it is necessary for a Bishop to be something of a statesman. Such was Bishop G. J. Mountain. The time was fast approaching when the Church must become absolutely self-reliant. The S.P.G. had notified the Bishop, in 1856, that the Society would have to decrease the amounts paid to the clergy—the first year from £100 sterling to £80, the next three years to £50, after which the grants would cease altogether. This was a grave moment, for no reliance whatever could be placed any longer upon State aid. The Crown and the Church had parted company.

In this severance between Church and State, the Church did not suffer an absolute loss. In 1857 the Canadian Government paid over in debentures to the Diocese of Quebec $53,341.59 as compensation money for those clergymen who had been relying upon State aid, the clergy having themselves presented the amount to the Church, they to receive their incomes as usual. This was placed under the management of a committee known as "The Clergy Trust," with the provision that as the clergymen who were receiving incomes from the interest on it should die (or as the fund might otherwise admit of it) other clergymen taking their places might receive a like benefit.

The ever-liberal S.P.G. also handed over to the diocese in this year $75,000, a balance of "Clergy Reserve" revenue which that Society was entitled to use to recoup itself for its expenditure upon its missions in the Province of Quebec. Instead of keeping it, the Society generously handed it over to Quebec as an episcopal endowment fund. This was a timely provision for the days of scarcity at hand, when with the death of Bishop G. J. Mountain the episcopal income was to cease.

Now that the days of ecclesiastical independence were at hand, the Bishop, by means of correspondence with the Home authorities and others, at last secured an enactment by which the Church might assemble her members in synod and transact her own temporal affairs. In this matter he was following the example of the Diocese of Toronto, whose clergy and laity met together for the first time in Synod in the year 1857, under the presidency of the Hon. and Right Rev. Dr. Strachan, Bishop of the diocese.

All preliminaries having been at last settled, the Bishop called the clergy and lay representatives of the parishes and missions together for the first meeting of Synod, on July 6th, 1859. The address of the Bishop on that occasion was a masterly production. Indeed, there were few men who could deliver more able addresses than he.

Though over seventy years of age, the Bishop commenced, in 1861, his eighth and last triennial circuit in

January, and encountered some hardships of travel which, at his advanced age, were of serious import. His wife, too, his partner of forty-seven years, died on the 23rd of August. Still, though shaken in health, he continued his duties. To his own Synod in 1861 he gave his clergy and laity a useful caution as to the election of their bishop—for their next bishop would have to be chosen by their own votes—and he expressed a hope that all canvassing and caballing would be not even named among them. The good Bishop's caution was needed. Episcopal elections were henceforth to be the rule in Canada as in the United States. They have not always, however, been free from the very actions which this saintly Bishop of the old school so much feared. Yet another diocese was formed in Upper Canada, in that of Ontario; and now the time had come when the dioceses of Upper and Lower Canada were to meet together in Provincial Synod, by means of equal representation from each. It was a day much to be remembered. Here were assembled the Bishops of Montreal (who had been constituted Metropolitan of Canada), Quebec, Toronto, Huron, and the Bishop-elect of Ontario, together with twelve clergymen and twelve laymen from each diocese. The clergy that represented Quebec were: Rev. Dr. Falloon, Rev. G. V. Housman, Rev. Dr. Nicolls, Rev. Armine W. Mountain, Rev. E. C. Parkin, Rev. C. P. Reid, Rev. S. S. Wood, Rev. H. Roe, Rev. Charles Hamilton, Ven. Dr. Hellmuth, Rev. A. J. Woolryche, Rev. E. W. Sewell. The lay representatives were: Lt.-Col. Rhodes, Right Hon. Lord Aylmer, Dr. F. D. Gilbert, and Messrs. B. T. Morris, W. G. Wurtele, W. R. Doak,

G. Irvine, H. S. Scott, C. N. Montizambert, G. Okill Stuart, J. B. Forsyth, and Philip Viberts. All these were present except Rev. E. C. Parkin and Messrs. Stuart and Viberts. The venerable Bishop of Quebec was now so feeble that he could not take his place in the procession to the cathedral; but to him, as was most fitting, was allotted the task of preaching the sermon, which, it is needless to say, was suitable to the important occasion.

After this we still find the aged Bishop at his work, confirming and ordaining. He was present at Kingston (Upper Canada) at the consecration of the Bishop-elect of Ontario in March, 1862, but before the end of that year he was prostrated with an illness that proved to be his last. He lived, however, long enough to see the establishment of a diocesan board (consisting of an equal number of clergy and laity) for the administration of the funds of the diocese. The S.P.G., by special arrangement, agreed to pay the amount of money represented by the salaries of the missionaries supported by it to the Society *en bloc*. This led to a system of management for the support of country parishes which in time proved to be most successful, and which has made Quebec the admiration of other dioceses. But the faithful old Bishop lived only to see its establishment. It came into operation on January 1st, 1863. Five days later the beloved Bishop died. He died quietly, like an infant, in his son's arms, on January 6th (the festival of the Epiphany, 1863), at the age of seventy-four, full of hope of a blessed immortality. And thus passed away one of the noblest workers, one of the most devoted Churchmen, one of the kindliest spirits, one of the gentlest souls that ever lived. He lived as he died, and of his death Bishop Feild, of Newfoundland, remarked, " I have never heard of any person's departure respecting which I could more earnestly and sincerely say and pray, ' Let my last end be like his.' "

The Sorel Church of Early Days.

The above is a picture of one of the earliest churches built in Canada. Sorel was originally in the Diocese of Quebec, but it is now in that of Montreal. The church represented above served a good purpose till it was replaced, in 1843, by the building which now stands in Sorel.

7. The Hon. and Right Rev. John Strachan, D.D., LL.D., First Bishop of Toronto.

JOHN STRACHAN was born at Aberdeen, in Scotland, on April 12th, 1778. His father, John Strachan, was an overseer of granite quarries near Aberdeen.* His mother was a rigid Presbyterian. Her maiden name was Elizabeth Finlayson. Though his father seems to have been rather inclined to Scotch Episcopalianism, the son was certainly brought up a Presbyterian. He was only fourteen years old when his father died, and the burden of supporting his mother made him thoughtful beyond his years. The best way to support her, as he thought, was to qualify himself for school teaching. With this end in view, he entered the University of Aberdeen at the age of sixteen, and during the long vacation earned money by teaching. After holding one or two situations as a teacher he was offered a position in Upper Canada by the Governor, to take charge of an academy there at a stipend of £80 sterling a year. He arrived in Canada, as he himself used to put it, "on the last day, of the last week, of the last month, of the last year, of the last century." He arrived, however, only to meet with a great disappointment. The scheme for the proposed college had failed. The poor young Scotchman found himself a stranger in a strange land, with

* See "Memoir of the Rt. Rev. John Strachan." By Bishop Bethune.

only about twenty shillings in his pocket. He made a friend, however, in Richard Cartwright, Esq., who engaged him as private tutor in his own house. This brought him other pupils.

At this time there were only three clergymen in the whole of Upper Canada. The Rev. John Stuart was at Cataraqui (Kingston); Rev. John Langhorn was at Ernest Town, on the Bay of Quinte; Rev. Robert Addison was at Niagara.* But others were destined very soon to be added. The Rev. George Okill Stuart (son of Rev. John Stuart) was appointed to York (Toronto) in 1800, and Rev. J. S. Rudd to Cornwall in 1801. Mr. Rudd, who was a B.A. of Queen's College, Cambridge, removed to Sorel in 1803, where he died in 1808, after having buried his wife and all his children save one.† These clergymen received about £100 a year, paid partly by Government and partly by the S.P.G.

The four places mentioned are of historic interest. At Niagara (called at first Newark) the first Government of Upper Canada was formed under Governor Simcoe.‡ This shortly afterwards was moved to York (Toronto).¶ It must be borne in mind that they were all mere villages, nestling amidst the trees of a primeval

---

*A very interesting account of these pioneer clergy is to be found in "The Church in the Colonies, Toronto," by Rev. Ernest Hawkins. The Rev. H. C. Stuart, in his "The Church of England in Canada, 1759-1793," makes it quite evident that, in addition to these, a Rev. Mr. Bryan had ministered at Cornwall somewhere about 1786 or 1788 (see pp. 88, 89). There is no mention, however, of Mr. Bryan in the "Digest of S.P.G. Records." It would be interesting if some one could throw some light upon his history.

† Digest of S.P.G. Records.

‡ "Life and Times of Governor Simcoe." By D. B. Reid.

¶ Rev. Dr. Scadding, in his "Toronto of Old," makes it very evident that "Toronto" was the ancient name of this historic place. An attempt was made to change it to York, but the old name, fortunately, was soon reverted to.

forest. The first church built at York was one of primitive simplicity, constructed of wood and surrounded by trees.

Such was the state of the country when Mr. John Strachan was tutoring children at Kingston. His intercourse with the rector, Rev. Dr. Stuart, and with other Churchmen of strict integrity and noble mind, soon led the young Scotchman to incline to his father's predilections and to claim the Episcopal Church as his own. He studied for Holy Orders, and was ordained by the first Bishop of Quebec (Dr. Jacob Mountain) in 1803, and was appointed to Cornwall at £130 a year. Here he opened a grammar school, which for nine years was the seminary of higher learning in Canada. He taught in a little wooden building, which, scarred with the initials of the pupils—many of them afterwards men of renown in Church and State in Canada—still stands in Cornwall.*

In 1807 he married the young widow of Mr. Andrew McGill, of Montreal. She was the daughter of Dr. Wood, a physician of Cornwall, and being possessed of an annuity in her own right was able to be of considerable assistance to her husband in his work. In Cornwall Mr. Strachan built a church of wood, and this primitive building he always regarded with much affection.† In 1811 his own University of Aberdeen conferred upon him the degree of Doctor of Divinity, and in that year his old and valued friend at Kingston, Rev. Dr. John Stuart, the pioneer clergyman of Upper Canada, died.

* The writer saw this venerable building in 1889. It was then used as a cow stable !

† This, since his death, has been replaced by a substantial stone structure known as the " Bishop Strachan Memorial Church."

Dr. Strachan hoped to succeed him at Kingston, but Rev. G. O. Stuart, the rector's son, received at the hands of the Bishop (Dr. Jacob Mountain) the position, somewhat to the doctor's disappointment. However, he contented himself with accepting the rectory of York

The Original St. James' Church, Toronto.

(Toronto), which in the end proved to be by far the better appointment.

This was early in 1812, the year of the war between Great Britain and the United States. The new rector at the capital showed himself equal to the circumstances of the country, even to heroism. In 1813 he was appointed a member of the Executive Council of Upper

Canada. This honour was bestowed upon him on account of "his zealous and valuable services during the late war." When peace was established the work of the Church went on. Dr. Strachan, as was his wont, opened a school; and thus, with all the irons he had in the fire, his hands were full. York was but a small place, yet it was a city in miniature, having within itself all classes of people, from the representatives of royalty to the poorest in the land, with here and there a red man of the forest to remind all of its primitive condition. In the little square wooden church, painted as it was of a bluish tint, was the Governor's pew, and when occupied by such personages as Sir Peregrine and Lady Sarah Maitland—zealous Church people—was a place indicative of some power both in Church and State. The church had no vestry; the clergy robed under the pulpit in full sight of the people.

In 1820 there were only sixteen clergymen in Upper Canada, classified by districts, corresponding with dioceses afterwards formed, as follows:

Huron.—Romaine Rolph, Amherstburg; R. Pollard, Sandwich.

Niagara.—Ralph Leeming, Ancaster; R. Addison, Niagara; Wm. Leeming, Chippawa; Wm. Sampson, Grimsby; B. B. Stevens, Queenston.

Toronto.—Joseph Thompson, Cavan; William Macaulay, Cobourg (then Hamilton township); J. Strachan, Toronto.

Ontario.—John Stoughton, Ernestown (Bath); John Leeds, Brockville (Elizabethtown); G. Okill Stuart, Kingston; F. Myers, Matilda.

Ottawa.—S. J. Mountain, Cornwall; M. Harris, Perth; J. G. Weagant, Williamsburg.

There was a memorable gathering of these clergy in this year (1820), when the Bishop (Dr. Jacob Mountain) visited Upper Canada.

In 1824 Dr. Strachan went to the old country, and had the great happiness of seeing the land of his birth and childhood. But the affairs of the Church in Canada occupied his attention. The struggle regarding the "Clergy Reserves" had begun. The land which was set apart for the maintenance of the Church in every township was claimed by the Presbyterians as belonging to them as well as to the Church of England; and a similar claim was soon made by all denominations of Protestants. This arose from the loose wording of the Act which designated the beneficiaries as "a Protestant clergy," and it became a very vexed question, and involved Dr. Strachan in much political dispute and agitation.

General Simcoe, first Governor of Upper Canada, as far back as 1792 had two great objects in view for the benefit of the new colony. One was the appointment of a bishop, and the other the establishment of a university. Dr. Strachan, thirty-two years afterwards, felt how pressing these two needs were. The university received his earliest attention. Like all true Churchmen, he knew that education and religion should go hand in hand. Largely by his exertions, grammar schools were established in various places, and in 1826, after having paid a visit to England for the purpose, he had the proud satisfaction of having a university promised for Toronto. It was to have a royal charter, and was to bear the title of King's College. In 1827 Upper Canada was divided into two archdeaconries, York in the west, and Kingston in the east. The archdeacons respectively were Dr. Strachan, of York, and Dr. G. Okill Stuart, of Kingston. Sir John Colborne became Lieutenant-Governor in succession to Sir Peregrine Maitland in 1828. Through him Upper Canada College was established. Sir John was favourable to the claims of the Church, and in his time fifty-seven parishes were formed into rectories, with suitable endowments. This led to the exhibition of much rancour throughout the country on the part of those opposed to the Church.

Some of these parishes failed to comply with the necessary preliminary steps, and therefore lost their endowment, but the others have retained it to the present day.

The rectories that obtained their glebe lands in 1836, arranged in districts corresponding to the present dioceses, are as follows:

Toronto.—St. James', York Mills, Mimico, Cobourg, Peterborough, Cavan, Thornhill, Port Hope, Markham, Darlington, Barrie, Newcastle.

Huron.—Woodhouse, Woodstock, London Township, St. Paul's (London), Warwick, Adelaide, Amherstburg, Malden.

Ontario.—Kemptville, Picton, Prescott, Elizabethtown, Kingston, Belleville, Napanee, Adolphustown, Fredericksburgh, Bath.

Niagara.—Grimsby, Ancaster, Wellington Square, Niagara, St. Catharines, Stamford, Chippawa, Guelph, Thorold, Bertie (Fort Erie), Louth (Dalhousie).

Ottawa.—Perth, Cornwall, Williamsburg, Richmond, Beckwith (Carleton Place).

Sir John Colborne was succeeded in 1836 by Sir Francis Bond Head, whose first Government was so intensely Conservative that the Radicals and Liberals of the country resented it. What is known as "the rebellion" broke out in 1837. When this was over the new Governor exerted himself on behalf of the formation of Upper Canada into a separate diocese, and this was at last effected in 1839. Early in that year the newly-erected Church of St. James was destroyed by fire, to the great grief of the Archdeacon. He was, however, cheered with the fact that Toronto was to be formed into a diocese, and that he was to be the first bishop.

The Diocese of Toronto was set apart without any endowment. That was to be an after consideration. The Archdeacon was to have his present income, about £1,000, less what he might have to pay for an assistant in the parish.

In the summer of 1839 Dr. Strachan was consecrated in England, by Archbishop Howley (Canterbury), Bishop of Toronto, and with him was consecrated Dr. Aubrey G. Spencer, Bishop of Newfoundland. On his return to Toronto the Bishop found his church rebuilt and restored; the body being of stone, the tower of wood. Such was the first cathedral of Toronto.

Dr. Strachan, at the age of sixty-one, began his active career as first Bishop of Toronto.* In 1840 the much-vexed question of the Clergy Reserves was for the

* The diocese at this time numbered seventy-one clergymen. Jubilee Volume, Diocese of Toronto, p. 140.

time settled by Act of Parliament, the Church of England receiving benefit to the extent of two-thirds and the Church of Scotland one-third of a portion of the property involved, the remaining portion, which was half of the unappropriated lands, to be devoted by the Government to purposes of public worship and religious instruction in Canada.*

In 1844 an elaborate tabulated statement was made, showing the clergy with their parishes and missions in the diocese at that time. It is interesting to compare it with the list of 1820. It is as follows, divided into districts corresponding with the dioceses afterwards formed. A clergy list changed from seventeen to one hundred and five in twenty-four years showed a large increase in the population of the country, and also a fair amount of Church energy and work:

Huron.—Wm. Bettridge, Woodstock; D. E. Blake, Adelaide; M. Boomer, Galt; C. C. Brough, London Township; M. Burnham, St. Thomas; R. F. Campbell, Goderich; J. Carey, Walpole Island; H. C. Cooper, Usborne, Biddulph, McGillivray, etc.; B. Cronyn, London; Adam Elliot, Tuscarora; F. Gore Elliott, Colchester; Francis Evans, Woodhouse (Simcoe); Richard Flood, Caradoc (Muncey); John Hickie, Blenheim, etc.; W. H. Hobson, Chatham; F. Mack, Amherstburg; W. Morse, Paris; A. Mortimer, Warwick; A. Nelles, Mohawk; G. Petrie, Burford; A. Pyne, Moore; T. B. Read, Port Burwell; W. Ritchie, Sandwich; J. Rothwell, Ingersoll, Oxford, etc.; James Stewart, Tyrconnell; J. C. Usher, Brantford.

* See Bishop Bethune's "Memoir of Bishop Strachan," p. 179.

Algoma.—F. A. O'Meara, Manitoulin Island, Sault Ste. Marie, etc.

Niagara.—James L. Alexander, Binbrook; John Anderson, Fort Erie; G. M. Armstrong, Louth (Port Dalhousie); A. F. Atkinson, St. Catharines; T. Creen, Niagara; T. B. Fuller, Thorold; J. G. Geddes, Hamilton; G. Graham, Nassagaweya; Thos. Greene, Wellington; G. R. F. Grout, Grimsby; B. C. Hill, Cayuga, etc.; W. Leeming, Chippawa; W. McMurray, Ancaster and Dundas; F. W. Miller, Chippawa Forces; J. Mockridge, Elora, etc.; A. Palmer, Guelph; A. Townley, Dunnville; G. W. Warr, Oakville.

Toronto.—S. B. Ardagh, Barrie; Samuel Armour, Cavan; A. N. Bethune, Cobourg; W. S. Darling, Scarborough; Thomas Fidler, Fenelon Falls; John Gibson, Georgina; H. J. Grasset, Toronto, Assistant; George Hallen, Penetanguishene; R. Harding, Penetanguishene; G. S. J. Hill, Chinguacousy, Tullamore, etc.; A. Jamieson, Brock, Uxbridge, etc.; T. S. Kennedy, Darlington, Bowmanville; R. J. McGeorge, Streetsville; John McIntyre, Orillia; J. M. A. McGrath, Springfield; V. P. M. A. Meyerhoffer, Markham; George Maynard, North Gate (Toronto Township); G. Mortimer, Thornhill; F. L. Osler, Tecumseth; H. B. Osler, Lloydtown; J. Pentland, Whitby; T. Phillips, Weston; W. H. Ripley, Toronto, Trinity; C. Ruttan (Assistant), Cobourg; A. Sanson, York Mills; H. Scadding (Assistant), Toronto; Wm. Shaw, Colborne; Jonathan Shortt, Port Hope; Bishop Strachan, Toronto; G. C. Street, Newmarket; R. J. C. Taylor, Peterborough; John Wilson (Curate), Cobourg.

Ontario.—W. A. Adamson, Amherst Island; T. H. M. Bartlett, Kingston Garrison; Ph. G. Bartlett, Carrying Place; Robert Blakey, Prescott; Job Deacon, Adolphustown; E. Denroche, Brockville; S. Givens, Napanee; John Grier, Belleville; W. H. Gunning, New Dublin; W. F. S. Harper, Bath; Catechist, Marysburgh; W. Herchmer (Assistant), Kingston Township; W. Macaulay, Picton; E. Morris, Lansdowne, etc.; H. Patton, Kemptville; R. V. Rogers, Kingston; Paul Shirley, Camden, Loughboro, etc.; Ven. G. Okill Stuart, Kingston.

Ottawa.—E. J. Boswell, Carleton Place; John Flood, Richmond; M. Harris, Perth; M. Ker, March; J. G. B. Lindsay, Williamsburg; H. Mulkins, Pakenham; J. Padfield, Franktown; R. Rolph, Osnabruck; S. S. Strong, Bytown (Ottawa); A. Williams, Cornwall.

This amounts to 105, viz., Huron 26, Algoma 1, Niagara 18, Toronto 32, Ontario 18, Ottawa 10.

The detail of visitations in all parts of Upper Canada for the next twenty years, when some relief was granted by the subdivision of his enormous diocese, presents a picture of energy and perseverance that crown with glory a consecrated old age. There are some people still living who remember the short yet sturdy frame of the Bishop, as he drove about in his own carriage over rough roads and log bridges, and his appearance at distant missions to confirm the candidates awaiting him. His Aberdeen accent never left him, though there were times when he himself fancied that it had; but without those well-known northern tones the good old Bishop would not have been Bishop Strachan.

During his triennial visitations of the diocese, there were many things of a public nature which caused him hard and unceasing toil. Some method had to be adopted for enabling the diocese to do the work of the Church on proper systematic and business lines. This was done by the formation, in 1842, of the "Church Society," which, until the establishment of a diocesan synod, and even for some time after it, was the great means by which all Church work in the diocese was done.

St. James' Cathedral was again destroyed by fire in the great conflagration of 1849, but the result was the erection of a building somewhat in keeping with the growing size and importance of Toronto. It still stands a monument of the zeal and good taste of the Bishop and the congregation. It also remained a parish church, though other churches in the meantime had been built throughout the city; but the Bishop had placed his chair there, and had made it the cathedral church of the diocese.

Bishop Strachan in his work was doomed at times to many disappointments. King's College, for instance, which he had hoped he had secured as a Church university, was pronounced the property of all denominations, and therefore was lost to the Church.

Nothing daunted, the Bishop called upon the Church people of the diocese to subscribe towards a new university, heading the list himself with a subscription of £1,000 ($5,000); and, at seventy-two years of age, crossed the Atlantic Ocean, made appeals to the societies in England and to individuals there, and secured sufficient encouragement to enable him, on his return, to establish a Church university, so guarded and protected that it could not be alienated from the purposes for which it was formed.

This was the origin of Trinity University. Up to this time a divinity school, established in 1841 at Cobourg, was the only means in the diocese for training young men for the ministry.

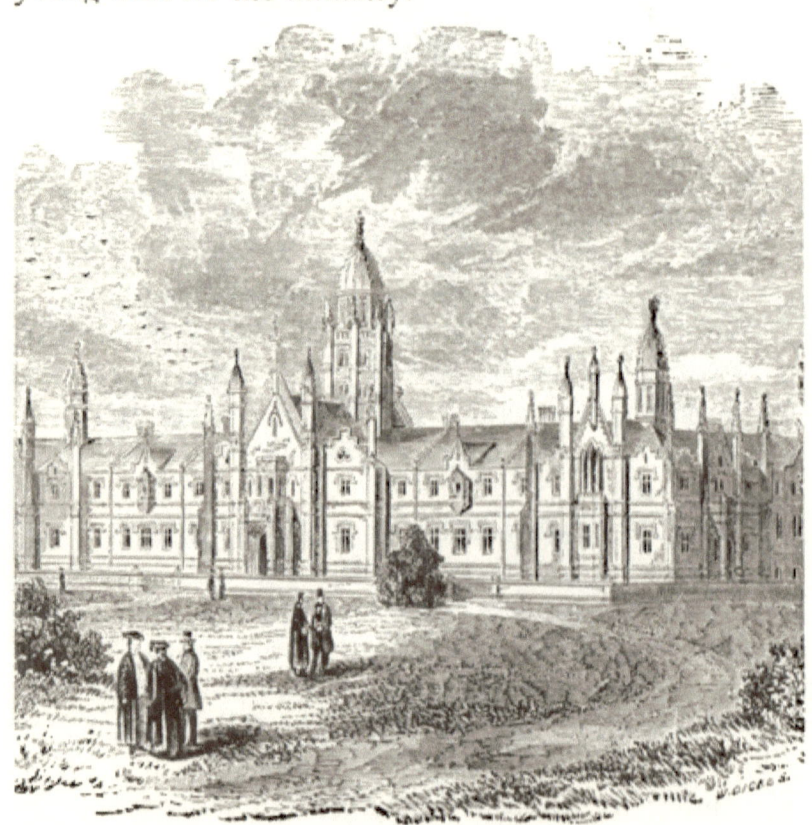

Trinity College, Toronto, in Early Days.

In the year 1851 the first Diocesan Synod was held in Toronto. One hundred and twenty-four clergymen and one hundred and twenty-seven laymen assembled in the Church of the Holy Trinity on Thursday, May 1st. On Thursday, January 15th, 1852, Trinity University was formally opened, with the Rev. George Whitaker as Provost.

In 1854-5 fresh struggles arose over the Clergy Reserves; the Provincial Parliament could not rest till every vestige of Church and State was removed from Canada; hence the renewed agitation, which was finally settled by a compromise. The Government, for the future, would pay no more stipends to the clergy, except to those already on their list. It was then that the happy expedient was hit upon of asking the Government for a gross amount to be paid to the clergy in lieu of the promised incomes. To this the Government consented, and handed over £188,342 (not far from a million dollars) to the Church Society of the diocese.

The clergy, with one exception, agreed to leave this large sum as an endowment for the Church, they individually to receive the interest on their own proper share during their lifetime. The Bishop spoke highly of this "noble and disinterested" act, which was to their "lasting honour," and by it they had "merited the gratitude of the Church in Canada forever, and won for themselves the cordial admiration of true Churchmen throughout the world."*

In September, 1861, Bishop Strachan was present at the first meeting of the Provincial Synod of Canada, an event which marks an epoch in the history of the Church. The delegates appointed to attend this meeting from the Diocese of Toronto were as follows:

* For the names of these clergy, see "History of Church and State in Canada." By Rev. E. R. Stimson.

St. James' Cathedral, Toronto.

Clerical.—Rev. James Beaven, D.D.; Ven. A. N. Bethune, D.D., D.C.L.; Rev. T. B. Fuller, D.D.; Rev. G. Whitaker, Rev. S. Givins, Rev. E. Denroche, Rev. W. S. Darling, Rev. E. H. Dewar, Rev. H. T. Holland, Rev. Stephen Lett, LL.D.; Rev. J. G. Geddes, and Rev. T. S. Kennedy.

These were all present except the Provost and Dr. Lett.

Lay.—Hon. J. H. Cameron, Hon. G. W. Allan, Dr. Bovell, Hon. J. Patton, Hon. George Boulton, Judge Boswell, and Messrs. S. B. Harman, T. C. Street, R. B. Denison, J. W. Gamble, and E. G. O'Brien.

Judge Boswell and Messrs. Campbell, Street, Patton, and Harman were not present.

By the subdivision of the diocese into Huron, on the west, in 1857, and Ontario, on the east, in 1861, Bishop Strachan, in his old age, found himself responsible for a much smaller territory than had hitherto fallen to his lot. But his strength was visibly beginning to fail. In 1865 the Synod made provision for the election of a coadjutor bishop. A school for boys, under Rev. C. H. Badgley, was also established at Weston. In that year the Bishop sustained a great loss in the death of Mrs. Strachan, who, for fifty-eight years, had been his valuable assistant in all his work.

The synod of 1866 elected the Venerable Archdeacon A. N. Bethune coadjutor, with the title of Bishop of Niagara. Bishop Strachan, to his great grief, was obliged to decline the invitation to attend the Pan-Anglican conference of bishops, which, for the first time, was appointed to be held on the 24th September,

1867, at Lambeth. He did this on account of his failing strength—he was just entering upon his ninetieth year.

He had the satisfaction of seeing a Church school for girls started about this time in Toronto, and was pleased to give his permission that it should be called " The Bishop Strachan School." It has continued an efficient school for girls ever since.

Bishop Strachan died on All Saints' Day, November 1st, 1867. His little town of York had become a great city, and was known as the " Queen City of the West," and its inhabitants turned out in great force to pay the last marks of respect to him whose name had been connected with the history of Upper Canada from its earliest days.

He was buried in a vault expressly constructed for the purpose, beneath the chancel of St. James' Cathedral.

The good Bishop was short in stature; his face wore that resolute expression which was but an index to his character; he was one on whom men would instinctively rely in any time of anxiety or danger; he knew nothing but duty; when lumbering over rough roads, sometimes he would not stop, after confirmation service, even for dinner, if by doing so he would be late for the next appointment. The rector's wife and daughters might have ready their very best dinner, the savory odors whereof might float ever so temptingly into the room. " Na, na!—we must move on," was the inexorable order, and his hungry and disappointed chaplain, or chaplains, had to forego the expected repast for several hours more rough shakings on the country road, winding its way in and out of the woods, because "the Bishop must not be late."

The Bishop, though apparently stern in manner, was kind at heart. Nor was he without a sense of humour. When a number of gentlemen who had been his pupils at school gave a dinner to their aged Bishop —they themselves at the time being well advanced in life—they instinctively, yet laughingly, came to order when his lordship, in his old schoolmaster-voice, said, on coming to the table, "Boys, tak' your places!"

Many anecdotes are told of his life and dealings with men, but upon these we cannot dwell. Our space has permitted us to do little else than speak of his active life and work, and that only in a condensed form; but many monuments of Church work throughout Ontario still remain to mark the devoted spirit and heroic soul of the first Bishop of Toronto.

A Schoolhouse of Early Days in Canada.
(Such buildings were often used for Divine Services.)

8. The Right Rev. Aubrey George Spencer, D.D., First Bishop of Newfoundland.

AUBREY GEORGE SPENCER was the son of the Hon. William Spencer. He was born in England in 1795, and was educated at Greenwich. He served for a time in the Royal Navy, but, not liking the sea, he returned, gave what money he had earned to his mother, and somewhat late in life entered Magdalen Hall, Oxford. Here he won two prizes for poems, one of which, entitled "The Colisseum," was said to be of great merit.

Having received Holy Orders, and after a year's work as curate in England, he resolved to go abroad as a missionary. The field chosen was Newfoundland.

In 1819 this gifted young Englishman left the genial surroundings of English home life to undergo all the fatigues and dangers of a missionary in a distant land; but after a couple of years' work in the rigorous climate of that island, he was obliged, for his health's sake, to remove to Bermuda, where, while Rector of Paget and Warwick, he exercised his missionary spirit by endeavouring to improve the condition of the negroes.

The Bermudas are a group of islands lying between six and seven hundred miles to the south of Newfoundland, about in line with the State of Georgia. They were discovered, shortly after the time of Columbus,

THE RT. REV. AUBREY GEORGE SPENCER, D.D.
First Bishop of Newfoundland and Second Bishop of Jamaica.

Born, 1795. Consecrated, 1839. Resigned Newfoundland, 1843, Jamaica, 1855. Died, 1872.

by a Spaniard named Bermudaz. But little was known of them till early in the reign of James I., 1609, when a vessel was wrecked close to them, and all the ship's company, who were on their way to the new colony of Virginia, numbering one hundred and fifty, were cast upon them. Among them was a lovely island, twenty-five miles long and three wide, of which they took possession in the name of King James. In time these islands were all occupied by English people, and were divided into five Church "livings." These livings have had rectors since the year 1622. They are situated six hundred miles from Newfoundland, and, possessing a tropical climate, form a lovely place of refuge for the Bishop of Newfoundland in the winter.

Newfoundland[*] is the oldest of the British colonies, its history dating back to the reign of Henry III.; but nothing is recorded in a missionary way until the S.P.G. was formed in 1701.

In 1702 there were two clergymen working in Newfoundland. In 1704 it is reported as having "several settlements of English, with many occasional inhabitants, such as workers, mariners, etc., at fishing seasons to the number of several thousands, but no public exercise of religion except at St. John's (the capital), where there is a congregation, but unable to sustain a minister."

Bishop John Inglis, as already related, appointed Mr. Spencer Archdeacon of Bermuda, and visited the island in 1826. He also visited Newfoundland in

---

[*] It is a large island, about the size of England, and not unlike it in shape. Its northern part lies close to Labrador (Quebec), and its southern part not far from Nova Scotia.

1827. In 1839 Newfoundland and Bermuda were set apart by the S.P.G. as a diocese, and Archdeacon Spencer was appointed the first bishop. He was consecrated in England, in 1839, side by side with Archdeacon Strachan, the bishop-designate of Toronto, by Archbishop Howley (Canterbury). The S.P.G. helped Bishop Spencer generously with its funds, the inhabitants of Newfoundland being able to do little or nothing to help themselves.

The Society undertook the full payment of the clergy, offering £200 a year as a stipend for each mis-

Off the Coast of Newfoundland.

sionary. The result of this was a considerable increase in the clerical staff of Newfoundland. Bermuda, except among the negroes, offered no field for missionary work. The parishes were supported by glebe lands and by Government. Bishop Spencer made heroic efforts to subdue the difficulties of his enormous mission field, but too long visitations by sea, for the most part in open boats, coupled with severity of climate, difficulty of locomotion, having no mission ship at his command, seemed to dishearten him.*

Still he visited not only the northern parts of Newfoundland, but also the coast of Labrador. He founded a small theological institution, maintained principally by the S.P.G., for training men specially for work in Newfoundland. In 1842 there were twenty-seven missionaries and sixty-four churches and chapels in Newfoundland. In Bermuda there were nine clergy and eighteen churches and chapel schoolhouses. In 1843 Bishop Spencer was offered by Lord Stanley the bishopric of Jamaica, and, owing to his weak state of health, he accepted it. He had the will to do the work in Newfoundland, but not the physical power. In his own words, "A missionary in Newfoundland must have a strength of constitution to support him under a climate as rigorous as that of Iceland; a stomach insensible to the attacks of sea-sickness; pedestrian powers beyond those of an Irish gossoon; and the ability to rest occasionally on the bed of a fisherman, or the hard boards in a woodman's hut."

He was allowed to work for nearly ten years in Jamaica, when his physical strength again gave way, and he was obliged to retire to England. For a time he assisted some of the English bishops in their work, but was obliged to remove to the genial, soft climate of Torquay for quiet and rest. Here he won the love of all who crossed his path. He died on St. Matthias'

* See "Life of Bishop Feild." By Rev. H. W. Tucker.

Day, 1872, in the seventy-seventh year of his age, leaving his wife, who had been his companion for fifty years, to mourn his loss. A cross was erected to his memory in Collaton churchyard, Devonshire, on which he is described as " Beloved pastor, faithful friend, true poet. His songs were the songs of Zion. His memory blest in many lands." A handsome three-light window is erected to his memory in St. Andrew's Church, Halfway Tree, Jamaica, and is designed to show the varied character of his work. On one side is a tropical scene, with the radiant sun and palm trees, and, on the other, the cold northern seas, with their icebergs.

Labrador Waters.—Seal Boats Escaping from the Ice.

THE RT. REV. EDWARD FEILD, D.D.
Second Bishop of Newfoundland.
Born, 1801.   Consecrated, 1844.   Died, 1877.

9. The Right Rev. Edward Feild, D.D., Second Bishop of Newfoundland.

EDWARD FEILD was of a distinguished and ancient family. He was born at Worcester on June 7th, 1801. At Rugby and Oxford he received his education. He passed his University with first-class mathematical and second-class classical honours. He was made a deacon on May 21st, 1826, and ordained priest in 1827 by Bishop Lloyd, and served as curate at Kedlington. He proved himself a pastor able to grapple with the practical questions of the day, and when he was appointed Rector of English Bicknor he put forth this ability with energy and zeal for ten years. Those were days when workmen were resisting the introduction of machinery, on the grounds that it would diminish the prospects of labourers. Mr. Feild reasoned strongly with them, and to good purpose, showing that machinery would greatly help labour by the largely increased manufacture of articles of every description, in which a correspondingly increased number of labourers would be required. The clergy are of more use to the State in such matters than is generally known.

Mr. Feild manifested his love for children, for which he was always noted, by establishing day and Sunday schools, and supporting them at his own cost. It was highly suitable to his disposition when he was appointed Inspector of Schools in the Diocese of Salisbury.

In 1844 he was offered the bishopric of Newfoundland, and, to the great grief of his parishioners, he accepted it. He was consecrated at Lambeth on the 28th of April, and sailed from Liverpool on the 5th of June. He arrived first at Halifax, where he spent a short time conferring with the Bishop of Nova Scotia, Dr. John Inglis, from whom he gained much valuable information regarding the nature of his future work.

On his arrival at St. John's he was taken much by surprise by the imposing reception given him. A boat containing the clergy of St. John's (two in number), with their churchwardens and others, and another from H.M.S. *Eurydice*, having on board the Governor's son and Private Secretary, met the ship. In this latter he and the clergy were taken to the wharf, where he found companies of soldiers with their officers drawn up to receive him, which they did by presenting arms.

Bishop Feild, by his actions, soon showed that he understood what the life of a missionary bishop ought to be. His income was £1,200 (about $6,000) a year —£500 from the S.P.G., and £700 from parliamentary and colonial funds. He did not live, however, in accordance with this income. His furniture was of pine, and of the simplest kind. He had no looking-glasses, except a few small hand mirrors, which were fastened to the walls. He had no carpets upstairs. His living was of the plainest kind. Beer or wine he never used. He used to say that a man who worked hard must live plainly. We are told that he offered to give up £500 a year of his salary to the S.P.G., if it would be the means of procuring for him five additional clergymen.

He found the little theological seminary in a very poor condition, but his energy soon gave a new impetus to it. His demand of the S.P.G. was for more men. Two clergymen he maintained himself, and supported two students at the college. Never was man better fitted for missionary work, both physically and mentally, than Bishop Feild. As a boy he had been a good athlete; he had taken his part in the exercises of town and gown days. A good swimmer, a good sailor, patient and cheerful, he learned to love his work, and was thankful that God had called him to do it. Instead of complaining of the hardships and rigorous climate of Newfoundland, he was always ready to state that even on the Labrador coast it was a healthier climate than England, and this in a country where patches of snow were frequently to be seen lying on the fields in July! In 1846 he was cheered by the sympathy of Queen Adelaide, who, on hearing that the church at Placentia Bay had fallen into decay, generously restored it. This church had been built by Prince William (afterwards William IV.) in 1785. But in that year Newfoundland met with a great disaster in the almost complete destruction of

Theological College, St. John's, Newfoundland.

the capital, St. John's, by fire. In this conflagration the parish church was destroyed. Upon this the Bishop went to England with a view to building at St. John's a fine cathedral church. Money to the extent of $35,000 had been promised towards this object, and Sir Gilbert Scott presented Bishop Feild with the plans for the future building. He returned to his work greatly cheered at the prospect of being able to build the church. He had also been promised in England a mission ship, which was to be his own, to enable him to do effective work in his aquatic dioceses. In 1847, when the first sod was turned for the cathedral, the mission ship arrived, " a bonnie wee thing," presented by the primus of Scotland, and called *The Hawk ;* yet she was none too small, for she was quite equal to a voyage across the Atlantic, and was destined to cross more than once.

With this the Bishop was as pleased as a child with a toy. She was fitted up so that her hold formed a long room, which served as a church. With a chaplain and a couple of students who were thus being trained for their future work, Bishop Feild, every other year, sailed this ship in and out of the harbours and coves of Newfoundland. Sometimes he ran great risks from being ignorant of the waters and having no pilot, but as time went on this danger was diminished by his experience. This ship brought many a blessing to a long-neglected and isolated people, and the Bishop, while thankful to have been able to impart some spiritual gifts, would be full of sorrow at his inability to do more. Bishop Feild saw, with true wisdom, that people ought to be trained to support their own clergymen to as great an extent as possible. There were two things that he saw that militated against this. One was relying too much upon endowments, and the other receiving too much support from English societies. With the former of these he was not much troubled, but, as to the latter, he requested the S.P.G. to diminish the salaries of the missionaries by one-half, and to treat his own in the same manner. Bishop and clergy threw themselves upon the generosity of the people, and did not do so in vain. The S.P.G. was thus saved a large sum of money annually, and the people of Newfoundland, poor as they were, were provided with the best possible endowment for the Church in the future by the inculcation of that spirit of liberality and independence which forms the best support for church and congregation anywhere.

In 1847 Bishop Feild was gladdened by the arrival of Rev. Jacob George Mountain, great grandson of the first Bishop of Quebec. His father, the grandson of the Bishop, was Rev. Dr. J. H. Brooke Mountain, Rector of Blunham, Bedfordshire, England. Mr. Mountain was stationed first at Harbour Briton, in Fortune Bay, on the southern coast of Newfoundland.*

In 1848 Bishop Feild visited the dreary coast of Labrador, where, as a rule, a few shivering Indians alone are to be found.

He met here with a worthy couple who had been married by their Roman Catholic servant, whom they caused to read the marriage service to them out of

---

*An interesting account of Mr. Mountain's work in Newfoundland is given in "Lives of Missionaries in North America." S.P.C.K.

the Anglican Book of Common Prayer. Indeed the Bishop and his missionaries frequently met with good, honest couples who, after having their children baptized, asked for the blessing of holy matrimony, which hitherto they had been unable to procure. Such had been the spiritual destitution of this rugged sea-girt mission.

Bishop Feild, though glorying in privations and discomforts himself, had such a tender heart that he never sent a missionary to a lonely spot without feelings of sympathy amounting to sorrow. He said of a Mr. Gifford, whom he left at Labrador, " Here he must stay alone, among utter strangers, common fishermen, without house or home, with no probability of retreat or escape, no prospect of seeing a friend, or even getting a letter for nearly a year. He must eat fish, and little else, in a small kitchen. What a contrast to an English curacy !"

When the Bishop went to Bermuda, where everything was on a very small scale, he delighted in paying personal visits to parishioners of the clergy. He once rode nine miles to see a poor old man who had desired to see him.

In 1850 the nave of the cathedral, which was to be known as that of St. John the Baptist, was completed. Though it was the fashion of those days to sell the pews of a newly-erected church, Bishop Feild was able to open his cathedral with the seats all free.

Long journeys were an easy matter for Bishop Feild. We are not surprised, therefore, to find him at Quebec, the guest of Bishop G. J. Mountain, attending the conference of bishops held in Quebec in 1851.

The Metropolitan, Bishop Fulford of Montreal, Bishop Strachan of Toronto, and Bishop Medley of Fredericton, were also present.*

St. John's Cathedral, St. John's, Newfoundland.

In 1854 cholera visited Newfoundland, and the Bishop, with his clergy, worked heroically through it. So many children were left orphans by it that the

* Some account of this conference has already been given on page 71.

Bishop started the Church of England Orphanage for boys and girls, which afterwards grew into two separate establishments. He had in mind the education of young Eskimo, who should be sent as missionaries to their own people; but he was never able to carry this out to any great extent.

In that year (1854) the Bishop induced the Rev. Jacob G. Mountain, who for seven years had been a hard-working missionary at Harbour Briton, to move to St. John's, to be Principal of the Theological College. In July of that year, Mr. Mountain went to England and married a lady whom he had known in early life; but they were destined to live together only for a short time. Early in 1856, Mr. Mountain was made Rector of St. John's Cathedral, but in the autumn he was attacked with typhus fever and died.

In 1857 the Bishop asked the S.P.G. for a coadjutor bishop. He offered to give up all his salary, if necessary, and he added, with sweet humility, "I should be quite willing, and in some respects prefer, that another bishop, as Bishop of Newfoundland, be appointed, and I act as his coadjutor, without any stipend, save that of a missionary." One would imagine from offers of this kind that Bishop Feild was a man of ample private fortune, but this was not the case. He had little or nothing of his own.

In 1858 the Bishop was enabled to establish a Widows and Orphans' Fund for his diocese, and received subscriptions for it to the amount of about four thousand dollars. By 1864 this had been increased to ten thousand dollars.

Bishop Feild was continually moving about in his mission ship. In 1861 he had the great pleasure of encountering in the Strait of Belle Isle Bishop G. J. Mountain and his son (and future biographer), Rev. A. Mountain. Bishop Mountain, as Bishop of Quebec, was also upon a visitation in his part of Labrador. It was delightful for these two missionary Bishops to meet thus in the dreary waters of Labrador. The Bishop of Newfoundland entertained his unexpected but warmly welcomed guests upon his ship, and only on the third day would he let them depart. The day following this departure was the Bishop of Quebec's seventy-second birthday.

In 1866 Bishop Feild was in England, and in the spring of 1867 he was married to the widow of his former missionary and rector in Newfoundland, Rev. Jacob Mountain. In that year also he procured the appointment of his Archdeacon, Ven. J. B. Kelly, as his coadjutor, who came to England for consecration, and, with his Bishop, attended the Lambeth Conference.

On his return to Newfoundland, Bishop Feild made another voyage of visitation in *The Hawk;* but this vessel, which had done such faithful service for twenty-five years, was, in time, pronounced dangerous, and sold. Another ship, the *Star*, had been lost, but in 1872 Lieutenant Curling, officer of engineers, admiring the life, labours, and character of Bishop Feild, presented for Church work in Newfoundland his own splendid yacht, the *Lavrock*, and along with it the giver gave himself as a missionary in one of the roughest fields of Newfoundland.

In 1870 the Bishop was able to form an endowment fund for the bishopric of Newfoundland, which to him was a great source of satisfaction, as a large portion of the episcopal income would die with him.

Bishop Feild tried to keep pace with his age. It was an age when synods were beginning to be formed. In 1871 he was able to preside over his own first synod. Feeling the end of his days approaching, the Bishop retired to Bermuda, where he died on the 8th June, 1877. He was buried in Bermuda, much to the regret of the Church people of Newfoundland, who would have deemed themselves highly honoured if the remains of such a man could have rested with them.

Bishop Feild was a man of indomitable courage and perseverance. A greater man for work probably has never been known. He would encounter dangers which he would not allow others to meet. Towards the close of his life a dangerous journey had to be taken by a young missionary. The Bishop would not let him go, but declared he would go himself, and when the annoyed clergyman asked for an explanation of this the Bishop told him that he was young yet, and had many years of usefulness left in him for the Church, but as for himself his days were nearly ended, and, should he perish, it did not matter. He was a High Churchman, and never sought to disguise the fact, but he always took great pains to show reasons for everything that he did. He was not a ready speaker. When told of the sudden death of the great Bishop Wilberforce (in 1873), he said: "Think of my inability to address a congregation of even poor fishermen with readiness and effect, but the stammering tongue may speak when the dead is silenced forever." He was a man who walked with God by a constant round of devotion and prayer. If he could not obtain privacy for his devotions, as upon the deck of a vessel, he would not omit them because of the presence of others, but aloud he would repeat them, because they brought him nearer to God. He was frequently heard at night repeating his psalmody and prayers, when he supposed that all near him were asleep.

His energy was great. He left fifty clergy where he had found but twelve. He had established a good theological college, raised a Widows and Orphans' Fund, and an Episcopal Endowment Fund (of about $60,000). He had also built a cathedral, which for many years was the pride of all Newfoundland. Fire has since destroyed it, but it stood for years as he left it, the rudiments of the most imposing specimen of pointed architecture on this side of the Atlantic.

A Mission Station in Newfoundland.

10. The Most Rev. John Medley, D.D., First Bishop of Fredericton and Second Metropolitan of (Eastern) Canada.

INTO the wilderness of New Brunswick came, in 1783, and afterwards, many thousands of loyal British subjects, seeking a refuge from the oppressions of rebellion in the United States. Many of these were Church people; some of them, indeed, were clergymen. As already noticed, parishes were gradually formed by these people, and, as time went on, the Church gathered strength. But it was left for many years practically without episcopal supervision, for, though it formed part of the Diocese of Nova Scotia, it received at first but little benefit from the Bishop, owing to the enormous territory of which it formed a part; and what little benefit it did receive was soon discontinued. For the last ten years of the life of Bishop Charles Inglis that distinguished prelate was unable, through failing strength, to take any active supervision of the diocese; and for seven years the second Bishop of Nova Scotia, at the very beginning of his episcopate, was obliged to reside in England. It was not till Dr. John Inglis, the third Bishop of Nova Scotia, commenced his work that the diocese began to realize that there was a hand at the helm.

The division of New Brunswick into a separate archdeaconry, coupled with occasional visitations by the

THE MOST REV. JOHN MEDLEY, D.D.
First Bishop of Fredericton and Second Metropolitan of Canada.
Born, 1804. Consecrated, 1845. Died, 1892.

Bishop, gave a new and vigorous impetus to Church work within its bounds. The Archdeacon of New Brunswick, the Venerable G. Coster, was a practical leader, and under him a Church Society was formed on September 8th, 1836, the first systematic attempt made in a British colony for the more full and efficient support of its own Church.*

At this time there were in New Brunswick eighty parishes, twenty-eight clergymen, and forty-three churches or chapels. A great many parishes, therefore, were vacant, and the few clergy that occupied positions were supported almost entirely by the S.P.G. In 1843 this Society voted the munificent sum of £20,000 (nearly $100,000) towards the endowment of a bishopric in New Brunswick.

In the meantime, the Chief Justice, the Solicitor-General, and other leading persons in the colony itself, had managed to raise over $10,000 towards the same object.† Thus was the proposed diocese liberally and substantially endowed from the very outset. The position was offered by the Archbishop of Canterbury to the Rev. John Medley, Vicar of St. Thomas' Church, Exeter, and Prebendary of Exeter Cathedral.

Born on December 19th, 1804, deprived of his father, Mr. George Medley, of Grosvenor Place, London, when he was a little child, he was early taught to lean upon his mother, in whom he had a safe and pious guide. From her journal it transpired that he began Latin when he was six years old, Greek when he

* "Annals of the Colonial Church." By Ernest Hawkins.

† "The Life and Work of the Most Rev. John Medley, D.D." By Rev. Canon W. Q. Ketchum, D.D.

was ten, and Hebrew when he was twelve. He was educated at Wadham College, Oxford, where he graduated with honours in 1826. In the hall of this college there is a life-size painting of him as Bishop in his robes. He was ordained deacon in 1828, and priest in 1829. He served as curate at Southleigh, Devonshire, incumbent of St. John's, Truro, and vicar of St. Thomas', Exeter. He was consecrated Bishop of Fredericton (the capital of New Brunswick) on the 4th May, 1845, at the chapel of Lambeth Palace, London. At this time he was a widower, his wife having died in 1841, leaving six children to her husband's care. His eldest daughter, who succeeded to the management of his house, had also died; and, strange to say, his mother, who broke up her own home to take care of his, was killed by being thrown from a carriage, while seated by her son's side. Thus it was an afflicted man who accepted the bishopric of Fredericton. Indeed, the entire change from English life to hard missionary labours in New Brunswick may have been hailed by him as a blessing.

The newly appointed Bishop arrived in Fredericton on St. Barnabas' Day, 1845, and met with an enthusiastic reception. In the autumn of that year he prepared to build a cathedral. Fresh from Exeter, he had a natural desire to reproduce in his distant diocese some grand edifice that might, alike, remind him of his home and form a centre of Church activity and power. A site was presented, the stone promised, and £4,500 (in five years) subscribed. The foundation stone was laid on the 15th of October, 1845, in the presence of the Lieutenant-Governor, members of the Legislative Council, the officers of the 33rd Regiment, and many others. The work, however, went on slowly, for the people did not show much enthusiasm about it.

In 1846 the Bishop paid an extended visit through his diocese. There were no railways, and but few steamers, yet we read that he travelled 2,859 miles in that year. He also ordained five deacons and two priests, confirmed 504 candidates, and consecrated two churches. Full and graphic descriptions of his journeys are to be found in the reports of the S.P.G.

He was delighted with his new work, and had no hard words to say of his life in the wilderness. He expressed admiration for the climate, which, though hotter and colder than that of England, yet had none of the chilly, starving feeling of cold and wet together. "The sunshine on the snow" was a thing of great beauty to him.

In 1847 the number of his clergy had increased from twenty-nine to forty-three, and in that year he divided the diocese into seven deaneries, a rural dean for each being appointed by the clergy.

But funds were needed for the building of his cathedral, and for travelling missionaries; candidates were needed for Holy Orders, and books for his cathedral library. To procure aid toward all these objects he went to England in 1848. His family accompanied him. He received aid for his cathedral to the extent of about $15,000, chiefly through the Society for the Promotion of Christian Knowledge. £350 were granted by the S.P.G. for additional missionaries, and the University of Oxford gave £100 towards his cathedral library—besides which he received many gifts in books. He also procured an organ for his chapel.

Bishop Medley was not only a good scholar, but he was also a man of refined tastes and many accomplishments. He was much interested in architecture, and was a good musician. Church music was beginning to change, from the style of Tate and Brady to that which produced Hymns Ancient and Modern; and the Bishop did all he could to promote this improvement in his own diocese. A special hymn book was prepared, which served for use in the diocese until replaced by Hymns Ancient and Modern. Many chaste anthems and services were composed by him. He was well pleased, on his return to Fredericton, to place the organ in the chapel. In 1851, Bishop Feild, of Newfoundland, visited Fredericton. The two Bishops then journeyed together to Boston and to Montreal, where they were met by Bishop Strachan, of Toronto. The three Bishops then went to Quebec, where the venerable Bishop, Dr. G. J. Mountain, warmly welcomed them. From there Bishop Medley proceeded alone to New York, Philadelphia, and other places in the United States.

The object of his journey seems to have been to collect money for the cathedral, for we read that the Bishop, through the liberality of many friends, especially in New York, secured £180 for that purpose. The work of the cathedral went on very slowly. At one time it came to a standstill—there was no money. The Bishop betook himself to prayer, spending a whole night in supplication, that he might be able to finish the work which he had begun. In those days the English mail came but once a month. On the morning after this night of prayer it arrived, and brought him a cheque for £500, accompanied merely by the words, "To the glory of God, and for the completion of Fredericton Cathedral. F.S.M." This turned the scale; more money came in; the cathedral was completed. On a stone in the southwest pier of the tower arch are the

The Anglican Cathedral, Fredericton, N.B.

letters "F.S.M." This was the first stone laid after the Bishop's prayers were so signally answered. The

Bishop became personally responsible for the remaining debt, and the cathedral was consecrated on the 31st of August, 1853. At this service the venerable Bishop G. J. Mountain, of Quebec, was happily present. Fredericton had been his first charge after his father had ordained him to the sacred ministry.

Before the close of the year 1854, by subscriptions and money received from England, the Bishop was relieved of the personal responsibility he had assumed. In connection with this there is a very pleasing incident related of an old Sunday-school pupil of the Bishop's. His name was George Hatherley. Being a traveller for a tea merchant in Bristol, he carried with him wherever he went a subscription book for his old Sunday-school teacher's cathedral, and pleaded so earnestly that he was able to send contributions to the Bishop amounting to about $2,500.

On the 19th of December, 1854, the Bishop wrote these words: "On my birthday received a letter from Mr. Hatherley, who has collected sufficient to pay off all the cathedral debt, for which great mercy all praise be to God. Thus is the year of trouble and perplexity joyfully ended through the never-ending goodness of my God."

The Bishop, though apparently stern, was uniformly kind, and especially so towards those who differed from him in their views. A clergyman of well-known evangelical views, on hearing the Bishop preach on one occasion, accused him of not preaching Christ; on which the Bishop sat down beside him and explained matters so gently and clearly that the clergyman was ever afterwards his true friend. Another said to him once, rather boastfully, "You know, my lord, I am a Low Churchman." "I hope, sir," said the Bishop, "that you are a humble one." The Bishop also was not without a sense of humour. On one of his voyages across the Atlantic, a lady—one of the autograph-hunting type—besieged the Bishop for his signature. For the sake of peace he wrote in her book, "J. Fredericton." Not satisfied, the lady, handing the book to him again, said: "I want you to say what you are"; whereupon the Bishop wrote beneath his name, "A miserable sinner."

His mode of life at Bishopscote (his residence, close to the cathedral) was exceedingly plain and simple, and in this way money was saved for the poor and for the Church. Yet there was ever a warm welcome at the See house, where high culture and good taste were always evident. Bishop Medley did not readily take up the idea of forming a diocesan synod. One was formed, however, in 1862, and was incorporated by the Provincial Legislature.

We have stated elsewhere that the dioceses of Quebec, Toronto, Huron, Montreal, and Ontario formed a Provincial Synod in 1861, with the Bishop of Montreal as Metropolitan. This Provincial Synod met again in 1865, 1868, 1871, 1872, and 1873; but by this time the word Canada had been enlarged so as to embrace the whole of British territory in America, extending from the Atlantic Ocean on the east to the Pacific Ocean on the west. This led, naturally, to an extension of the Provincial Synod, and the dioceses to the east of Quebec, namely, Nova Scotia and Fredericton (Newfoundland not having been included in the

Dominion of Canada), were invited to send delegates to this Synod.

Accordingly at the eighth session held in Montreal, from the 9th to the 16th of September, 1874, delegates from Nova Scotia and Fredericton were present.

The clergy from Fredericton were Rev. F. H. J. Brigstocke, Rev. Canon de Veber, Rev. Canon Medley (son of Bishop Medley), Rev. Canon Scovil, Rev. Canon Ketchum, Rev. John Pearson, Rev. F. Partridge, Rev. T. E. Dowling, Rev. G. M. Armstrong, Rev. Dr. Jarvis, Rev. G. G. Roberts, and Rev. G. Schofield.

The laity appointed were Hon. Chief Justice Ritchie, Hon. R. D. Wilmot, Lieutenant-Colonel Maunsell, and Messrs. H. W. Frith, C. W. Weldon, G. Sydney Smith, W. Carman, Hurd Peters, W. Wilkinson, R. T. Clinch, D. Street, and G. W. Whitney.

All these were present except Mr. Peters. With these, of course, came the Bishop of Fredericton and the Bishop of Nova Scotia, who took their seats in the Upper House.

In the year 1878, the Bishop of Fredericton, being the senior bishop of the Ecclesiastical Province of (eastern) Canada, was appointed by the House of Bishops, Metropolitan, and in that year he attended the second meeting of the Lambeth Conference in England. The first meeting of the Provincial Synod under his presidency was opened in Montreal on September 8th, 1880, on which occasion the Synod presented His Lordship with a handsome crozier, or metropolitan staff, which for several sessions afterwards preceded his venerable form in the processions connected with them.

In 1881 the venerable Metropolitan began to feel the weight of years, and, fearing that his diocese might suffer through that, he asked his Synod to give him a coadjutor. The Synod expressed its willingness to do so, and, by the recommendation of the Metropolitan, the choice fell upon the Rev. H. Tully Kingdon, Vicar of Good Easter, Essex, his own city. The Metropolitan made over the half of his income for the support of Bishop Kingdon.

In 1885 Bishop Medley completed the fortieth year of his episcopate, to mark which event the clergy and laity of the diocese subscribed about $6,000 towards what they knew would please him best, the assistance of candidates for the ministry in their college course. It was called "The Bishop Medley Scholarship Fund."

At the age of eighty-four the Metropolitan attended the third Lambeth Conference, which met in July, 1888. He returned safely to his diocese in the September of that year.

On the 25th of August, 1889, the Bishop's second son, Charles (the Rev. Canon Medley), died a painful death from cancer of the throat. He had been his father's companion and right-hand man in the many years of his long episcopate, and his melancholy death had a visible effect upon his aged father, yet he persevered in his work. He sprained his right hand, but, with characteristic energy, he learned to write with his left hand.

On the 17th July, 1892, he preached in St. Paul's Church, St. John, a touching and impressive sermon, which was heard distinctly in all parts of the church. In a few days he returned to Fredericton, where he was taken ill, but lingered until the summer began to pass away. He frequently became unconscious, but the cathedral bells chiming for evensong always revived him. "Why, there are my bells! Yes, they are my bells," he would say, with a pleased expression upon his face. His last connected words were, "O Lamb of God, that taketh away the sins of the world, grant me Thy peace." He died on Friday, September 9th, 1892, at half-past eight in the morning, at the advanced age of eighty-eight.

The Old Trinity Church, St. John, N.B., as enlarged in 1856.

It has since been replaced by the present splendid church of which the Venerable Archdeacon Brigstocke is the rector.

THE RT. REV. DAVID ANDERSON, D.D.
First Bishop of Rupert's Land.
Born, 1814.   Consecrated, 1849.   Resigned, 1864.   Died, 1885.

11. The Right Rev. David Anderson, D.D., First Bishop of Rupert's Land.

THE term Rupert's Land was originally a very extensive one. It embraced that enormous territory which Captain Sir W. F. Butler, in the fascinating book which he wrote on the subject, so aptly termed " The Great Lone Land." It was discovered by Hudson in 1610, and his name is still connected with that great northern sheet of water well known as Hudson's Bay. In the reign of Charles II., in the year 1670, an incorporated body known as the Hudson's Bay Company was formed in England by letters patent under the great seal of England, with Prince Rupert at its head. In these letters patent it was ordained that the territories granted to the company should be " reckoned as one of the King's plantations and colonies in America called Rupert's Land." This company formed trading posts in different parts of the wide territory, for the purpose of trading with the Indians. The officers and clerks of this company were content to live very lonely lives. The only news they received from the outside world was on the arrival of the Hudson's Bay ship from England once a year. Latterly some letters were brought in by the Governor of Rupert's Land, Sir G. Simpson, when he came in spring from Montreal by canoe to attend the Counci of Rupert's Land.

It is related of one of the chief factors or managers of this company that he, being a subscriber to the *Times*, was content to receive a whole year's supply of the paper—over three hundred copies—at once! He managed the reading of all this literature, however, quite systematically. His instructions to his servants were to put one paper on his breakfast table every morning, in the strict order of the dates, beginning at the first even unto the last, and there in the lone wilderness this contented man read his newspaper every day, quite regardless of how old the news might be. He knew he had a year for it all, and it might as well dawn upon him gradually.

By trading in valuable furs, and other commodities of a cold region, much wealth was amassed; but for two hundred years nothing was done in a spiritual way either for the people connected with the fort, or for the aborigines. The prayers of the Anglican Church, it is true, were read at the Hudson's Bay forts, and occasionally an officer interested himself in the people at his post. In 1815 the Governor of this country, Major Semple, reported on this subject as follows: "I have trodden the burnt ruins of houses, barns, a mill, a fort, and sharpened stockades, but none of a place of worship, even upon the smallest scale. I blush to say that over the whole extent of the Hudson's Bay territories no such building exists." Five years after this the company itself sent out a chaplain, the Rev. John West. Mr. West was also appointed a missionary by the C.M.S. He proceeded to the Red River Settlement. Here he built a church and a schoolhouse on a lot set apart for Church purposes by the Hudson's Bay Company, which has been since known as St. John's Church lot, and is within the city of Winnipeg. He visited several Hudson's Bay posts, and ministered, in addition to the company's officers and servants, to a small Scotch colony and to retired servants of the company and their families of mixed blood. But he took great interest in the Indian natives. He had brought down with him from York Factory two Indian boys, one of whom, after fourteen months' instruction, he baptized and named Henry Budd, after his rector in England, the Rev. Henry Budd, one of the founders of the C.M.S. This society sent out another missionary, the Rev. David Jones, in 1823, who agreed to fill the place of Mr. West during a visit he paid to England. But on Mr. West remaining in England, the Rev. D. Jones was appointed as chaplain by the Hudson's Bay Company, and the C.M.S. then sent out in 1825 another missionary, the Rev. A. Cochrane. Mr. Jones built at Image Plain a church, which is now St. Paul's Church. Mr. Cochrane settled at the Grand Rapids of the Red river, now known as St. Andrew's, where he built a church, the third church of the settlement. This able missionary was everything to these people, " minister, clerk, schoolmaster, arbitrator, peace-maker, and agricultural director." In 1832 Mr. Cochrane established a mission further down the river among the Indians. Though up to this time there had been no direct effort on any Indian tribe, there had been a number of Indian pupils received and instructed in the Mission House at St. John's, and careful attention and instruction given to the large body of at least 1,500 halfbreeds who had settled in the districts round the missions. Visits had also been paid to the nearer tribes. In 1841 the Rev. Abraham Cowley joined the mission. It was no easy matter either to reach the Northwest in those days, or to live in it. He came to Quebec with his wife, hoping to join an expedition to the Northwest, but found that, after all, his shortest route would be to return to England and take the first vessel bound from thence to Hudson's Bay. So back to England he went, and from thence to Hudson's Bay, from which he and Mrs. Cowley journeyed for 800 miles by canoe, and at length reached Red River.

Such was the state of things when, in 1844, Bishop G. J. Mountain, of Quebec, paid, at the request and by the arrangements of the C.M.S., his memorable visit to the Red River Settlement. The total population of the Red River was then 5,143, of whom 2,798 were Roman Catholics.[*] Bishop Mountain found four churches attended by 1,700 persons, and nine schools with 485 scholars. Including halfbreeds and Europeans, 846 persons were confirmed. The number of communicants was 454, but in two of the churches "there was no communion table, and no place reserved for it."

In his report of this visit, the Bishop makes an incidental reference to the "Leith bequest."[†] This was a sum of money £12,000 ($60,000) bequeathed by Mr. Alexander Leith, a chief factor of the Hudson's Bay Company, for missionary purposes. The trustees

[*] S.P.G. Digest., p. 178. See also under Bishop G. J. Mountain, p. 68.
[†] See "Journal of Bishop of Montreal," C.M.S.

of Leith's charity obtained a decree from the Court of Chancery, approving of a scheme for the due administration of the funds of the charity, and carrying into effect in the way that seemed most fitting the charitable purposes designed by Mr. Leith's will. This scheme for establishing a bishopric was aided by the Hudson's Bay Company binding themselves at the same time to contribute £300 ($1,500) per annum towards the Bishop's stipend. When Bishop G. J. Mountain heard of this he wrote to the S.P.G., "I bless God to learn that my prayers have been heard on behalf of Red River."

The bishopric was offered to the Rev. David Anderson and accepted by him. He was born in 1814, and was educated with Archibald Campbell Tait, late Archbishop of Canterbury, as one of his classmates at Edinburgh Academy. He became a scholar of Exeter College, Oxford, from which he graduated in honours in 1836. In 1841 he married the eldest daughter of James Marsden, Esq., of Liverpool. His wife died in 1848, leaving him with three sons. He was consecrated at Canterbury Cathedral on the 29th of May, 1849, and arrived at York Factory (Hudson's Bay) on the 16th of August. He was accompanied by his sister, Miss Anderson, and his three sons. His sister was his constant companion in all his work. They reached the Red River Settlement on the third of October.

On the very day of his arrival, Rev. John Macallum, who for years had successfully carried on, under the name of the Red River Academy, the school established by the Rev. D. Jones, died, and the Bishop, being an accomplished scholar, immediately took up his work as that which first came to his hand. The first church the Bishop preached in was the old one at St. Andrew's. The Bishop said of it : " The appearance of the congregation is very devotional ; they respond well ; they sing with heart and soul. The first burst of music, when they all joined in the psalm of praise, quite upset and overpowered me ; indeed, I have not heard any sound sweeter in my ears since I left England." A glance at a map of North America will show what an enormous territory had fallen to his lot as a diocese. In the "Great Lone Land" he was "monarch of all he surveyed."

The winters were long and dreary, and travelling tedious—in summer by canoes or boat, in winter by dog-sleighs. The Bishop's first confirmation took place in May, 1850, the candidates numbering nearly four hundred. At his second ordination, also in that year, Mr. Henry Budd, the native Indian already mentioned, was ordained deacon, and proved to be for years a most useful and faithful pastor. He had already been a most successful catechist.

At the request of the Bishop, in 1850, the S.P.G. sent Rev. W. H. Taylor, of Newfoundland, to take charge of a small settlement on the Assiniboine river, now St. James' parish, a great part of which is in the city of Winnipeg.

He thus speaks of his journey: "We had been six weeks or more journeying over the extensive prairies which lie between the United States and this country. We had been in the wilderness exposed to the savage hordes of Indians, and the wild beasts, scarcely less fearful; and the sight of neat and quiet dwellings, with their apparent safety and comfort, was most pleasing. So we travelled down the Assiniboine to the settlement on the Red river; we could see the little farms on the river's side, and the banks filled with stacks of corn and fodder, with vast herds grazing at large in the plains. Then the French church, the fort, and in the distance the English church and the Bishop's house, told us that we were again in a land where the true God was known and worshipped."

Here, near Fort Garry, within sight of the scalps suspended over the graves of the dead on the very spot where for years the heathen revels had been performed, was built in due time, by the Society's aid, a temple to the living God. In May, 1852, before either church or parsonage was finished, a devastating flood swept over the surrounding district, and the parsonage and glebe became a place of safety for a homeless, houseless population, including the Bishop and his family.

When the Bishop arrived in his diocese there were only five clergymen in it. In 1851 there were nine; four having parochial charges, and the others being purely missionaries. In 1852 he visited the shores of James' Bay. The journey was made in a birch-bark canoe, and occupied twenty-six days and a half. Here he ordained to the diaconate Mr. John Horden, who had been sent out by the Church Missionary Society to labour at Moose Fort, in the region of Hudson's Bay, and before his departure for home he ordained him priest. This was the future Bishop of Moosonee. In 1853 Mr. (afterwards Archdeacon) Cochrane was sent out as a missionary to Portage la

Prairie, where, with the aid of the Bishop, the Governor, and other friends, he built a church, and there he remained till his death in 1865. In 1855 the Rev. Mr. Taylor's mission became the organized parish of St. James', Assiniboine. The church was consecrated on the 29th of May, and lent its aid in raising the tone of public worship in the diocese.

Bishop Anderson had worked at the school unexpectedly cast upon his hands by the death of Mr. Macallum. The Bishop thus referred to it in his primary charge: "Dying the day of my entrance into the Red River, his wish was that the first offer of it should be made to me by those whom he had left behind; and God seemed to direct me not to refuse. It has laid upon me more of labour, but that labour has been its own reward. To it, in anticipation of the future, I have given the name of 'St. John's Collegiate School.' Should I be permitted to rebuild the church there, it would be St. John's, my own cathedral church, called so after the apostle of whom we think to-day. Near it would be rebuilt, then, if circumstances permit, with more of architectural plan, the collegiate school. As a part of it at present, and hereafter it may be a separate building, would be the institution for the training of a native ministry, St. John's College; and over all, whether the youth training in wisdom's ways and growing daily in earthly knowledge, or those to be prepared in theological study for the service of the sanctuary, I would write as the motto of duty and hope, 'In Thy light shall we see light.'" The Bishop later on gave the school the name of St. John's College, and formed a College

Board; but after some years the college was closed, and remained closed for about nine years.

In 1856 Bishop Anderson visited England, where he secured some money to help him build a cathedral and further other missionary work. The Hudson's Bay Company subscribed £500 towards the cathedral,

St. John's Cathedral, Winnipeg.

and a similar amount was given by the Society for the Promotion of Christian Knowledge. The building was erected according to English plans that were reduced, but through imperfect workmanship proved a failure. The tower, being unsafe, had to be taken down. The cathedral is still used as such, but is quite different from what was contemplated; yet its cost was out of all proportion to its real value. In 1862 the S.P.G. formed a mission at Fort Ellice, or Beaver Creek, two hundred and forty miles west of Winnipeg, on the

Assiniboine river, where the Rev. T. Cook, a native of the country, ministered to the Indians, as well as to the few English settlers in reach of him, and to half-breeds.

Of the labours of Bishop Anderson we cannot speak in detail. By 1864 his clergy had increased to twenty-three. In that year he returned to England, where he remained, resigning the see on the 4th of October. He was a man of sympathetic and gentle nature. The Indians were special objects of his anxious care. He was known to them as their great praying father; he rejoiced in their conversion; he grieved over their sad condition as heathen.

The accounts of his journeys throughout his boundless see are deeply interesting. All signs of improvement were to him a great joy. By his gentle, pious, and devoted life he witnessed in the midst of his clergy and people, for fifteen years, a good confession, which left its impression long after his bodily presence was removed from their midst. On his resignation of the diocese his old friend, Bishop Tait, then Bishop of London, made him Chancellor of St. Paul's Cathedral. He subsequently became Vicar of Clifton. A sad and lingering illness, which deprived him of all power of thought and speech, attacked him in 1878, and in this condition he lingered till 1885, when he passed quietly away to his eternal rest.

THE MOST REV. FRANCIS FULFORD, D.D.
First Bishop of Montreal and First Metropolitan of Canada.
Born, 1803. Consecrated, 1850. Died, 1868.

12. THE MOST REV. FRANCIS FULFORD, D.D., FIRST BISHOP OF MONTREAL, AND FIRST METROPOLITAN OF (EASTERN) CANADA.

WHEN Jacques Cartier, in 1535, sailed up "the goodly great gulf full of islands, passages, and entrances," on St. Lawrence Day, he gave for all time to the noble river the name of the saint commemorated; and on his journey halted at the promontory since called Quebec, but then known as Stadacona. Here he met some Indians whose chief was Donnacona, "the lord of Canada"; but he did not linger long; before him lay the noble river which he greatly desired further to explore. He pushed westward until, on the 3rd of October, 1535, he reached the Indian village of Hochelaga, a mere collection of cabins, surrounded by palisades, and built amid fields of Indian corn. Here dwelt fully a thousand natives, who extended to the bold navigator a cordial welcome. Cartier called this place Mount Royal, and hence its name Montreal.

Seventy-three years afterwards (in 1608) Champlain laid the foundation of the present city of Quebec, and one hundred and five years afterwards (in 1640) a few houses were built on the site of the Indian village of Hochelaga, and formed the commencement of the city of Montreal.

From the very beginning it became noted as a trading post. In 1720 it was said to have had a population of 3,000. When Quebec was captured by General Wolfe, in 1759, Montreal in the following year was taken possession of by the British troops. But its former occupants, the French, were treated with a liberality not usually granted to the vanquished, with the result that the city has ever been as it is now, in point of numbers, more French than English. The S.P.G., therefore, sent the Rev. David Chabrand de Lisle, a French-speaking clergyman, a native of Switzerland, to minister to French and English as best he could in Montreal. This did not prove to be a very good policy, for the British did not like Mr. de Lisle's broken English, and the French did not care very much for his religion.

The first service was held in a church which formerly belonged to the Jesuits' college, on December 20th, 1789. This church was called Christ Church, at the suggestion, it is said, of Bishop Charles

Old Christ Church, Montreal.

Inglis, of Nova Scotia. In it ministered Rev. Mr. de Lisle, then Rev. Mr. Tunstall, and in 1801 Rev. Dr. Mountain, brother of the first Bishop of Quebec. In 1803 the church was burned, and in 1805 the foundation stone of a new and substantial Christ Church was laid, but the church was not opened for worship till 1814.

In 1815 Dr. Mountain died, and was succeeded by his curate, Rev. John Leeds. In 1820 Montreal was made a rectory by royal letters patent, and Rev. John Bethune (who had been a pupil at Cornwall to Rev. Dr. Strachan, afterwards Bishop of Toronto) was appointed first rector.

Early in 1836 Dr. G. J. Mountain was consecrated Coadjutor Bishop of Quebec, with the title of "Bishop of Montreal," but it was a mere title. The Bishop of Quebec (Dr. Stewart) died almost immediately afterwards, and Bishop Mountain succeeded him. At that time (1836) the parishes and missions in the Montreal part of the diocese were Montreal, Sorel, Abbotsford, Chambly, St. John's, Clarenceville, Frelighsburg, Philipsburgh, Stanbridge, Dunham, Shefford, Rawdon, St. Andrews, Grenville, Hull, and Coteau du Lac.

Bishop G. J. Mountain's ardent desire to see Montreal formed into a separate diocese was at length, after much patient waiting, gratified. In 1849 Rupert's Land was formed into a separate diocese largely by his exertions, and in the following year he received intimation that Her Majesty had been pleased to form a new diocese with Montreal as its see city. The clergyman chosen for the position was Rev. Francis Fulford, minister of Curzon Chapel, Mayfair. He was the second son of Baldwin Fulford, Esq., of Great Fulford, England, and was born at Sidmouth on the 30th of June, 1803. He graduated from Exeter College, Oxford, in 1824, and was made a deacon in 1826, and a priest in 1828. He occupied successively the rectories of Trowbridge (Wiltshire) and Croydon (Cambridgeshire) before he was minister at Mayfair.

He was consecrated Bishop of Montreal in Westminster Abbey on the 25th of July, 1850, at the age of 47. It was at a time when great burning questions began to agitate the Anglican Church. The Oxford movement was causing intense excitement, not only at home, but abroad. It was felt in Canada as elsewhere. The men who originated that movement were contemporaries of Francis Fulford. The arrival of the new Bishop was, therefore, eagerly looked for. This took place on the 12th of September, 1850, when His Lordship and Mrs. Fulford, with their son and daughter, took up their abode in the city of Montreal.

Hard work lay before the new Bishop, but from it he flinched not. A month after his arrival the Church Society of the Diocese of Montreal was formed. Soon he held visitations of his clergy, and the general work of diocesan machinery began to tell for good upon the Church.

In 1856 the old Christ Church, which had been made the cathedral church of the diocese, was totally destroyed by fire. At first this was looked upon as a disaster; but it eventuated in the construction of another building on a different site—a structure which was somewhat worthy of the fine city of which it was to be the cathedral. It stands to-day a fitting monument to the memory of the first Bishop of Montreal and a bright ornament to the city. When, however, the cost

Christ Church Cathedral, Montreal.

of this building came to be counted up, it was found that a very heavy debt rested on it, to lessen which the

Bishop cut off all possible expenditure in his household, moving to a small dwelling and submitting to the discomfort of rigid economy. Thus do clergymen often submit to personal sacrifice on account of burdens which a wealthy laity could easily relieve. The Bishop lived, however, to see much reward for his self-denial, as the debt was greatly diminished before his death.

Bishop Fulford wielded considerable influence over all men in his diocese. He was not allied to any particular party in the Church, but gave himself to the general welfare of the great body in which he was an important officer. His prudence, firmness, and devotion made him a good and wise ruler; and many a dispute and misunderstanding was quietly repressed by his own unostentatious exertions. He was unwearying in his journeys, in holding meetings and devising plans for the welfare of his diocese. He spoke readily and earnestly when addressing the young people at his confirmations, and his sermons were usually characterized with much force and fervour. Under his rule the Church exhibited signs of life and activity it had never possessed before.

In 1859 the diocesan synods of Quebec, Toronto, and Montreal petitioned the Queen to appoint one of the Canadian bishops to preside over the general assemblies of the Church in the province, the result of which was that Bishop Fulford was appointed Metropolitan of Canada, with Montreal as the metropolitical see; and in 1861 the first Provincial Synod was organized and held in that city. The delegates appointed to represent the Diocese of Montreal at that Synod were as follows:

Clergy.—The Very Rev. John Bethune, D.D. ; Rev. Joseph Scott, D.D. ; Rev. William T. Leach, D.C.L., LL.D. ; Rev. Charles Bancroft, D.D. ; Rev. E. DuVernet, M.A. ; Rev. William Anderson, Rev. G. Slack, M.A., Rural Dean ; Rev. D. Lindsay, M.A. ; Rev. Gerald de C. O'Grady, M.A., Rural Dean ; Rev. W. B. Bond, Rev. J. Flanagan, Rev. J. C. Davidson.

Laity.—Hon. George Moffatt, Hon. Judge McCord, Major Campbell, C.B. ; Hon. Hiram Foster, M.L.C. ; Hon. Philip H. Moore, M.L.C. ; and Messrs. Edward Carter, Hugh Taylor, J. Armstrong, L. S. Huntingdon (M.P.P.), Charles Smallwood (M.D.), R. A. Young, and William Barrett.

The Metropolitan presided over this meeting with dignity and ability. His address to the Synod was worthy of the occasion. It may be interesting, as a matter of history, to recall a few of his opening words :

"There are two of my Right Reverend brethren who, from their age and long and active labours, no less than their office, may in an especial manner be looked upon as fathers of the Church in Canada, and of many of its important institutions Our senior prelate, the Lord Bishop of Quebec, in an address he made to his own synod last year, spoke of the commencement, within the recollection of some aged men still living, of the episcopate of the first Anglican bishop in this country, with but five clergymen in the whole province, with which his diocese was co-extensive. Though the clergy had been largely increased, yet still they were but few and widely scattered when my Right Reverend brother himself succeeded as the bishop of the same undivided diocese, now upwards of a quarter of a century ago; while my Right Reverend brother of Toronto has stated that at the time of his ordination by the first Bishop of Quebec, in 1803, he made but the fifth clergyman in the whole of the Upper Province. We are assembled here as the representatives of five separate dioceses (reckoning that of Ontario), with not less than three hundred and fifty clergy officiating in them."

The first suggestion to hold a "Pan-Anglican" Synod—a synod which was to embrace representative Churchmen of the Anglican communion throughout the world—came from the newly-formed Ecclesiastical Province of Canada. In this great assembly, which was duly held in England, the Metropolitan of Canada took a prominent part; but on his return to Montreal in 1868 he gave unmistakable signs of failing health, and on the 9th of September, 1868, while the Provincial Synod was in session, the good Bishop, at the close of the day, quietly passed to his place in the Church at rest. He had arrived in Montreal on the 12th of September, 1850, and on the same day, eighteen years afterwards, his remains were placed in the quiet earth. All classes of people mourned his loss. The tolling of the bell of the Anglican cathedral was answered by the tolling of the great bell of the Roman Catholic Church of Notre Dame, as a sorrowing procession followed his remains to the cemetery of Mount Royal.

THE RT. REV. HIBBERT BINNEY, D.D.
Fourth Bishop of Nova Scotia.
Born, 1819.   Consecrated, 1851.   Died, 1887.

13. THE RIGHT REV. HIBBERT BINNEY, D.D., FOURTH BISHOP OF NOVA SCOTIA.

ON the death of Bishop John Inglis, the Rev. Hibbert Binney was appointed by the British Crown to succeed him. His father, Rev. Hibbert Binney, was of New England descent, the Binney family having moved to Nova Scotia from Massachusetts. He graduated from King's College, Windsor, in 1811, and received from that college, in 1827, the degree of D.C.L. He was stationed at Granville, Sackville, and finally at Sydney and Arichat, in Cape Breton Island. He married Henrietta Lavinia, daughter of the Honourable Richard Stout, of Cape Breton. While in Cape Breton Island his son, the future bishop, was born—on August 12th, 1819. His father soon afterwards returned to England, where, in 1838, he became rector of Newbury, in Berkshire.

The younger Hibbert received his education at King's College, London, and afterwards at Worcester College, Oxford. From here he graduated, in 1842, with first-class honours in mathematics. He became a fellow of his college and tutor, and was also appointed bursar.

In 1842 he was made deacon, and in the following year he was admitted to the priesthood. At the age of thirty-two he received the appointment to the bishopric of Nova Scotia, and was consecrated on the festival of the Annunciation (March 25th), 1851, in Lambeth Chapel, by Archbishop Sumner of Canterbury, assisted by Bishops Blomfield of London, Wilberforce of Oxford, and Gilbert of Chichester. He arrived in Halifax on July 21st, 1851, and on the following Sunday preached in St. Paul's.

It was a flattering position for this young Nova Scotian to return to his native land with the sacred trust of a diocese placed in his hands. Possessed of good bodily health and sound English training, his career, in every sense of the word, promised to be a successful one. Almost immediately upon his arrival he found himself plunged into the ever-recurring business of a large diocese.

His attention was first drawn to King's College, Windsor, which, from a Church point of view, was not in a satisfactory condition. It was under the rule of a political governing body, seven of whom belonged to the Church of England, three were Presbyterians, and one " not a member of the Church of England." This, for a Church of England institution, was considered anomalous. Strenuous efforts, therefore, were made to place the college in the hands of its own natural friends. This was finally effected through the local legislature in 1854, and by it it was enacted that the Bishop was to be president of the governing body, and that all the governors were to be members of the Church of England.

Bishop Binney opened a chapel known as "Salem," largely at his own cost. It was to be a church for the poor, and came to be known as " Bishop's Chapel."

It was placed in the charge of Rev. J. C. Cochran, whom he afterwards made a canon.

The Bishop held strong views regarding the distinctive claims of the Church of England as a branch of the ancient Catholic Church of Christ, and this led him to encounter some difficulties and anxieties. From the first moment of his landing he experienced the most bitter opposition from most of those from whom he should have received support.* On his arrival he continued to use St. Paul's Church for the cathedral church of the diocese, as his predecessors had done, and as was fitting and proper. St. Paul's was the old historic church—the mother church of the diocese, and in it was the proper place for the Bishop's chair. But the new Bishop had an objection to the use of the black gown in preaching, and also to the placing of the elements of the Holy Communion on the Lord's table before the beginning of the office. These seem small matters now, but then they were questions on which there were very strong feelings. His wishes were opposed at St. Paul's, and also at his own chapel at Salem.

In the meantime a "chapel of ease," which had been struggling for existence in the southern part of the city for several years, and which had been consecrated by Bishop Binney a few months after his arrival in Halifax, and in 1856 had been set apart as a parish church under the title of St. Luke's, seemed to afford the Bishop an opportunity of worshipping where the service could be rendered somewhat in

---

* See article by Rev. Dr. (now Very Rev. Dean) Partridge in *The Canadian Church Magazine and Mission News*, June, 1887.

accordance with his wishes. This church was made into a separate parish in 1858, and in 1865 Bishop Binney constituted it the cathedral of the diocese,

St. Luke's Cathedral, Halifax.

and set up a dean and chapter connected with it. The Rector of St. Luke's, Rev. W. Bullock, was was appointed the first dean. St. Luke's is but a plain wooden edifice, and, as a building, can put in no claim whatever to be a cathedral. But the same, indeed, may be said of St. Paul's, which, though larger than St. Luke's, is but a plain wooden structure.

Bishop Binney all his life had a great longing for a cathedral, some building that should be worthy of the Church and city that it was to represent. When Salem had to be given back to the Congregationalists, to whom it belonged, the Bishop purchased a disused Methodist building, with a view to providing a place of free worship for the poor, but afterwards abandoned this idea, and built Trinity Church by his own contributions and those of his immediate friends. This building, however, "in the interests of peace," he gave up to St. Paul's.

There seemed at one time a prospect of having a cathedral in the southwestern part of the city. Judge Bliss had given a magnificent site for it, and ten thousand dollars were promised if a cathedral was begun within a certain time. This did not lead to the construction of a cathedral, but close to the site the Bishop built a chapel which might be used, on the erection of the cathedral, as a chapter house and synod hall. This came to be known as "Bishop's Chapel," and in it regular services were held, the Bishop himself providing a chaplain and ministering there when his other duties would admit of it.

Bishop Binney always had a great desire to increase the funds of his diocese. The Diocesan Church Society had been fourteen years founded when he arrived, and had an income of $3,884. Before his death this had increased to within the neighbourhood of $9,000. To this also he added a Church Endowment Fund, which is much the same as a diocesan mission fund, and this by degrees grew till it had an income of about $7,000 a year. A Widows and Orphans' Fund and a Superannuation Fund were also formed, both of which are in a position to yield what may reasonably be demanded of them.

The Bishop was strongly in favour of the formation of a diocesan synod. As early as February, 1854, he expressed a wish to have one established in his diocese, but this met with an unexpected opposition, chiefly on the grounds of the proposed admission of the laity to the councils of the Church. Pamphlets were written against it, and a general agitation kept up, which caused the Bishop much anxiety. But his great learning and strong logic enabled him to show the undoubted superiority of his position. Application was made to the Provincial Legislature for an act of incorporation, but through the opposition given to it it was rejected. In 1864, however, another application was made, and this time consent was obtained, but it was through the personal exertions of the Bishop. He could not find a lawyer willing to undertake the matter, so he appeared before the bar of the Legislative Council himself, and pleaded his cause with such ability that his point was carried. A lawyer remarked, "If the Bishop had been brought up a lawyer, he would have beaten us all." "Clearly," was the response, "for he has beaten you all as it is."

The utility of the synod has since abundantly proved the wisdom of the Bishop. The Synod of Nova Scotia, however, as in Quebec, meets but once in every two years. The Bishop was a good chairman, and kept every matter before the synod well in hand. His rebukes sometimes were stern, but they fell mercilessly upon friend and foe alike.

In September, 1874, Bishop Binney, with twelve representative clergymen of his synod and as many laymen, presented themselves as members of the Provincial Synod which met in Montreal. The members were as follows:

Clergy.—Rev. Dr. White, Rev. J. J. Ritchie, Rev. T. Maynard, Rev. Canon Townshend, Rev. J. Ambrose, Rev. P. J. Filleul, Rev. H. L. Owen, Rev. J. A. Kaulbach, Rev. Dr. Nichols, Ven. Archdeacon Gilpin, Rev. J. B. Richardson, Rev. John Abbott.

Laity.—Col. Wood, Hon. W. B. Vail, Dr. J. R. De Wolf, and Messrs. Peter Lynch, E. P. Archibald, W. Gossip, W. C. Silver, G. Reading, E. Kaulbach, A. M. Cochran, P. C. Hill, and C. Bullock.

Many churches were built during Bishop Binney's episcopate, and always with an improved style of architecture. His visitations throughout the diocese, especially in the early days, were long and laborious, yet he spared no effort to keep his diocese visited.

On September 22nd, 1871, the Collegiate School at Windsor was destroyed by fire. It was not until 1877 that the new and present building was erected. It is built of wood. In 1875 the president of King's College, Rev. Dr. McCawley, resigned, and Rev. John Dart was appointed his successor. In 1878 the Hensley Memorial Chapel was built, close to the college. The greater portion of the cost ($14,000) was generously met by the late Edward Binney, a near relative of the Bishop. In 1881 the Government grant ($2,400) was withdrawn altogether from King's, and the Alumni, with the encouraging support of the Bishop, resolved,

Hensley Memorial Chapel.

if possible, to add $40,000 to the further endowment of the institution. Of this amount $16,000 was paid in. But besides this, a Mr. Roach, of England, contributed £500 on condition that no confederation between King's and Dalhousie colleges should ever take place. A contingency legacy (in time to revert to the college) of about $30,000 was also left by the late Rev. E. W. Hodgson.

Bishop Binney had tried to establish at Halifax a school for girls, but in this he met with some difficulties which caused him much trouble—in the midst of which he unexpectedly died on the 30th of April, 1887, at the age of sixty-eight, and after an episcopate of thirty-six years. He died in New York, while on a visit to the city, but his remains were brought to Halifax and buried there on May 6th, 1887.

In 1855 Dr. Binney married Mary, daughter of the Hon. William Blowers Bliss, first puisne Judge of Nova Scotia. She and three children, Rev. Wm. Hibbert Binney, M.A., Oxon., Vicar of Wilton, Cheshire; Miss Binney, and Mr. John Edward Binney, B.A., Oxon., survived him.

The Bishop was possessed of ample means, and at times the diocese and the poor felt substantial benefit from it.

He had looked forward to the centennial celebration of the Nova Scotia episcopate, Bishop Charles Inglis, the first colonial bishop, having been consecrated in 1787. There was to be a grand celebration of this event in Halifax, and then the foundation stone of a new and grand cathedral was to be laid. It was to be a monument of the growth of the Anglican episcopate throughout the world.

But a few months before the time the Bishop died. The first Bishop was consecrated in 1787; the fourth Bishop died in 1887. The whole projected celebration was overcast with gloom, and the prospects of the new cathedral seemed as far away as ever.

Library and Convocation Hall, King's College, Windsor.

14. THE RIGHT REV. BENJAMIN CRONYN, D.D., FIRST BISHOP OF HURON (LONDON, ONT.).

IN the old maps of Upper Canada (now the Province of Ontario), the western part of the colony was divided into the London and Western districts, and contained the counties of Essex, Kent, Middlesex, Oxford, and Norfolk. As far back as 1700 there was a village of Mohawk Indians established on the banks of the Grand river, east of the Oxford district, by the New England Company, the oldest society for the welfare of the Indians known. Its charter dates back to 1661. Here there stood, as early as 1711, a little mission chapel, to which Queen Anne at that date presented a set of communion plate of solid silver. This church was replaced by another and a better one in 1773, through the exertions of the celebrated Indian Tyendenaga, or Captain Joseph Brant. When it was first built the country for miles around was a dense forest. Now it stands in the centre of a richly cultivated district, crowned by the beautiful city of Brantford. This is the oldest church in Western Ontario, and still remains a link between the present and the past.

Another place of early mention is Sandwich, on the St. Clair river, in the extreme west. In 1797 Sandwich was then the chief town of the western district, as Niagara, Kingston, and Cornwall were of the

THE RT. REV. BENJAMIN CRONYN, D.D.
First Bishop of Huron (London, Ontario).
Born, 1802. Consecrated, 1857. Died, 1871.

districts lying eastward. At these four points Governor Simcoe, in 1797, hoped to establish grammar schools.*

In the memory of people still living, the western portion of "Upper Canada" was a wilderness. The steady flow of immigration, the rapid felling of trees, the hasty building of log houses, the frequent "clearances," the constant smoke from the burning up of "underbrush," the fencing of newly-made fields, the gradual formation of roads, villages, and towns, was a leading characteristic, not many years ago, of this region, now a magnificent territory, with several large towns (four of them cities†), farms of the very best quality, and villages numerous.

In 1825 the Hon. and Rev. Mr. Stewart, when on an extended missionary tour, visited the Mohawk church. He says: "On my arrival at the Grand river, on the land of the Six Indian Nations, I found that a new village of British inhabitants had sprung up in their neighbourhood. It is Brantford, and is two miles from the Mohawk church."‡ In 1828 Dr. Strachan, at that time Archdeacon of York, visited Brantford, Burford, Oxford, and the River Thames. He speaks of Sandwich and of Chatham, and of the extensive property owned by Colonel Talbot. It was a feature of this new colony that many gentlemen of the old country, chiefly retired officers from the army and navy, were found living in the wilderness, hoping

* "The Church in the Colonies," Toronto, Hawkins, p. 183.

† London, Brantford, Stratford, and St. Thomas.

‡ "The Church in the Colonies," Toronto, Hawkins, p. 69.

soon to become a landed gentry—a hope which, owing to the rigorous toil involved in it, was never realized, except in a few cases.

In 1838 Bishop G. J. Mountain, of Quebec, reported that "in travelling from the town of London (on the Thames, in Middlesex county) to Goderich (then in a very distant region on the banks of Lake Huron), he passed through a tract of country sixty miles in length, in which there was not one clergyman or minister of any denomination." He speaks of the same destitution between "Wodehouse," on Lake Erie (near the town of Simcoe), and St. Thomas (about seventeen miles south of London), a distance of about fifty miles.

In 1842 Bishop Strachan, of Toronto, speaks of visiting the Mohawk church and Tuscarora, where "there are two excellent missionaries, Rev. Adam Elliot and the Rev. Abraham Nelles." In that visitation he mentions Dunwich, Paris, and Galt as mission stations. In 1847 there is the further mention of Westminster (near London), Malahide, Woodstock, Blenheim, Wilmot, Stratford, and Zorra; and also of Owen Sound, far up in the north on the banks of the Georgian Bay; and of Simcoe, in Norfolk county.

Among the many places of this most interesting part of "Upper Canada," it was soon very evident that London was destined to outstrip them all in population and importance. In 1822 the Hon. and Rev. Dr. Stewart speaks of "the very rapid progress in wealth and population of London," where, on Sunday, July 28th, he ministered to a congregation of nearly 250 persons. He earnestly recommended the Society (S.P.G.) to send a missionary to London.*

Yet it was ten years before a missionary arrived, and then it was apparently more by accident than design. Of this missionary it becomes us now to speak.

Benjamin Cronyn was the son of Thomas Cronyn, Esq., of Kilkenny, Ireland, and was born in that place on July 11th, 1802. He was educated at Trinity College, Dublin, where he graduated in 1822; in 1824 he was divinity prizeman, and took his master's degree in 1825, in which year he was admitted to the diaconate by the Bishop of Raphoe. He was priested by His Grace the Archbishop of Tuam on Trinity Sunday, 1827. In 1832, at the age of thirty, he resolved to emigrate to Canada, and with his wife (the daughter of J. Bickerstaff, Esq., of Lislea, Longford, Ireland) and two small children he set sail. He carried with him many good wishes, and among them those of Rev. Peter Roe, Rector of Kilkenny, who gave him a letter on his departure full of friendship and good wishes.

It was a long, tedious journey by sea and by land. His destination was Adelaide, in the west of Upper Canada. Through the woods in a rough "lumber wagon"—lumbering, indeed, over roads that did not deserve the name—for days he toiled on, till, his wife becoming tired and ill, he was obliged to stop.

* "Annals of the Colonial Church," Quebec, Hawkins, p. 74. This does not agree with the statement made by a contributor in Dr. Langtry's "Eastern Canada and Newfoundland" that the first house had been erected in London in 1827. In "Canada Past and Present"—W. H. Smith—it is said that London was first laid out (surveyed) in 1826. There must have been many houses in it by that time, so that Dr. Stewart's report (which was made by himself to the S.P.G.) must have been correct.

The place where he halted was London, or "The Forks," as it was sometimes called. It was only twenty-six miles from Adelaide, but the emigrants for the present could travel no further.

Though, twenty years before this, the Hon. and Rev. Dr. Stewart spoke of London as a place of size and wealth, his words must be understood in a comparative sense only, for in 1832 London was but a hamlet. Yet it was growing, and there were many Church people in and about it. When it was noised abroad that a clergyman was in their midst, there were many baptisms, and weddings, and services that kept Mr. Cronyn busy. How great had been the neglect of the Church! He officiated here on Sunday in a farm house which had served as a court house.

Here, then, Mr. Cronyn remained. He had many hard experiences as a pioneer clergyman. On one occasion, shortly after his arrival, he started on foot for Adelaide with his friend, Colonel Curran, the two carrying between them a quarter of beef for a needy settler. They lost their way at night in the woods. Wolves, attracted by the smell of the beef, hovered near them. They were found in the morning by some people who, expecting them, had gone to look for them. They were nearly exhausted by their adventure.

A good horseman, a bold swimmer, a practical farmer, architect, and engineer—sufficient for backwoods purposes—he proved himself of great use to the community, both in a temporal and spiritual way. He taught the farmers how to improve their pigs and cattle, and how to enrich the soil of their farms; and himself, more than once, accepted the position of pathmaster, that he might do something to improve the vile roads, in the mud of which he and his weary horse often had to pursue a monotonous and tardy way.*

London grew, and as it grew the inhabitants determined that it should be London. The river hard by was the Thames; the bridges, Westminster and Blackfriars; the market, "Covent Garden Market"; the county, Middlesex—a slice of the old world in the bush—and when, in 1835, a church was built, of course it was called St. Paul's, destined to be St. Paul's Cathedral. This was a frame building, and was pronounced "one of the finest, and certainly one of the neatest, churches in the province." In 1836 London was made a rectory.

St. Paul's Church and Rectory, London.

This pioneer church was destroyed by fire in 1844, and very soon afterwards a good substantial brick building was erected, and was "the largest church west of Toronto." In 1852 a beautiful chime of bells was placed in the tower.

In the meantime great improvements were taking place in all the western portion of the province. The original five counties were increased by those of Lambton, Huron, Bruce, and Grey in the west and northwest, Elgin (in the south of Middlesex), and of Brant, Perth, and Waterloo in the Oxford and Norfolk

---

* See an interesting account by a contributor in Dr. Langtry's "Eastern Canada and Newfoundland."

region, making in all thirteen. The Diocese of Toronto had become unwieldy in the extreme. The formation of two new dioceses, one in the west and the other in the east of " Upper Canada " (Ontario), was imperative, and resolved upon.

The necessary endowment was raised (chiefly by subscription) in the western section first, and the thirteen counties mentioned were formed into a diocese, with London as the see city. The name of the new diocese became a question. There could not well be two bishops of London, it was thought. The name " Huron " was finally chosen, probably because of the great lake of that name which washes its northern and northwestern shores.

A new state of things had set in for the Church of England in Canada. The Crown was to have nothing more to do with matters ecclesiastical. The people must learn to support the clergy, and the clergy must learn to govern the Church as best they might. Bishops were no longer to be Government officers. If the clergy and laity wanted bishops, they must devise some plan of procuring them irrespective of politics or governments. The only plan that could be devised was the primitive one of election. This was settled. The clergy were to meet in London, and with their lay representatives from the different parishes to elect a bishop.

This led to the canvassing of names. The Rev. Benjamin Cronyn had received from his Irish *alma mater* the degree of D.D. He was rector of the first church in the new district. He had been a hard-working missionary, and was a man of good ability and genial, kindly spirit. But he was of "pronounced evangelical views," and this caused some of the clergy and laity to look elsewhere. In the eastern portion of the province was the Venerable Dr. Bethune, Archdeacon of York, whose views were known to be of an opposite character. He was selected as one who many thought would make a good bishop. The evils of the elective system showed themselves in things that were said and done on behalf of the two "candidates" by their ardent supporters. The election was held in St. Paul's Church, London, on July 9th, 1857, the Bishop of Toronto (Dr. Strachan) presiding. On the first ballot Dr. Cronyn received twenty-two clerical votes and twenty-four lay votes, and Archdeacon Bethune twenty clerical and ten lay. Dr. Cronyn was therefore declared first Bishop of Huron. Such was the result of the first episcopal election in Canada.

The parishes and clergy of the diocese at that time were :—

Galt, Rev. M. Boomer ; London Township, Rev. C. C. Brough ; Woodstock, Rev. W. Bettridge ; Bayfield, Rev. F. Campbell ; St. Thomas, Rev. A. St. George Caulfield ; London, Rev. B. Cronyn, Rev. H. O'Neill ; Sandwich, Rev. M. Dewar ; Goderich, Rev. M. Ellwood ; Tuscarora, Rev. A. Elliott ; Colchester, Rev. F. G. Elliott ; Simcoe, Rev. F. Evans, D.C.L., Rev. R. S. Birch ; Huntingford, Rev. F. D. Fauquier ; Delaware, Rev. R. Flood ; Dawn or Zoan Mills, Rev. J. Gunn ; Saugeen, Rev. T. P. Hodge ; Tyrconnell, Rev. H. Holland ; Port Burwell, Rev. H. P. Jessop ; Morpeth, Rev. C. C. Johnson ; Walpole Island, Rev.

Andrew Jamieson ; Ingersoll and Beachville, Rev. J W. Marsh ; Amherstburg, Rev. W. Mack ; Port Stanley, Rev. J. Mockridge ; Adelaide, Rev. H. Mortimer ; Owen Sound, Rev. A. H. R. Mulholland ; Mohawk, Rev. A. Nelles ; Grand River, Rev. J. Kennedy ; Stratford, Rev. E. Patterson ; Burford, Rev. J. Padfield ; Haysville, Rev. W. B. Rally ; Eastwood, Rev. T. B. Robarts ; Sarnia, Rev. G. J. R. Salter ; Moore, Rev. A. Williams ; Chatham, Rev. F. W. Sandys ; Warwick, Rev. T. Smyth ; Mount Pleasant and Waterloo, Rev. E. R. Stimson ; Paris, Rev. A. Townley ; Brantford, Rev. J. C. Usher ; St. Marys, Rev. A. Lampman ; Dereham, Norwich, and Otterville, Rev. Mr. Young.

Dr. Cronyn proceeded to England, and was consecrated at Lambeth in 1857 by the Archbishop of Canterbury. In 1858 the first session of the Diocesan Synod was held, and a constitution adopted.

The diocese began its career with forty-one clergymen. In 1860 these had increased to sixty-nine. Of these, twelve were chosen as representatives to the first Provincial Synod, or, as they termed it, "General Assembly," held in Montreal in September, 1861. The twelve were : Rev. M. Boomer, LL.D., the Venerable Archdeacon C. C. Brough, Rev. E. L. Elwood, Rev. R. Flood, Rev. W. Bettridge, Rev. B. Smythe, Rev. F. W. Sandys, D.D., Rev. J. W. Marsh, Rev. St. G. Caulfield, LL.D., Rev. A. Nelles, Rev. J. Padfield, Rev. J. C. Usher—all of whom were present except Mr. Padfield. The lay representatives were Messrs. L. Lawrason, A. Shade, W. Watson, J. Johnson, I. Cottle, H. Johnson, G. Kains, W. D.

Allan, J. Keefer, I. Farrell, H. Ingles, and Dr. Dewson. Messrs. J. and H. Johnson and J. Keefer were absent.

The whole of the territory forming the Diocese of Huron is composed, almost without exception, of the very best farming land in Canada. The result is that commercial prosperity has always marked its course. The rapid change from forest and hamlet to splendid farms, villages, towns, and cities, is amongst the brightest pages of Canadian history. Bishop Cronyn had the pleasure of seeing marked improvements in the parishes under his care—and a frequent subdivision of them, which taxed his ability to the utmost to keep them supplied with men. To Ireland, his native land, he went again and again to get men, and to his exertions are due the importation to Canada of men like the present Bishop of Algoma (Dr. Sullivan), the present Dean of Montreal (Dr. J. Carmichael), and the present Bishop elect of Niagara (Canon DuMoulin). These all began work under Bishop Cronyn, who frequently expressed himself as well satisfied with "his boys," except, perhaps, when they left him at comparatively early dates for higher positions elsewhere.

In the early days of his episcopate Bishop Cronyn became involved in a controversy regarding the teaching of Trinity College, Toronto, which he considered unsound. The corporation of that institution placed these charges before the other bishops of the "Province," viz.: The Metropolitan (Dr. Fulford), the Bishop of Toronto (Dr. Strachan), the Bishop of Ontario (Dr. Lewis), and the Bishop of Quebec (Dr. Williams), all of whom upheld the teaching of the College ; but the Bishop of Huron was not satisfied, and therefore exerted himself to establish at London a college over which he himself could exercise more immediate control. This led to the formation and partial endowment —through subscriptions made for the purpose—of Huron College, which was opened in 1863, under the presidency of Rev. Isaac Hellmuth, D.D., about whom we shall hear more presently.

In 1864 the clergy of the diocese had increased to seventy-nine, and thirteen students had matriculated at the college; but the funds of the Church Society (which had been continued as begun in the Diocese of Toronto) had fallen off a little—a fact which the Bishop deplored in his charge of 1865; but steady growth, nevertheless, continued to characterize the diocese. A great domestic affliction fell upon the Bishop in the death of Mrs. Cronyn. The kind sympathy which he received on that occasion the Bishop touchingly referred to in his address to Synod in June, 1867. In that year (1867) the clergy in the diocese numbered eighty-eight, and the churches 145. Indeed, the Bishop found it very difficult to keep his diocese supplied with pastors, for at this time there were twelve vacant missions. In that year (1867), also, Bishop Cronyn attended the first Lambeth Conference in England, the expense of his journey being met by an assessment on the parishes of the diocese. The Bishop, on his return, viewing matters from his own standpoint, did not draw a very glowing picture of the condition of the Church in the motherland.

Bishop Cronyn, from his consecration, had retained the rectory of St. Paul's, London; but on his return from England a see house was purchased for him, in which he resided with his second wife, a lady of culture whom he had married in the Old Country.

The S.P.G., which had helped the diocese in its infancy, now began to expect the child to stand alone; and, in the prospect of losing support from it, a sustentation fund was formed, subscriptions to which in 1869 amounted to $30,000, and to double that sum in 1870. In that year the clergy had increased to 93, and it became evident that the rapid growth of population in the diocese was beginning to make it a matter of great moment as to how the Church was to keep pace with it—and all the more so because the health of the Bishop began to fail. In June, 1871, he said to his Synod that his medical advisers had informed him that to continue the same course of over-exertion that he had done in the past would be little short of suicide, and that he was unable any longer to perform those duties of the episcopate which required constant physical exertion; and hoped the Synod would take some steps to provide for the discharge of the more arduous labours of the episcopal office for the future.

In accordance with this request, a special meeting of the Synod was held in Bishop Cronyn Hall, London, a few weeks after the regular meeting, viz., on the 19th of June, for the purpose of electing a coadjutor bishop. The choice fell upon Dr. Hellmuth, who had risen to the position of Dean of Huron. He took the title of Bishop of Norfolk. In a few months, however, he was called upon to be Bishop of Huron, for on the 22nd of September (1871) Dr. Cronyn died of heart disease.

The Bishop left three daughters and two sons. The oldest daughter married Colonel Burrows; the next, Edward Blake, Esq.; and the youngest, S. H. Blake, Esq. The sons are Benjamin, now living in the United States; and Verschoyle, Chancellor of the Diocese of Huron.

. His family and friends erected to his memory the church known as the Bishop Cronyn Memorial Church, now in charge of Rev. Canon Richardson. A hall for Synod purposes was also erected in the grounds of St. Paul's Church, and was called " Bishop Cronyn Hall."

The Mohawk Church, near Brantford. Built about 1773, through the instrumentality of Brant, the celebrated Theyend'enaga.

THE RT. REV. GEORGE HILLS, D.D.
First Bishop of Columbia.
Born, 1816. Consecrated, 1859. Resigned, 1892. Died, 1895

15. THE RIGHT REV. GEORGE HILLS, D.D., FIRST BISHOP OF COLUMBIA (BRITISH COLUMBIA).

ON the distant Pacific coast lies a beautiful, yet rocky and mountainous island, two hundred miles long, and from ten to seventy miles broad. The ownership of it lay between England and Spain. George Vancouver, master of a ship out on an exploring expedition, claimed it for England. Bodega y Cuadra, in command of a Spanish vessel, claimed it for Spain. The two commanders, sitting amicably together on the island, in 1792, agreed to call it for the present Cuadra and Vancouver Island. The Spanish part was soon dropped, which meant that the island had passed into the possession of Great Britain. The bold, rocky mainland of North America adjacent to it also became British territory. This island remained for many years what it had been for ages before, the home of roving Indians and wild animals of the forest.

Then came the fur trader and the officers of the Hudson's Bay Company. The southern part of Vancouver Island, with its excellent and well-protected harbour, was selected as an admirable spot for a fort and trading post. The natives called the place Camosun, and here James Douglas, an astute Scotchman of the Hudson's Bay Company, erected the plain wooden buildings, well and substantially fortified, that were to stand for many years. The greater portion of it was built by the year 1844, and was called Fort Camosun, but in 1845 the name was changed, with much loyal ceremony, to that of Fort Victoria.

About three miles from it was an Indian village called Esquimalt, where was another harbour even better than that of Camosun, and great trading ships used to arrive from England on the business of the

A Hudson's Bay Post.

company. By degrees land was cultivated, and the fort was well supplied by the produce of the island itself. It was soon found that coal also was to be obtained on this new domain, and this led to further investigation and to the establishment of other places on the Island, such as Fort Rupert, Ellenborough, and Nanaimo.

These people, exiled a very long distance from the Old Country, were not altogether without the ministrations of the Church, for the Hudson's Bay Company at times had a chaplain, one of whom, Rev. R.

J. Staines, of Trinity Hall, Cambridge, tried to teach the people to establish homes for themselves, and so to induce colonization. This, however, did not receive the support of the company, whose business was best served by keeping the place, as long as possible, a wilderness. The first governor of the colony was Richard Blanshard, who was appointed in 1850, but on his arrival he found there was little to govern, and soon resigned the charge.

In the following year, James Douglas, chief factor of the fort, was made governor. Victoria was laid out as a town, but it lacked population. In 1856 the Island was divided into four districts, viz., Victoria, Esquimalt, Nanaimo, and Soke, and seven men were appointed to represent these places in an assembly which Her Majesty's Government required Governor Douglas to set up. There were then on the Island only about two hundred and fifty white men.

About this time, in October, 1857, Mr. William Duncan arrived from England, sent out by the C.M.S. as a missionary to the Indians on the North Pacific coast. His work will be noticed elsewhere.

In 1858 it was noised abroad that there was gold in Vancouver Island and British Columbia.* Then took place an extraordinary influx of people. From California and elsewhere they came—twenty thousand of them—with eager faces, to seek their fortunes. Three thousand of them arrived in Victoria in one day, and encamped round the fort. Things were changed. The *terra incognita* became suddenly known.

* In this year this term was applied for the first time, in the Imperial Parliament, to this territory; but it did not include Vancouver Island, which remained a separate colony, with its own Governor and Assembly.

The cry of gold has a wonderful attraction for the masses. Many of the gold-seekers, it is true, returned to their homes disappointed, but fresh arrivals for several years took their places, and many villages and towns sprung up throughout the hitherto silent and unoccupied land.

In 1859 the colony was separated entirely from the Hudson's Bay Company, and Douglas, who had been serving in the dual capacity of governor of the colony and chief factor of the great trading monopoly, had to resign one or the other. He elected to remain governor of the colony. In this year the Rev. R. Dowson, sent out from England by the S.P.G., arrived in Victoria to open up work among the "heathen Indians." He found but one small village situated near Victoria, and the men were "idle and diseased";* but he started on a voyage of discovery in a vessel of the Hudson's Bay Company, touched at Nanaimo, where he found a wretched little village, built of wood, "amongst mud and stumps," and having a population of 160 whites and halfbreeds, with a few hundred Indians camped about it. Here Mr. Dowson held service in a room which had been used as a school, established by the Hudson's Bay Company. At Fort Rupert, two hundred miles further north, where there were only six white people, he found encamped a thousand Quackolls, the most blood-thirsty of all Indian tribes on the Northwest coast.

Plenty of heads and other human remains lay on the beach. A prisoner taken captive in war was landed

* Digest of S.P.G. Records, p. 181.

among them. They all rushed down from their houses and ate the poor wretch alive.

On Mr. Dowson's return to Victoria, he endeavoured to teach the wretched Indians something about God and the soul; but he met with no encouragement, either from the whites or themselves; yet within a year he had won the hearts of many of the poor savages, who said to him, "You teach Indian good—Indian's heart good to you." In the same year, 1859, a second missionary, Rev. J. Gammage, was sent out by the S.P.G., who began work among the miners on the mainland.

It was about this time that the S.P.G., through the munificence of Miss (now Baroness) Burdett-Coutts, who endowed a bishopric and two archdeaconries for Columbia to the extent, in all, of about $120,000,* was enabled to send a missionary bishop to Victoria. The man selected for this pioneer work was the Rev. George Hills, an Englishman, born in the year 1816 at Egthorne, Kent. He was the eldest son of the late Rear-Admiral Hills, and received his education at the University of Durham, where he took the successive degrees of B.A., M.A., B.D., and D.D. Admitted to the diaconate by Bishop Bowstead, of Lichfield, in 1839, and subsequently priested by Bishop Maltby, of Durham, he served as curate at North Shields, Northumberland, and at Leeds, under Dean Hook. He was, also, incumbent of St. Mary's, Leeds, and of Great Yarmouth, Norfolk, and, in 1850, received the appointment of Honorary Canon of Norwich Cathedral. He was consecrated "Bishop of Columbia" in West-

* "Stranger than Fiction." S.P.C.K.

minster Abbey on St. Matthias' Day (Feb. 24th), 1859, by Archbishop Sumner, of Canterbury. Bishop Feild, of Newfoundland, and Bishop DeLancey, of New York, assisted at the consecration, as well as Bishop Tait (London), Bishop S. Wilberforce (Oxford), and Bishop J. T. Pelham (Norwich). After spending several months in England, collecting money for his diocese, the new bishop set sail for the distant West. He arrived in 1860, just as the Rev. Mr. Dowson, through the illness of his wife, returned to England.

Victoria he found a strange mixture of almost all nations and tribes under the sun; white people of all nationalities and tongues, blacks from Africa, Mongols, Chinamen, Polynesians, Malays, Americans, Mexicans, Indians, and many others were there to greet the Bishop with wondering looks as he sauntered through the busy little streets. In 1863 Governor Douglas, who had seen the very beginnings of Victoria in 1843, retired from his position. In doing so he received the honour of knighthood, and, with every mark of respect shown by the people he had governed, he left as Sir James Douglas, K.C.B. He was succeeded in 1864 by Captain Kennedy, at which time the white population of Vancouver Island was about 7,500.

Such was the community in which Bishop Hills had undertaken to live. He had two colonies under his charge, comprising a territory as large as France and England put together. Rough miners, keen speculators, wretched Indians, many of them without even the glory of savagery, but degraded with the white man's rum and the white man's diseases—a motley, wretched, excited crowd, either wallowing in wretchedness or moving ceaselessly on to some place in the wilderness where had been set up the all-powerful cry of gold.

How to reach these was the great care of the pioneer Bishop. He found substantial assistance in the ever-ready S.P.G., which, between the years 1860 and 1865, added twelve missionaries to the Bishop's slender staff, and Victoria, Nanaimo, Esquimalt, and

Bastion of Old Hudson Bay Forts, Nanaimo, B.C.

Saanich, on Vancouver Island; Lilloet, New Westminster, Hope Sapperton, on the mainland (or " British Columbia "), with other stations, were regularly supplied with services. The Rev. A. C. Garrett helped among the Indians at Victoria; Rev. R. C. Lundin Brown tried the thankless task of work among the miners.* Rev. John B. Good toiled long and earnestly among the Indians at Victoria, Nanaimo, and elsewhere. The Rev. John Sheepshanks ministered at New Westminster—the fast rising capital of the mainland—and so, with here and there a missionary, the work went on. The Bishop himself travelled continuously from post to post, by canoe, by Hudson's Bay steamboat, or on horseback. Long, solitary journeys he took as he went about "confirming the churches." Great were the hindrances that he met with from the elements above, the sparse accommodation and the uncouth jargon of the Indians (called the Chinook), which, through an interpreter, formed the only means by which he could make known the message which was ever ready to break from his lips; yet he persevered, though the progress was unsatisfactory and slow. The typical missionary—described by the Bishop himself—was " a man with stout country shoes, corduroy trousers, a coloured woollen shirt, a leather strap round his waist, and an axe upon his shoulder, driving a mule or horse laden with packs of blankets, a tent, bacon, a sack of flour, a coffee pot, a kettle, and a frying-pan."†

In this manner, halting at intervals for rest and cooking, which involved the making of his own bread, the missionary would travel for hundreds and hundreds of miles to minister to Indians and miners only.

* His book published by the S.P.C.K. (England), "Klatsassan, or Life in British Columbia," is very interesting.

† "Under His Banner." By Rev. H. W. Tucker, M.A.

And to visit the haunts of the miners—what sanctified courage it meant! Often it was pandemonium—often 'twas like the mouth of hell. Yet the missionary, finding sometimes no one willing to attend his service, stands outside a drinking saloon and boldly denounces the wickedness of the people. It may be—and such has happened—that one at least of the carousing gamblers will listen and stand firmly by the man who dares to tell the truth in such a dangerous place. Bishop Hills himself spent weeks at a time among men of this description. Such was British Columbia, and such it remained for several years.

In 1865 the Bishop married Maria Philadelphia Louisa, eldest daughter of Admiral Sir Richard King, Bart., K.C.B.

In 1866 Vancouver Island was united to the mainland, and the two colonies were henceforth to be known as one, under the title of British Columbia. Bishop Hills, however, still retained for the diocese the title of Columbia only. In 1867 the "British North America Act" was passed, whereby the colonies could unite at will in a confederation to be known as the Dominion of Canada. But British Columbia did not join this confederation till 1871. One of the conditions of its joining was that a railway was to be built connecting the Pacific coast with the Atlantic. It was commenced in 1871, and completed in 1885. This marked a new era in this distant colony. It was henceforth to be known as the Province of British Columbia.

The Church in this province had a favourable start. It was provided with a bishop in its very early days. In fact, the bishop was almost the first among the missionaries. It had a good endowment from the beginning and received aid from two great missionary societies, and has met with a fair amount of progress; yet it has not been without its troubles.

The Bishop had set up his cathedral in Victoria, and the Rev. Edward Cridge was made dean; but

Christ Church Cathedral, Victoria, B.C.

troubles arose which ended in the disaffection of the Dean, and in his putting himself at the head of the Reformed Episcopal movement.

Two new dioceses were formed on the mainland— one in the north in 1879, and the other in the south in 1880. Bishop Hills was thus confined to Vancouver Island, which is still called the Diocese of Columbia.

It started its fresh career in 1880, with eleven clergymen. In 1885 the Canadian Pacific Railway—one of the greatest triumphs of the age—was finished, and the Pacific province brought much closer to the rest of the Dominion, of which it formed an important part. Victoria gradually became a city of no mean proportions or appearance. Its population in 1881 was 5,925; in 1891, 17,000.

Bishop Hills thus spoke to his Synod in June, 1892, of the progress of the Church:

"From the census of 1891, it appears that the Church of England has made greater progress in British Columbia than any other religious body, the progress being thirty-one per cent. of the whole increase of population during the decade. Considering how peculiarly cosmopolitan, from special circumstances, the Pacific province has always been, its population having been gathered from all points, rather than direct from the mother country, this result is an encouragement to both clergy and laity of the Church of England."

In that year, 1892, Bishop Hills resigned his work and returned to England. On account of his wife's ill-health he had contemplated resignation some years previously, but, her death removing the cause of his proposed retirement, he bravely settled down to his work again; but in 1892 his failing strength warned him that his active days were over. He said good-by to a people loath to lose him. He had seen great changes. He had seen a wilderness grow into a province, a diocese subdivided into three, a staff of two clergymen enlarged to seventy, a little wooden town for his see city expanded into a beautiful city, the Pacific

Ocean, which bounded his diocese, connected by a trans-continental railway with the Atlantic, and then he went back to his native land. Shortly after his arrival he was stricken with paralysis, from which, however, he slowly recovered. He returned to his old diocese of Norwich, whose bishop was now Dr. Sheepshanks, who had been one of his clergy in the wilderness of British Columbia.

It was a graceful act which led the former priest to give his old Bishop a quiet little English living, where he spent, in calm retirement, the rest of his days. He sank to rest on Tuesday, December the 10th, 1895, at Parkham, Suffolk, at the age of seventy years.

A writer in an English paper * thus speaks of him :—

"He could create enthusiasm in his workers and draw out their strong affection. This was partly due to his fine presence, his magnificent voice and his rare powers of conversation, but chiefly to his wonderful energy, his great gifts of organization, and his unwavering faith that if a work was God's He would make it grow in His own time."

* Quoted in *The Canadian Church Magazine and Mission News*, Feb., 1896.

THE MOST REV. JOHN TRAVERS LEWIS, D.D., LL.D.
Archbishop of Ontario and Third Metropolitan of (Eastern) Canada.
First Bishop of Ontario (Kingston).
Born, 1825.   Consecrated, 1862.

16. THE MOST REVEREND JOHN TRAVERS LEWIS, D.D., LL.D., ARCHBISHOP OF ONTARIO AND THIRD METROPOLITAN OF (EASTERN) CANADA; FIRST BISHOP OF ONTARIO (KINGSTON).

WE have already seen that the eastern part of "Upper Canada" was the cradle of Church work in what is now known as the Province of Ontario. Here it was that the early pioneer clergymen, John Stuart and John Langhorn, commenced their work, the former at Cataraqui (now Kingston) in 1786, and the latter at Ernestown (now Bath) in 1787. Dr. Stuart was "commissary" for Upper Canada, which was under the episcopal control, first, of Bishop Charles Inglis, of Nova Scotia, and from 1793 of Dr. Jacob Mountain, first Bishop of Quebec. In April of that year a small wooden church, forty by thirty-two feet, was built at Kingston, and dedicated to St. George. One of the churchwardens at the time was Captain Robert Macaulay, father of Hon. John and Rev. William Macaulay. St. John's Church, Bath, was opened for divine service on June 3rd, 1795, and still exists. Cornwall, in the extreme east of the district, was occupied by the Rev. John Strachan in 1803.

In or about 1808, the Rev. John G. Weagant, Lutheran minister at Williamsburgh, on the St. Lawrence, not far from Cornwall, connected himself with the Church, bringing his congregation with him. In 1814, Elizabethtown and Augusta were formed into a parish under Rev. John Bethune, brother of Alexander Neil Bethune, afterwards Bishop of Toronto. In 1823, Augusta was separated from Elizabethtown (or Brockville), and was placed in charge of the Rev.

St. George's Church (afterwards Cathedral), Kingston, Ontario.

Robert Blakey. About the same time Adolphustown and Fredericksburgh, on the Bay of Quinte, were detached from Ernestown, and placed under Rev. Job Deacon, the Rector of Ernestown being Rev. John

Stoughton. In 1827, a new stone church, of the Queen Anne style of architecture, replaced the wooden structure at Kingston. For many years this remained the chief ecclesiastical edifice of that city. In that year the Rev. William Macaulay was sent to Hallowell (Picton), in Prince Edward County—a lovely county, almost an island, lying between Lake Ontario and the Bay of Quinte.

This portion of the province was divided into districts and counties, as follows:

The *Eastern District*, containing the counties of Glengarry, Stormont, and Dundas, on the St. Lawrence.

Ottawa District, containing Russell and Prescott, on the Ottawa.

Johnstown District, containing Grenville and Leeds, on the St. Lawrence.

Bathurst District, containing Carleton, on the Ottawa, and Lanark, extending north to the Ottawa.

Midland District, containing Frontenac, Lennox (and Addington) and Hastings, on Lake Ontario and the Bay of Quinte, and Prince Edward, lying between the lake and the bay.

The County of Victoria also lay within the Midland District, but was not separated from the Diocese of Toronto.

Other parishes were formed, such as Belleville, Camden, Tyendinaga, or Mohawk mission to the Indians, in the Midland District; Lamb's Pond (as distinct from Brockville) and Osnabruck, in the Johnstown District; and Bytown (afterwards Ottawa), March, Richmond, Beckwith (or Franktown), and

Perth, in the Bathurst, or, as would be better understood at the present time, the Ottawa District. The population of this district in 1824 was 10,000, and in 1832 it had increased to 32,000.

In 1834 Carleton Place was opened in the Bathurst District, and Murray, or Carrying Place, in Prince Edward County, on the narrow neck of land between it and the mainland.

Thus, when Upper Canada was formed into a separate diocese under Bishop Strachan in 1839, the eastern portion of his diocese was composed of twenty-one parishes, with a population of 150,000.

By 1849 ten new parishes were added, or one for each year since Bishop Strachan took charge of the work. These parishes were all in the neighbourhood of Kingston, viz.: St. James' and St. Paul's, Kingston, Barriefield, Wolfe Island, Amherst Island, Napanee, Marysburg; west of Kingston was Trenton; in Grenville County, Merrickville; and in the Bathurst (Ottawa) District, Pakenham.

In 1850 the parish of West Hawkesbury, beautifully situated on the Ottawa river, in the County of Prescott, in a line directly north from Cornwall, was formed, and the Rev. John Travers Lewis placed in charge of it. This accomplished young clergyman was born in 1825, at Garry Cloyne Castle, County Cork, Ireland. He was the son of Rev. John Lewis, M.A. Having received his primary education at Hamblin and Porter's school, Cork, he entered Trinity College, Dublin, from which he graduated in 1847, after a very distinguished career, in which he carried off the highest honours, being senior moderator in

Ethics and Logic, and gold medallist in Mathematics. He also obtained honours in Classics.

Receiving his Divinity Testamur in 1848, he was made deacon by the Bishop of Chester (Dr. John Graham), acting for Archbishop Beresford, of Armagh, and admitted to the priesthood by Right Reverend Dr. Knox, Bishop of Down. After a curacy of two years at Newton Butler, he emigrated to Canada in 1850, and, as we have seen, was appointed to West Hawkesbury. Here he met with true missionary work, for he was practically travelling missionary for a large portion of the Ottawa district. In 1851 Mr. Lewis married Anne Henrietta Margaret, daughter of the Hon. Henry Sherwood, sometime Attorney-General for Upper Canada.

Mr. Lewis soon showed himself to be, not only a brilliant scholar, but an able and fluent speaker—not of the impassioned kind, but of that deliberate and calm style which indicated a sound and logical mind. He came to the province at a time when men of ability were needed, and when opportunities were opening for the use and display of their powers. Bishop Strachan summoned a conference of the clergy and lay representatives of the various parishes in April and May, 1851, to prepare the way for regular synodical meetings. At this meeting the Rev. "J. T. Lewis, A.B.," was present—the last name on the list.

In 1854 the travelling missionary of Hawkesbury was promoted to the rectory of Brockville, a rising town on the frontier. In the autumn of that year the first Synod of Toronto was held, at which, as rector of Brockville, Mr. Lewis was present. In 1855 he received the degree of LL.D. from his University, and soon after he proceeded to the degrees of B.D. and D.D.

In the Synod of 1856 very encouraging reports were given from the west (Huron) regarding the raising of funds for the endowment of a new see ; but those from the east were not so favourable. There seemed to be a hesitancy to subscribe until it should be made quite clear that the clergy and laity were to be allowed to choose their own bishop. The necessary endowment was not made up till the year 1861. In the meantime Rev. Dr. Lewis had taken a good position in the Synod of Toronto. He was a member of the Executive Committee, and first among the delegates elected to the first Provincial Synod, which was soon to meet.

Since West Hawkesbury had been formed in 1850, the following parishes were added to the list : Smith's Falls (1851), Stirling, Hillier, Loughborough, Portsmouth, Mountain (all in 1853) ; Gananoque (1854), Mission in Renfrew (1855), Osgoode (1856), Newboro (1857), Huntley (1858), Roslin, Lansdowne Rear, Matilda (all in 1859) ; and North Gower, 1860.

On the 12th of June, 1861, at the call of Bishop Strachan, the clergy and laity of the newly-formed diocese met in Kingston for the purpose of electing a bishop.

At this Synod there were 53 clergymen present, and 112 laymen, representing 41 parishes. On the first ballot the Rev. Dr. Lewis received 31 clerical and 39 lay votes, Archdeacon Bethune one clerical and one lay, and Rev. W. Macaulay one lay vote. Upwards of 20 of the clergy seem to have withdrawn or to have abstained from voting. This made a two-thirds vote of the clergy present a necessity, provided also that a quorum (37 at least) were present. The roll of the clergy, therefore, was called, and 38 answered to their names. Dr. Lewis accordingly was declared elected. The name of the new see was left to Bishop Strachan, who designated it "Ontario"—probably because of the lake which washed part of its shores, as Lake Huron did part of the recently formed diocese in the west.

In September of that year (1861) the first Provincial Synod was held at Montreal. The following were the members appointed to represent the new diocese :

Clerical.—Ven. George Okill Stuart, D.D.; Rev. J. A. Mulock, Rev. W. B. Lauder, Rev. J. S. Lauder, Rev. T. H. M. Bartlett, Rev. W. Bleasdell, Rev. R. L. Stephenson, Rev. J. G. Armstrong, Rev. C. Forest, Rev. F. R. Tane, Rev. H. Mulkins, Rev. H. Patton, D.C.L.

Lay.—Hon. J. Shaw, Hon. G. Crawford, Hon. J. Hamilton, Sheriff T. Corbett, and Messrs. T. Kirkpatrick, G. P. Baker, W. B. Simpson, W. Ellis, D. B. O. Ford, E. J. Sisson, S. G. Chesley, and D. F. Jones.

These were all present but Rev. J. S. Lauder, Hon. J. Shaw, and Hon. J. Hamilton.

Owing to some delay in granting the "letters patent"—a piece of routine ever since dispensed with—Dr. Lewis had not yet been consecrated. He was appointed Secretary, however, of the Upper House, and therefore sat with the bishops.

It was not until March 25th of the following year (1862) that the consecration took place. Dr. Lewis was consecrated in St. George's Cathedral, Kingston, by the Most Reverend Dr. Fulford, Metropolitan of Canada, assisted by the aged Bishop Strachan (then 85 years old), Bishop G. J. Mountain (73 years old), the newly-elected Bishop of Huron, Dr. Cronyn, and Dr. McCoskry, Bishop of Michigan.

This was the first episcopal consecration held in Canada, and the Church had thus attained to a new era in her history.

Bishop Lewis was very young for a bishop, being only thirty-seven years of age; but his scholarship, executive and speaking ability, marked him as one well chosen for the position. He was called upon very early in his episcopate to declare his position ecclesiastically. The Bishop of Huron (Dr. Cronyn) had taken exception to the teaching of Trinity College, Toronto. The corporation of that institution placed the matter before the other bishops for their pronouncement upon it. They all declared in favour of Provost Whitaker's teaching. The reply of Bishop Lewis was characteristically brief, and showed that he allowed full play for differences of opinion in many matters of Church doctrine, but thought that these might be held without attaching blame to any one.

As to his diocese an herculean task lay before him. The country was growing rapidly. His own diocese, though new, was in point of territory immense, and was almost entirely a missionary field. The Bishop moved cautiously, though very anxious to build up the Church. He was able to announce to his Synod in

1864 that the clergy had increased from fifty-one to seventy-three, and he added : " It would have been possible to have added largely to this number if I had seen my way clear to the decent maintenance of additional labourers ; but it seemed to me better policy to increase our missionaries only in the ratio of our ability to support them, rather than run the risk of encountering afterwards all the disheartening effect of a reaction and a diminution in the number of the clergy, who would inevitably have been forced to leave the diocese."

In fact the Bishop began to realize how little Church of England people had been taught to give, but he did not feel that it was too late to begin the instruction. The total contributions for diocesan purposes for the twenty-two years previous to the formation of the diocese, and taken up within the territory comprised by it, amounted only to $24,580, or an average of $1,229 per annum.* The total amount subscribed for purely missionary purposes during the first five years of the existence of the new diocese was $86,228.40, or an average per year of $17,245.† Bishop Lewis, from time to time, urged the necessity of liberality on the part of the members of the Church as the only sure method of securing progress. He urged the formation of a Sustentation Fund and a Widows and Orphans' Fund, and was able to state to his Synod in 1865 that nearly $12,000 had been subscribed towards the $20,000 that he was anxious to

---

* Rev. Canon Spencer, in *The Canadian Church Magazine and Mission News*, June, 1887, p. 295.

† "Journal of Ontario Synod," sixth edition, p. 449.

raise for a Mission Fund or a Sustentation Fund for the diocese. The S.P.G. had promised $5,000 provided $20,000 should be raised within the diocese. This good beginning, however, does not seem to have been so well followed up, for it was not till 1870, apparently, that this fund reached $21,000.

Bishop Lewis was always very happy in his confirmation services. His able addresses contributed much to recommend the Church in every parish that he visited, for her distinctive doctrines were always forcibly dwelt upon. No one could fail to grasp the meaning of confirmation after listening to one of His Lordship's addresses. In calm, dignified language, without notes of any kind to rely upon, he would place before his hearers a train of scholarly, yet simple, reasoning that would defy refutation. He did much to show the importance of the Holy Communion, the reception of which, he always insisted, was the bounden duty of every member of the Church. This was at a time when quarterly, or, at the most, monthly, celebrations were largely the practice, and Bishop Lewis, in words which sometimes seemed startling, always pointed out the weakness of this practice. His great desire always was to make communicants of all the candidates confirmed by him, and, therefore, he almost invariably himself administered the Holy Communion immediately after the confirmation service. To see on a week day a crowded church, perhaps in some rural district; to see people listening earnestly, even wonderingly, to the Bishop, still a young man, tall and commanding in appearance, with a handsome, intellectual face, as he pleaded for obedience to the touching command of the Saviour, "This do in remembrance of me"; to see young people on whom he had just laid his hands in confirmation coming forward and kneeling to receive the blessed sacrament for the first time then and there, followed by their relations and friends, and then by others, till frequently the incumbent himself was often surprised at the number of communicants that received—all this was by no means an infrequent sight, and it was as encouraging as it was delightful.

In the "Journal of the Sixth Session" (1867) of the Ontario Synod, the Bishop says:

"Since we first met in synod five years ago, 6,007 persons have been confirmed, and, as the result, 5,500 new communicants added to the Church. This estimate of new communicants I believe to be below the truth, because I have been informed that on almost every occasion of confirmation persons who had been confirmed in former years came forward to communion for the first time, and of these persons I have not been able to keep any account. During the same period thirty-one new churches have been built, many of them costly and ecclesiastically correct. The total number of our church edifices is 216. Nor has the erection of parsonages been neglected. Fifteen new ones have been provided, in many cases with glebes attached, making a total of thirty-eight parsonages now in the diocese."

In this year (1867) the Bishop attended the Lambeth Conference, the expenses of the journey being met by the diocese. This great gathering of Anglican bishops from all parts of the world, which has since become a decennial feature of the Church, was first suggested by Bishop Lewis; or, if not so, he certainly was one of its original promoters.

The stand which the Bishop took relative to Church matters naturally raised some opposition to him on the part of those who differed from him; and there were those who had grave fears lest he had allied himself too closely with the High Church party; but, in 1869, he clearly showed to his Synod that he was not in favour of extreme ritual: "The session of the last Provincial Synod," he said, in his charge that year, "was rendered memorable by the passing of a resolution which has done much good in allaying alarm, caused by fear lest unlawful or obsolete practices should be introduced into the ceremonial of the Church." The resolution referred to was one disapproving of the elevation of the elements in the celebration of the Holy Communion, the use of incense, mixing of water with the sacramental wine, the use of wafer bread, lights on the Lord's table, vestments other than surplice, stole, and hood. Although this was not couched in the form of a canon, still it undoubtedly showed the mind of the Provincial Synod of the period.

The Bishop early developed much tact and ability in the management of his Synod. His plan usually was to give full scope for debate, and then, if he deemed it necessary, express his own views immediately before putting the question. This as a rule determined the fate of a measure, however strongly men may have differed regarding it. The weak points of the argument, as viewed by the chair, were mercilessly dragged to light, and the strong points skilfully marshalled so as to influence the vote about to be taken. The Synod, as a rule, stood by him by overwhelming majorities.

The patronage question may be cited as an instance of this. It is a misfortune that the Church in Canada has no settled method of filling up vacancies in parishes. In some dioceses, as Nova Scotia and Fredericton, the patronage lies in the hands of the congregations; in others, as in Montreal, a compromise is effected between bishop and people; in others, as in Toronto and Niagara, a "consultation" has to take place between the bishop and representatives of the people. This want of uniformity is much to be deplored. In the United States there is one undeviating law for the whole country, and with great advantage to the prosperity of the Church.

In Ontario the right of appointment to vacant parishes was put into the hands of the Bishop, without any restriction whatever. This led to occasional discontent; and attempts were made, from time to time, to alter the law, so as to give the people a voice in the appointment of their rector or incumbent; but they were always defeated by overpowering majorities.

A break, however, occurred in this influence of the Bishop over the Synod in the year 1871, and, to understand it, it must be borne in mind that there were within the Diocese of Ontario two prominent cities, Kingston and Ottawa, the latter having the immense advantage of being the capital of the Dominion. As early as 1868 a motion was made in Synod in favour of establishing a bishopric at Ottawa, and a committee, in the following year, reported a scheme for providing an episcopal income without an endowment; but, this not being adopted, it was moved in the Synod of June, 1870, that the Bishop be requested to remove the seat of the see to Ottawa. This was carried by the clergy, but rejected by the laity, and was therefore lost.

Somewhat to the surprise of many, however, the Bishop removed to Ottawa. The Synod was called together in the middle of winter, January 12th, 1871, to consider the question of electing a coadjutor bishop "to reside in Kingston," which meant that the Bishop had resolved to leave Kingston and remove to Ottawa. This Synod was largely attended, and splendid speeches were made. It was evident that men's minds were deeply stirred on the question. The Synod had already declared against such a step—was it now to approve of it? The Bishop used all his powers in favour of it, but in the end it failed. The clergy, by a majority of nine, supported the measure. The laity, by a majority of ten, were against it, and it was lost.

The Bishop, for the time being, had lost the firm hold that he once had upon the Synod. In the regular meeting which followed this somewhat disturbing Synod, viz., in June, 1871, the Bishop, though he had taken up his residence in Ottawa, made no allusion to the matter. His address was very brief, and simply referred to the business of the diocese. In it he stated that the average number confirmed in the diocese each year since its formation was 1,033. The funds of the diocese were in a satisfactory condition, with the exception of the Widows and Orphans' Fund, for which the Bishop made an urgent appeal.

Kingston was now without the bodily presence of a bishop, but the question of a coadjutor was still kept before the diocese, especially as about this time the health of Bishop Lewis began evidently to fail.

St. George's Church, Kingston, remained the cathedral of the diocese, but in Ottawa a chapel of ease to Christ Church, the old parish church of the city, was handed over to the Bishop as his church. Here, Sunday after Sunday, assisted by Rev. H. Pollard as his curate, the Bishop officiated, the building being called the "Bishop's Chapel."

In 1874, the number of the clergy having increased to eighty-six, the diocese was divided into two archdeaconries, that of Kingston and Ottawa, the former embracing the counties of Prince Edward, Hastings, Lennox, Addington, Frontenac, Leeds, and Grenville, and the latter comprising the counties of Renfrew, Lanark, Carleton, Russell, Prescott, Glengarry, Stormont, and Dundas; and at the same time a cathedral chapter was set up, and five canons were appointed. Thus there was a bishop, a dean, two archdeacons, and five canons, and the foundation laid for a new diocese, to consist of the archdeaconry of Ottawa.

In 1877 the Bishop urged upon his Synod the importance of dividing the diocese. It had become unwieldy, and he could no longer visit every congregation as he had hitherto striven to do, but must confine himself to visiting every parish only. Within the fifteen years previous to 1877 one hundred new churches had been built. The Bishop of Montreal was quite willing to give up a portion of his diocese towards helping to form a new see at Ottawa, and Bishop Lewis expressed the hope that an endowment for the purpose might soon be raised. The Synod appointed a committee to consider the matter.

In that year (1877) the Bishop attended the

second Lambeth Conference in England, at which one hundred bishops of the Anglican communion assembled from all parts of the world to confer together on matters affecting the welfare of the Church —the size and importance of which was becoming a matter of great congratulation. No Synod of Ontario was held in 1878, the Bishop being in the Old Country. In 1879 the diocese was divided into eight rural deaneries, five in the Kingston and three in the Ottawa archdeaconry. These were afterwards increased to eleven, six in Kingston and five in Ottawa. In that year the Bishop confirmed 1,645 people, 1,564 of whom received their first communion at the time of their confirmation. In the following year over 1,200 were confirmed. In 1881, owing to the Bishop's absence from home to recruit his health in Switzerland and elsewhere, the Synod did not meet till the month of December. In 1883 the Bishop again urged upon his Synod the division of the diocese, which he declared had outgrown his ability to perform the duties of as they should be done. He had a diocese of 20,000 square miles—a territory as large as Scotland—and the interests of the Church loudly called for its subdivision. Of this the Synod approved, and appointed a committee this time to arrange all preliminaries to the election of a bishop for the new diocese. Time, however, afterwards showed that the bull was not so easily taken by the horns as that. In that year also the Bishop called the attention of the Synod to the fact that the diocese did not own an episcopal residence. As the Bishop was still residing in Ottawa, the question of a see house was naturally a difficult one; but the people of Kingston began to show a willingness to secure a house provided the Bishop would come back to the original home of the diocese.

It was in 1883 that the Provincial Synod formed the Domestic and Foreign Missionary Society of the Church of England in Canada, and Bishop Lewis presided at the first regular meeting of its Board of Management. It was his suggestion that the Church should ask for at least sixty thousand dollars for the domestic and foreign work of the Church. That sum, however, has not yet been reached, though the contributions are creeping up towards it.

In 1885 the Committee on the Division of the Diocese reported a feasible plan by which an endowment of forty thousand dollars might be raised for the proposed see at Ottawa, and the Bishop was requested to arrange for contributions for that object from the English societies. In the following year (1886) the committee were able to report a small amount received —only a few dollars—towards the endowment of the new see, but still it was a beginning, and in that year the Bishop stated that "two new parishes, six new churches, and more than one thousand confirmed members have been added to the diocese every year for the last twenty-four years."

In 1886, the Bishop met with a heavy affliction in the death of Mrs. Lewis. The surviving children of this marriage are: Travers Lewis, of the firm of Chrysler & Lewis, barristers, etc., Ottawa, and Clement, also resident at Ottawa; Mrs. R. C. Hamilton, of Eastbourne, Eng., whose husband is a nephew of Bishop

Hamilton; Mrs. Llewellyn Lloyd, of St. Leonard's Forest, Horsham, Sussex, whose husband is of the family of Lord Overston, the great banker; and Eva, a professed sister in the Convent at East Grinstead. In his absence from home, consequent upon this great sorrow, confirmations were held in the diocese by Bishop Hamilton, of Niagara, and the Synod was not held till October. The Bishop was able to tell his Synod then that the Colonial Bishoprics' Fund in England, and also the Society for the Promotion of Christian Knowledge, had promised towards the endowment of the new see at Ottawa £1,000 each, conditionally on the sum of £9,000 being otherwise raised. He also reminded the Synod that on the 25th of March he had completed the twenty-fifth year of his episcopate. In that time the number of clergy had increased from fifty to one hundred and twenty, and a Sustentation Fund amounting to $34,500 had been secured.

In 1888 Bishop Lewis was enabled to attend his third Lambeth Conference in England, and in the following year (1889) he was married in Paris to Miss Ada Leigh, the celebrated head of charitable homes for English girls in the great French metropolis.

On his return to Canada (in 1889) he took up his residence in Kingston. Thus the wanderer had returned to his own see city. The Synod of that year enthusiastically congratulated His Lordship on the attainment of his sixty-fourth birthday, and most respectfully renewed the expression of affectionate confidence and esteem felt by its members towards His Lordship, earnestly hoping that, in God's good providence, their Right Reverend father in God might long be spared to preside over the diocese. The Bishop, with manifest emotion, acknowledged briefly this kindly act. His health to a great extent had been restored.

In 1890 the beautiful residence of Sir Richard Cartwright, in full view of Lake Ontario, was purchased for a see house at a cost of $12,000, the diocese assuming all necessary debt in connection with the purchase.

St. George's Cathedral, Kingston, enlarged.

In 1892, St. George's Cathedral, which had been undergoing enlargement and improvement, was completed and reopened for divine service. By the erection of a large dome, transepts, and chancel—all as an addition to the solid old church which had stood for so many years—a complete cathedral was constructed, a credit to Kingston and the diocese. It is in some respects a miniature St. Paul's.

In September (1892) the Most Rev. Dr. Medley, Metropolitan of Canada, died, and at the Provincial Synod which was held in Montreal, Bishop Lewis, as senior bishop, opened and closed the Lower House, and presided in the Upper House and House of Bishops. In January, 1893, Dr. Lewis was elected Metropolitan of Canada in succession to Bishop Medley, but there was some informality connected with the election, which caused the title to be deferred till the 13th of September of the same year.

This was the day before the opening of the first General Synod which met in the city of Toronto. It embraced all the dioceses of Canada, from the Atlantic to the Pacific. Fourteen bishops were present, viz.: eight from (Eastern) Canada, three from Rupert's Land, and two from British Columbia.

At this Synod it was resolved to bestow upon the Metropolitans in Canada the title of Archbishop. Dr. Lewis thus became His Grace the Archbishop of Ontario and Metropolitan of (Eastern) Canada.

The growth of the Diocese of Ontario is set forth clearly in tabular form in the Journal of 1895. We give below a comparison between its first year and its last:

	1863.	1895.
Number of parishes and missions	58	113
Diocesan collections	$5,618.52	$11,652.28
Domestic and Foreign Missions,	nothing	4,313.00

The completion of the endowment of the new Diocese of Ottawa was at last effected, and its formal separation from Kingston took place. On the 18th of March (1896) the new Synod met, and on the third ballot elected the Right Reverend Charles Hamilton, Bishop of Niagara, its first diocesan.

The Journal of Synod for the Diocese of Ontario for 1895 was therefore its last in its territorial form as originally set off from Toronto. The bishop then appointed has lived through its eventful history, and has had the satisfaction of seeing a new diocese formed from it and started on its way.

A View of Kingston, See City of the Diocese of Ontario.

17. THE RIGHT REVEREND JAMES WILLIAM WILLIAMS, D.D., FOURTH BISHOP OF QUEBEC.

WHEN Bishop George J. Mountain died at Quebec on the 6th of January, 1863, a link between the Canadian Church of the past and that of modern days was broken. He had come out with his father, the first Bishop of Quebec, in 1793, as a child. He had been intimately acquainted with the struggling Church of pioneer days. He had been largely instrumental in causing the Church to grow and to keep pace with a rapidly-increasing population. Diocese after diocese, to his great satisfaction, he saw established in territory of which he himself for several years was sole overseer. He had been, to a certain extent, a Crown officer. From the Crown he received his appointment, and from the Crown a great portion of his salary came. This died with him, and the era of self-support and self-management had set in for the now growing and important Anglican Church in Canada.

The Synod of "The United Church of England and Ireland" of the Diocese of Quebec assembled on the 4th day of March, 1863, for the purpose of electing a bishop. Forty clergymen were present, and a large number of laymen.

At the service which began at ten o'clock in the cathedral, the sermon was preached by Rev. J. W.

THE RT. REV. JAMES WILLIAM WILLIAMS, D.D.
Fourth Bishop of Quebec.
Born, 1825. Consecrated, 1863. Died, 1892.

Williams, M.A., Professor of Belles Lettres in the University of Bishop's College, Lennoxville, and rector of the Grammar School.

The first ballot showed that the Rev. A. W. Mountain commanded very nearly the requisite number of clerical votes; but the lay vote was not so strong. For any one person to obtain two-thirds of both orders was a difficult matter. It is said that Mr. Mountain himself was the means of having the law so made; if so, it was his own law which excluded him from the bishopric. As a son of the beloved old Bishop, his chances were good; but the first ballot showed that he was not likely to be elected. The second ballot, however, increased his clerical vote to 29 and his lay vote to 31—electing him by the clergy, but not by the laity. It was not till the eleventh ballot that an election was made. The choice then fell upon the Rev. J. W. Williams, who obtained the necessary number of clerical votes (28), and 52 lay votes, or ten more than the necessary number.

James William Williams was an Englishman, the son of the late Rev. David Williams, Rector of Banghurst, Hampshire, and was born at Overton, Hants, in 1825. The saintly Isaac Williams was his father's cousin, and he, with Archdeacon Sir George Prevost, who had married Isaac Williams' sister, were godparents to the infant. The father of Sir George Prevost had been Governor-General of Canada, and in the newly-born infant the connection between the two countries was destined to be continued.

At the age of seventeen, young Williams went out with a party of engineers to New Zealand. Here he had the good fortune to meet Bishop Selwyn, the apostle of the Pacific isles, and his intercourse with him was highly beneficial. After three years he returned to his native land, and graduated at Pembroke College, Oxford, where he read for Holy Orders, and was made a deacon by Bishop Wilberforce, of Oxford, in 1852. He was ordained a priest by Lord Auckland, Bishop of Bath and Wells, in 1853.

After serving as curate of High Wycombe, Bucks, and afterwards at Huish Champflower (where he married, in 1854, Maria Waldron, of Wiviliscombe, Somersetshire), he spent two years at Leamington, as assistant master in the college there, when he resolved to remove to Canada. He felt naturally drawn towards the education of boys, and for this he was greatly wanted in the Diocese of Quebec. The grammar school of Lennoxville had been closed for three years. In 1857 it was resolved to reopen it, and as Mr. Williams had just arrived in the country he was appointed to take charge of it. He and Mrs. Williams occupied for a boarding school a large house in the village square of Lennoxville, which for winter accommodation was none of the warmest. Mr. Williams was known to say that he used to go round early in the winter mornings to see if the water in the jugs, or perchance the boys, were frozen.[*]

As rector of this school Mr. Williams proved a great success. He knew how to deal with boys, and parents soon found that out. In a short time a large handsome new building was erected on the college grounds, between the rivers St. Francis and Massa-

---
[*] Rev. Dr. Adams, in *The Week*.

wippi, and in 1863 the school was filled to overflowing with one hundred and fifty boys.

At the episcopal election held in that year in Quebec, Mr. Williams, by appointment, preached the sermon. He preached from the words, " Stand ye in the ways and see, and ask for the old paths" (Jer. vi. 16). His sermon was a masterly exposition of the episcopal office, many quotations from Scripture and from the fathers being given to show the importance of it. It was no doubt this sermon which specially called the attention of the Synod to him, and led it, when the friends of Rev. A. W. Mountain and Bishop Anderson could not secure the end they had in view, to fix its choice on him. And events proved that the choice made was a good one.

Dr. Williams was consecrated in Quebec Cathedral on Sunday, June the 21st, 1863, by the Most Rev. Dr. Fulford, Metropolitan of Canada, assisted by Bishop Strachan of Toronto, Bishop Cronyn of Huron, Bishop Lewis of Ontario, and Bishop Hopkins of Vermont.

The Bishop commenced his career at the age of thirty-seven, and much hard work lay before him in the management of his large and somewhat discouraging diocese. It was large, for it was six hundred miles long ; it was discouraging because the French Roman Catholic population was always increasing, whilst English-speaking people in numbers were constantly decreasing. Perhaps the knowledge of this fact made the young Bishop brace himself for work, and throw all his influence in favour of providing for the Church in the future. Men work best when they pull against the stream. But whether or not, Bishop Williams soon proved himself a man for the times.

In the year after his consecration (1864), he held a visitation of his clergy at Lennoxville, at which he delivered a very able charge, which was printed and circulated. It dealt with some of the great questions of the day of vital importance to the Church. In speaking of preaching, he opposed the popular fallacy that clergymen, as compared with barristers, for instance, are wanting in powers of public speech. "Of the few eminently eloquent men of an age," he quietly remarked, "the fair proportion, it seems to me, are, and have been, ecclesiastics. And I have seen nothing tending to show that if all the occupants of the back benches of the court house were required to produce two original compositions, upon a limited range of subjects, for the same audience, for the rest of their natural lives, I have seen nothing tending to show that these productions, viewed as literary performances, would be in any way superior to the sermons now usually delivered." The Bishop was himself somewhat reticent in public meetings. He rarely spoke; but when he did speak there was often a force and quiet humour about his utterances, all the more noticeable, perhaps, because usually characteristically brief. The thought of true spirituality was always uppermost in his mind. "After all," he added, while speaking of sermons, "the most powerful element of preaching, the most persuasive and most instructive, is the spirituality of the preacher's character. The most eloquent of sermons is a holy life. It is useless to preach the Gospel unless we live it.

I speak not simply of the effect of example. What I mean is that if the utterance of the mouth is to be effectual, it must proceed from the fulness of the heart."

As to the diocese the Bishop remarked :

"Twelve months ago there were four vacant missions, and little prospect of filling them. I now see my way to the filling of them all, and filling them well. .... I have held confirmations in almost all the missions of the diocese, with the exception of those in the Gulf. The number of those confirmed amounts to 987."

The sum of money which, with proper foresight, had been secured by Bishop G. J. Mountain for an episcopal endowment fund had increased in 1864 to a little more than $100,000. This was yielding a handsome income, but, as a matter of justice, it was divided with Montreal, when a balance was left of $85,755. From this the Bishop received a stipend of $5,000 a year.

The Diocese of Quebec forms a remarkable example of funds carefully and well guarded, so that nothing has been lost ; and judiciously invested, so that an encouraging increase from time to time has been reported. A suitable provision for the country clergy was always a subject of much anxious thought, both on the part of the bishop and the various finance committees. In Quebec the rural work is unusually hard. The different stations are situated at long distances from one another, involving tedious drives. Large Roman Catholic churches are passed everywhere as the Anglican parson toils on to his modest little church with its handful of people. Thus it is in most places—in fact, nearly everywhere. The winters are long and trying. It is only the very strong who can do the work.

Yet, by a good system of finance, the missionary is not dependent upon the fitful and precarious "payments" of the people, but is paid regularly out of a common fund.

In 1867 a scale of payment, according to length of service, was adopted, by which a clergyman received for the first year's work four hundred dollars; for the next four years, five hundred; for the next twenty years, six hundred; and, after that, seven hundred. This was afterwards improved; but, even as it was, it was a wise and merciful provision. Whether a man might stay or go elsewhere, he was certain of *some* promotion—however small it might be.

In that year, also, a superannuation fund was started for providing pensions for aged and disabled clergy. Fifteen hundred dollars was secured and invested as a beginning.

But the care for these hard-working clergy did not cease here. A system of local endowment was commenced which has made Quebec famous among the churches. Every parish was encouraged to set apart a sum of money—however small—to be capitalized as an endowment for the future. At this juncture the right man appeared upon the scene, in Mr. Robert Hamilton, of Quebec, who, possessed of means, wanted to use them for God's glory and the advancement of His Church. Mr. Hamilton offered to present to each of a certain number of missions two hundred dollars, provided a like sum was raised by each, for a local endowment. This was afterwards extended, until $10,535 was spent by Mr. Hamilton in this way.

This endowment scheme was a great delight to Bishop Williams, who in 1876 made an urgent appeal on its behalf—an appeal which was responded to year by year with the very best results.

In 1877 the Rev. A. W. Mountain made over to the Church Society, as a gift from the Mountain family, eight thousand dollars as an endowment of one or more archdeaconries in the diocese, with the stipulation that, with the consent of the Bishop, it might be used as an endowment for a new diocese, if such should be formed. This sum was carefully invested, but not immediately made use of.

In this year Rev. Dr. Nicolls, who had been principal of Bishop's College, Lennoxville, for over thirty years, died. His is a name much to be remembered in the annals of the Diocese of Quebec. Many are those who knew his saintly character and faithful work in building up good and holy men for the work of the Church. The Rev. J. A. Lobley, Principal of the Montreal Diocesan College, was appointed principal in his place; but under him the headship of the Boys' School was combined with that of Bishop's College. Dr. Lobley was head over both institutions—an experiment which, we believe, worked well under him, and also ever since under his successor, Dr. Adams.

Bishop Williams was assiduous in visiting his diocese, even in the most remote parts of it. Some of the trips—on the Labrador coast and in the Gulf of St. Lawrence—involved at times positive danger. In an open boat, sometimes on a rough sea, appointments had to be kept. These trips were taken in the summer. To visit Labrador in the winter would have been a task of unnecessary toil and hardship, for then the missionary does his work on snow-shoes or by means of dog-sleighs; and often he has to contend with blinding snow-storms and numerous other discomforts and dangers. "He has the usual perils of the sea," the Bishop says, "to encounter in open boat along 275 miles of rocky coast in the summer, and the chance of being lost in a snow-storm in the winter."

About this time (1877) the grant of $9,661.10, hitherto paid in block sum to the Diocesan Board of the diocese to aid in the support of its country missions, was decreased to $8,709.99. This came at a time of considerable financial depression felt throughout the whole country; but a call was made by the Bishop upon the people of the country missions themselves to increase their assessment so as to make up the deficiency. This was done without any loss to the clergy; but some of the missions failed, through poverty, to make up what was required of them.

In 1879, at the earnest request of the clergy and laity of the Synod, Bishop Williams took a trip to Europe for a brief rest from his incessant toil. During his absence the Rev. Charles Hamilton acted for him as his commissary.

In 1881, the Bishop, writing to the S.P.G., says that he is anxious to get the co-operation of the other Canadian dioceses for the spiritual assistance of emigrants on their arrival. "I find," he remarks, "that in Upper Canada (where all the emigrants go) the

Church had gained, during the last ten years, twenty thousand, the Methodists a hundred and twenty thousand"; and adds with some force, "They did not come out in these proportions."

The Church Society Report for 1883 shows that the S.P.G. had made a further decrease in their grant, which was then $6,751.10. In this year the Bishop paid another of his visits to the coast of Labrador, where he heard the usual melancholy tale of dangers there in the winter. Inquiring for the man who had been his host on his previous visit, he was told that, having gone out to hunt, he had been lost in the snow. His body was found within a few yards of his house.

In 1884 progress was reported from Lennoxville College, which was prospering under Rev. Dr. Lobley. "During the last seven years," he writes, "the chapel has been enlarged, an organ placed in it, and two new special endowments made—the Harrold Fund, $25,000; and the Principal's Endowment Fund, $10,000. The formation of these funds is due principally to the liberality of Mr. Robert Hamilton, of Quebec, and the exertions of the Rev. Henry Roe, D.D., Professor of Divinity."

Dr. Lobley resigned the principalship of the College in 1885, and the Rev. Thomas Adams, M.A., D.C.L., of St. John's College, Cambridge, was appointed in his place. The memory of Bishop Williams, however, had never died away from Lennoxville. A permanent memorial of him was built by the "Old Boys" of that institution in 1888 in the Bishop Williams wing, replaced by the still handsomer Bishop Williams Hall of 1891.

By this time (1888) the Diocesan Board of Missions was able to adopt an improved scale of stipends for the clergy, which were to rise steadily from $600 to $850 per annum during twenty-five years of service.

The Church Society's Report for 1889 spoke very hopefully of the financial prospects of the diocese. The plan of local endowments began to show good fruits, and to enable the Board to look forward to the expansion of Church work, owing to the endowments of some parishes supported by it having become available. The principle of capitalizing a small sum of money works wonders as time goes on. Several new dioceses might have been formed in Canada had this principle been adopted. Bishop Williams always watched the progress of this fund with great satisfaction. It saved his diocese from ruin, and enabled it soon to sail out into clear water without any aid even from the faithful S.P.G.

To his Synod of 1888, Bishop Williams spoke of "the unwelcome conviction obtruding upon him that his faculties for sustained exertion were growing less," and added, "I shrink from the thought of hanging on with impaired powers, a weight and a drag upon the diocese," but concluded with the hope that the failure of his strength to work and his strength to live might come together. He was then sixty-four years old, yet we find him two years afterwards (in 1891) taking his usual long journey through the diocese. He is once more out upon the Labrador coast, tossing about in an open boat, ministering to the lonely people, who dearly loved to see him. From April to August his journeys were incessant. He returned home in August, having travelled in all about 2,800 miles.

This was his last prolonged trip. He died in
Quebec unexpectedly on April 20th, 1892, to the great
grief of the city, the diocese, and the Province of
Quebec.

He had the satisfaction of living long enough to
see his diocese placed on a good sound financial basis.
A short time before his death he wrote to the S.P.G.,
stating that very soon the Diocese of Quebec would be
able to do without any outside assistance whatever—
and this was carried out a few months after his death.
July the 7th, 1892, was the fiftieth anniversary—the
jubilee—of the Church Society. That date also was
within one year of the centennial of the foundation of
the diocese. Had the good Bishop lived, both these
days would have been days of proud satisfaction for
him. As it was, they were observed somewhat quietly;
but the Venerable Archdeacon Roe pointed out the
healthy growth which had taken place in all that had
to do with the sustentation and prosecution of Church
work. When Bishop G. J. Mountain died, the episcopal
income died with him. The income which came to
him as Rector of Quebec he distributed among the city
clergy. That, too, ceased. Beginning with almost
nothing in 1842, the Church Society had made such
good provision that it was able to face the battle for
life with good hope; and in 1892, when the grave of the
old Bishop's successor was but newly covered, the diocese had a clergy trust fund yielding $7,000 a year;
an archdeaconry fund yielding $600; a widows' and
orphans' fund sufficiently strong to pay each widow
$400 a year, and $50 for each child up to four in
number; besides the endowment of nearly all the weak

parishes, and a sustentation fund which enables the diocese to make a fair income to the clergy a certainty, according to length of service, no matter how poor his parish may be. The Church Society has, in all, a funded income of over half a million of dollars.

The spiritual tone imparted to the diocese by Bishop Williams showed that a higher consideration than that of finance rested upon his mind. This, emanating from him, influenced others. Free from all ambition, he dwelt among his own people, and seemed to care only to be known by them. Everything that he could do to promote their spiritual welfare was done by him. A great gloom fell over all when he was unexpectedly taken away. His wife, who had endeared herself to every one, and his son, Rev. Lennox W. Williams, Rector of St. Matthew's Church, were left specially to mourn his loss. As his chaplain, his son administered to him his last communion, and stayed with him till his gentle spirit had gone to the God who gave it.

A View of Quebec.

THE MOST REV. ROBERT MACHRAY, D.D., LL.D

Archbishop of Rupert's Land and Primate of All Canada.
Prelate of the Most Distinguished Order of St. Michael and St. George.

Born, 1831.   Consecrated, 1865.   Metropolitan, 1875.   Primate, 1893.

18. THE MOST REV. ROBERT MACHRAY, D.D., LL.D., ARCHBISHOP OF RUPERT'S LAND AND PRIMATE OF ALL CANADA.

WHEN Bishop Anderson resigned the see of Rupert's Land in October, 1864, the Rev. Robert Machray was asked by the Colonial Secretary to allow his name to be placed before the Queen ; but the offer of the bishopric from the Queen was not formally made till the following January.

Robert Machray bore the same name as his father, Robert Machray, Advocate, of Aberdeen, Scotland. He was born in 1831, and in due course became a student of King's College, Aberdeen. He was a prizeman in mathematics, natural philosophy, and moral philosophy, and on graduating in 1851 gained the Hutton prize (£65) for general scholarship and the Simpson prize (£60) for pure and mixed mathematics. In October, 1851, he entered Sidney Sussex College, Cambridge, being elected a Foundation scholar in December, 1851 ; Taylor scholar in May, 1852. He obtained various money prizes and exhibitions, being college prizeman in classics, mathematics, divinity, Latin theme, and English essay. He graduated as a Wrangler in 1855, and was elected three months later a Foundation Fellow, a position he still holds. He was ordained deacon in 1855, and priest the year after, by Dr. Thomas Turton, Bishop of Ely. In 1858 he was elected dean of his college. In 1860 and 1861 he was University Examiner, and in 1865 was appointed University Ramsden preacher. He assisted the Vicar of Newton and Hawton for three years, and in 1862 was collated by the Bishop of Ely to the Vicarage of Madingley, a small parish adjoining Cambridge, which he served from college. He at the same time filled various honorary offices, as Honorary Secretary, for the University, town, and county, of the Church Pastoral Aid Society, in which office he succeeded the Bishop of Madras; Honorary Secretary of the Army Scripture Readers' Society; Honorary Secretary of the Servants' Training Institution; and he took an active part in the work and classes of the Church of England Young Men's Society. He was consecrated at Lambeth on June 24th, St. John Baptist's Day, 1865. The prelates officiating were Archbishop Longley, of Canterbury; Bishop Tait, of London; Bishop Harold Browne, of Ely; Bishop Suther, of Aberdeen; and Bishop Anderson. He had previously received the degree of D.D. from the University of Cambridge, and LL.D. from the University of Aberdeen. His first episcopal act was the ordination, at the request of the Bishop of London (Dr. Tait), of Rev. W. C. Bompas to the priesthood. Mr. Bompas left at once for North America to serve as one of Bishop Machray's missionaries. His career will be noticed later in these pages.

Bishop Machray had to sail for his diocese within two months of his consecration. He made good use of this brief period in the interests of his new work. The Diocesan Fund formed by Bishop Anderson was exhausted. The new bishop must have a new fund. He therefore visited many places and addressed a number of meetings, procuring in this way £500 ($2,500), one-fifth of which he had subscribed himself.

Bishop Machray arrived at his destination on the 12th of October (1865), and on the 5th of December he held a meeting in " Bishop's Court " of all the clergy of " the settlement," with a view to establishing some system of self-help among them, and of promoting systematic giving. The offertory as yet had only been begun in the cathedral and three other churches. It was begun at the cathedral on Advent Sunday, the Bishop taking as his text, " Not because I desire a gift : but I desire fruit that may abound to your account " (Phil. iv. 17). It was now resolved to make use of it at all services. On the 11th of January following (1866) he set out to visit a portion of his diocese. He was out for seven weeks, in which time he made a circuit by Portage la Prairie, Westbourne, Fairford, Swan Lake, Cumberland, and the Nepowewin (near Prince Albert), returning by the Touchwood Hills, Qu'Appelle Lakes, and Fort Ellice. The distance travelled by dog-train must have considerably exceeded a thousand miles. In his own words : " We slept during seventeen nights by the camp fire in the open air. But the perfect comfort of this, when proper arrangements are made, although the thermometer may be lower than 40° below zero, is surprising to a traveller who first experiences it.

"At other times we slept in an old deserted log house or an Indian tent. The solitariness of the country in the interior must be felt to be realized.

During the whole journey we scarcely saw a dozen Indians in all, excepting those we met with in the immediate neighbourhood of a fort or mission station. At Fairford, and at the Pas, Cumberland, there were congregations of upwards of a hundred at both morning and evening service, but the bulk of the Indians, even in these stations, were in their hunting grounds. There were forty-eight communicants at the celebration of the Lord's Supper at the Pas. The offertory had been commenced there, and upwards of £3 was paid into my hands, being the first payment from the country to the Diocesan Fund. At Touchwood Hills, Assiniboia, I found a congregation of upwards of fifty. In other places I found but few Indians. They were scattered throughout the country, and are so always, with the exception of a few weeks twice in the year. The difficulty of missionary work is therefore very great."

On Wednesday, the 30th of May, 1866, the Bishop assembled the first conference of clergy and lay delegates of the Diocese of Rupert's Land. The clergy in the diocese, which was then the whole of the Northwest, were twenty-three in number; but, of these, two were only nominally connected with the diocese. They were in England, and did not return.

It was a brave attempt to hold a conference of clergy in a diocese so vast as Rupert's Land was then. Yukon was distant 2,500 miles; Mackenzie river, 2,000; Albany and Moose, 1,200; York Factory, 800; English river, 700; and this in a country where boats, canoes, and dog-sleighs, with perhaps an occasional Hudson's Bay steamer (for a few months in the year), were the only means of travel. But Bishop Machray meant work, and he got as many of the clergy as possible together. Ten clergymen were present, and eighteen lay delegates, representing nine parishes or missions. At this conference the Bishop spoke strongly about the low state of education in the "settlement." Nothing grieved him more than the state of the schools. "We must rise," he said, "to the effort of supporting our own schools," and His Lordship propounded an elaborate scheme whereby the whole community, Hudson's Bay people and all, might be benefited by the circulation of books and the establishment of parochial schools. The large population of heathen Indians in the dioceses greatly distressed the Bishop. From English societies, especially the C.M.S. and "The New England Company," he hoped to get large aid in missionary work among these poor children of the wilderness.

Bishop Machray knew well the value of a higher education for the clergy. He therefore lost no time in establishing a college in his wilderness which might be the means of supplying him with young men properly trained for the ministry. He was the right man for a new country. He saw what was needed, and rested not day nor night till the need was supplied. He now resolved to revive the old St. John's College. To the excellent library collected by Bishop Anderson he added by himself presenting seventy volumes, some of which were valuable works.

Bishop Machray had already engaged an old classmate of his—like himself, a Scotchman; a distinguished graduate of King's College, Aberdeen, a High Bursar and prizeman in Latin, Greek, Natural Philosophy, Moral Philosophy, and Chemistry—to be warden and theological tutor in the new institution. This was the Rev. John McLean, M.A., whom he also made Archdeacon of Assiniboine. At that time he was curate at St. Paul's Cathedral, London, Diocese of Huron. With himself as one of the staff, and with two others (besides the warden), he hoped to make a good beginning. The Bishop was not married. His whole energies, his income, his house, seemed always at the disposal of the Church. The old buildings at St. John's must be torn down, as they were quite uninhabitable, except the back part, which might be raised and a kitchen added; and for the rest the Bishop's own house might be available! For the proposed work the Bishop had already secured the necessary lumber. Immediately after the conference he accompanied Governor MacTavish by boat to Norway House, and from there proceeded to York Factory, where he held two confirmations, confirming fifty-six Indians. He found most of the Indians in that district professing Christians, and showing great propriety in their outward profession, frequently reading the Word of God in the syllabic character and maintaining regularly family prayer.

The second conference of clergy and lay delegates met in St. John's on May 29th, 1867, and unanimously resolved itself into a synod of the diocese.

He did not attend the Lambeth Conference in 1868, as he felt he had too recently left England to allow of this. But in this summer he visited the missions along James' Bay, confirming at Rupert's

House, Albany, and Moose Factory. The visit to Rupert's House was especially interesting. He spent a week examining, by the help of Mr. Horden, all the candidates for confirmation separately, and confirming some eighty adults. On his way back through Canada he laid the foundation stone of Hellmuth Ladies' College in London, and preached the sermon at the opening of the Provincial Synod of Canada. Passing on to New York he was present at the General Convention held there; and at the request of the presiding bishop, the Bishop of Kentucky, he consecrated at the great opening service in Trinity Church.

He met with much courtesy at the hands of the Governor of Rupert's Land and of the officers of the Hudson's Bay Company, some of whom subscribed handsomely to his funds.

By that time (1869) the Clergy Endowment Fund had reached $3,900, and was yielding an income of $200 a year; the Widows and Orphans' Fund had a capital of only $380, but still it was a beginning. The college he helped as a master, taking the mathematical department; his clergy he helped with his kind words and frequent visits; his people he helped by the strong hopes he had for the future; and all he encouraged to work for the Church which he was so anxious to establish on good, firm foundations among them. But there were most serious discouragements. A plague of grasshoppers had visited the country in their path as they swept on; and when everything was eaten they devoured one another, till heaps of corruption were left everywhere throughout the land. This the Bishop graphically described to his Synod in 1869, and deplored the severe blow that the plague had been to the country. The following year brought the rebellion, which caused much anxiety and trouble. But still for the Church he was hopeful. And when the Synod met again, which was not till 1873, he had better news to tell. Winnipeg, his " see city," from a place with but a few houses, had grown to be a village of 1,500 inhabitants, and other settlements had sprung up. The immediate territory in which it was situated was formed into a province, to be known as Manitoba, the fifth province to enter the confederation forming the Dominion of Canada. The Canadian Pacific Railway was in course of construction, and the amount of prosperity that this might bring to the country was naturally gilded with a glowing hope. And, besides that, the Bishop had been to England, and had had important interviews with the English societies, especially the C.M.S., with the result that three new dioceses were to be established in " Rupert's Land." Two of these were to be in the extreme north, one with its centre at Moose Fort (Moosonee), in the region of the Hudson's Bay, and the other with its centre at Fort Simpson, Mackenzie river, bordering upon the Arctic Circle. The missionaries already there, Mr. Horden at Moose Fort and Mr. Bompas at Fort Simpson, were to be the respective bishops. The third diocese was to be the immediate region of the Saskatchewan, extending far to the west, where the Rocky Mountains separate the " Great Lone Land" from British Columbia. Arrangements were being made for the endowment of this see. A canon was passed by the Synod dividing the diocese into the four dioceses of Rupert's Land, Saskatchewan, Moosonee, and Athabasca, determining their boundaries and arranging for the calling of a Provincial Synod. Through his own exertions in England, and the warden's in Canada, the endowment and equipment of St. John's College were considerably augmented by this year (1873), and the Bishop announced that he was gradually endowing a professorial chair himself. The funds had increased as follows: St. John's College, $30,000; Church Endowment, $7,000; Native Pastorate, $2,000; Widows and Orphans', $1,100.

When the Synod met again, on June 10th, 1875, the boundaries of Rupert's Land had been curtailed so that it consisted of the Province of Manitoba with the districts of Cumberland (except Fort la Corne), Swan River, Norway House, and Lac la Plaine, the three dioceses of Moosonee, Athabasca, and Saskatchewan having been formed. Seventeen clergymen were present at this Synod.

The Bishop's wise policy in securing land and endowments now began to show itself. He was enabled to found six canonries, four besides the two archdeaconries, which were to be more or less connected with the professorial work of St John's College. The position of dean was also being provided for, but till fully endowed was filled by the Bishop himself. In the Journal of Synod for 1895, after describing the endowment of these canonries, from about $1,000 to $600 each, we find the words:

" There is also a tract of over six hundred acres (including the hay privilege land) of very valuable land in the neighbourhood of the city of Winnipeg, from which in the course of a few years the cathedral may be expected to derive a considerable income."

Such was the progress that Bishop Machray's diocese made in ten years, with three new dioceses formed into the bargain. The four dioceses of the Northwest were formed in this year (1875) into a Provincial Synod, to be known as the Synod of the Province of Rupert's Land. It was to consist of two houses; the Upper House composed of the bishops, and the Lower House of delegates from their several dioceses. The first session was held in Winnipeg on August 4th, 1875. Bishop Bompas, of Athabasca, was not present. The other three bishops formed the first Upper House. The Apostolic Bishop Whipple, of Minnesota, preached the sermon.

At this meeting a letter was read from Bishop Anderson (then in England), in which he said: " Too grateful I cannot be to Almighty God for having spared me and permitted me to behold in the flesh and hear of so mighty a stride in what was as the wilderness, and which now in so many parts begins to bud and blossom. What a change in the half century! How great a change in the quarter of a century ! How migthy a one in your own ten years! Surely the Lord hath done great things, whereof we rejoice."

By the formation of the Provincial Synod, Bishop Machray became Metropolitan as well as Bishop of Rupert's Land. To the Diocesan Synod of 1887 the Bishop was able to speak of continued prosperity.

"We are no longer," he said, "isolated. By means of telegraphic communication connecting us with the States and Canada, newspaper enterprise presents us daily with the latest telegrams from all parts of the world. The telegraph already has been carried for about a thousand miles to the west of us."

St. John's College is a college in the University of Manitoba having a separate Faculty of Theology for conducting all the theological examinations required by its students for the degree of B.D. or D.D. There is also a literary examination conducted by the general examiner of the University. Colleges connected with other religious bodies may have the like privilege.

Besides St. John's Cathedral and College there was now in Winnipeg the Church of the Holy Trinity, under the Rev. O. Fortin. The College School (for boys) was flourishing under the Bishop as headmaster, with the Rev. Canon Grisdale, Rev. Canon O'Meara, and others, as assistants. What a parable on the importance of training a child in the way he should go, that the Bishop took charge of his boys' school himself!

In 1878 the Bishop attended the Lambeth Conference, and was assigned a seat along with the other Metropolitans by the side of the Archbishop of Canterbury. On his return he was presented by some of his clergy and laity with $800. This he afterwards gave to a fund for Machray exhibitions at St. John's College for sons of the clergy.

The second Provincial Synod was held in Winnipeg in 1879, at which the Widows and Orphans' Fund, which was for the whole original Diocese of Rupert's Land, was recognized as provincial, and, in accordance with a proposal of the Diocesan Synod of Rupert's Land, placed under provincial control, so that, as hitherto, the bishops and clergy of the whole province should be participants in the benefits of the funds.

To his Diocesan Synod of 1880 the Bishop described the change that had taken place within the short period of ten years. "Ten years ago," he said, "there was only one village in the country with about three hundred of a population. There was scarcely a house a quarter of a mile from Red river or the Assiniboine. To-day we have a country one hundred and twenty miles in breadth by two hundred miles in length, covered with small settlements, being dotted over with homesteads, and yet this country is but the gateway to the vast region of fertile land beyond. The village of three hundred people has become a city of twelve thousand inhabitants, with a business that is, perhaps, only exceeded now by six or eight cities in the whole Dominion. This past year has seen nearly three hundred houses wholly or partially built, at a cost of nearly a million of dollars. In 1870 there were established nineteen post offices. There are now nearly one hundred and fifty."

But all this made the Bishop feel more than ever the great responsibility resting upon him. The church of the city of Winnipeg was fairly well off with the help of endowments, but in the rest of the diocese—how was provision to be made for the needs of struggling settlers? This was the problem. Appeals were made to England and to the eastern part of Canada, with results somewhat disappointing to the Metropolitan, but at the same time every effort possible was made in the way of self-help. There was a debt also on St. John's College, incurred by continual additions made to the building—a debt of about $13,000, but still they must enlarge. For this they needed $20,000. There was also by this time established, chiefly through the liberality of Prebendary Wright, Hon. Secretary of the C.M.S., St. John's Ladies' College. Prebendary Wright gave $10,000, the Bishop gave about $8,000, and other friends contributed from $1,500 to $2,000.

The next year (1881) saw still greater progress in Winnipeg, especially in the rise of the value of land. The city was becoming a great railway centre. The C.P.R. was pushing its way to the west of it with an energy which meant not to stop till the Rocky Mountains were crossed and a way made to the shores of the Pacific Ocean.

The clergy list for 1883 showed a large increase to the clerical staff. They numbered forty-seven. The progress in the country still went on. The population had nearly doubled since the census of 1881. There was now railway communication from Lake Superior to the Saskatchewan, a distance of about 1,000 miles. Winnipeg, the hamlet of a few years ago, stood third in foreign importations in the list of Canadian cities. But all this meant anxiety for the Church. Fifty municipalities had been formed in Manitoba. Fifteen of these only had been provided with a resident clergyman. There was also the newly-formed Province of Assiniboia, to the west of Winnipeg, in the whole of which there were but three clergymen, viz.: two travelling missionaries and one permanently stationed at Regina.

The Provincial Synod also met in 1883, in the month of August. In 1884 the clergy list of Rupert's Land Diocese had grown from forty-five to fifty-two, though four or five were removed on account of the formation of the Diocese of Saskatchewan. The Diocese of Qu'Appelle was also formed that year, and Mackenzie River was separated from Athabasca.

When the Bishop took charge of the diocese in 1865, there were no endowments in money except the Bishopric Fund. There were only a few glebe lands, at that time of little or no value. In 1884 there were about thirty trusts or endowments, which had accumulated gradually, and were all held by the Bishop himself as a corporation sole. However, a considerable portion of this amount consisted of mortgages on Church land which had been sold in the time of the boom. The instalments due on those mortgages were not paid, and the land in time reverted to the Church for the foreclosure of mortgages or otherwise. By 1884, also, a new stone building had been erected for St. John's College, with the general structure of which all were well satisfied; but this raised the debt on that institution to about $55,000. The addition to the debt had, however, been contracted on the security of subscriptions which at the time were considered good and trustworthy, but which from the failure in means of so many were never paid. These subscriptions included sums of $1,000 and $500, that were regarded as absolutely safe. The sale of a valuable field of some fifteen acres, and other land belonging to the college and adjacent to it, could have greatly reduced this debt, but it was not considered advisable to sell. The canons of the cathedral are professors and instructors in the college.

But the reaction which many wise-headed men had foreseen, consequent upon the headlong rush into speculation caused by the "boom" in prosperity, had set in, and a change came over the spirit of the dream. The next year the Metropolitan deplored the scarcity of funds for the prosecution of his diocesan work, and the small amount of help received from Eastern Canada.

He urged the great necessity of liberality. This he could do with a clear conscience, for he had been most liberal with his own means. To St. John's College alone he had given from time to time much, besides the main portion of the endowment of the chair of Ecclesiastical History.

The Bishop was rejoiced by a gift to the college of $3,000 from Sir Donald A. Smith. This enabled him to receive the grant of $5,000 made by the S.P.G. on condition that $20,000 should be otherwise subscribed. But still the financial condition of the college gave the Bishop such anxiety that he went to England to get, if possible, some help for this small endowment fund of the college that was being raised, and for which $20,000 was yet required to secure the £1,000 promised by the S.P.C.K.; but in this he was not very successful. He secured, however, about $6,000 for various objects in his diocese. The expense of journeys of this kind Bishop Machray bore himself.

Archdeacon Pinkham, financial secretary of the diocese, and Canon O'Meara made excursions to Eastern Canada and collected some money for the Home Mission Fund. This became a regular institution, and brought to the diocese between three and four thousand dollars a year.

The Metropolitan was again in England in 1888 for two months, attending the Lambeth Conference, a full account of which he gave to his Synod. That year he received the unwelcome intelligence that the C.M.S. intended to reduce by degrees the grants made for the support of his missionaries. During this visit to England he preached the Commencement Sermon before the University of Cambridge, and received the degree of D.D. from the University of Durham.

In 1889 it was reported that six new missions had been formed in the diocese. The debt on St. John's College, however, was becoming a burden. It amounted to $61,618.85 in 1888, the addition being made by various additions and improvements in the college. All the debt, except a mortgage of $14,450, was due to some of the capitalized funds of the college. The college, of course, was paying these funds interest; but it was not satisfactory. The Bishop about this time ceased to be bursar of the college.

The Provincial Synod of Rupert's Land, which was held in Winnipeg in August, 1890, received a deputation from the various dioceses of (Eastern) Canada relative to the formation of a General Synod for the whole Dominion. The Bishop of Rupert's Land was always most favourable to this, and supported the proposition in every possible way in his diocese; but on the condition that the Provincial Synod should continue to exist, and that certain matters, for which he considered himself and his province in honour pledged, should remain with the Provincial Synod. His episcopate had grown, in a sense, with the growth of the whole Northwest itself; and the building up of an ecclesiastical provincial system with Winnipeg, his own see city, as its metropolitical centre, had called forth his energies and enlisted his warmest feelings; but the object had been realized only by the warm sympathy and cordial help of the English Church societies (especially of the C.M.S.) in their support of the bishoprics. The Bishop considered it both honourable and necessary to secure its interests. This he had already expressed to his own Diocesan and Provincial Synods. His Lordship received the deputation from the east with every mark of courtesy, and the joint conference between the representatives of the two provinces at which he presided came to an understanding regarding a basis on which a General Synod might be formed. This the Metropolitan of Rupert's Land stated, with evident feelings of satisfaction, to his own Synod, which met in October of the same year (1890).

In the end of 1890 a testimonial in money was presented to the Bishop by Churchmen of the diocese, on the completion of the twenty-fifth year of his episcopate. Of this money the Bishop gave $1,526 to the General Endowment Fund of St. John's College, and the balance he spent in purchasing a very fine massive eagle lectern for the cathedral. In 1891 the Diocese of Selkirk was formed from Mackenzie River. This made the eighth diocese formed out of territory once presided over by Bishop Machray alone.

To his Synod assembled in October, 1891, the Bishop was able to report a considerable increase in the diocesan Clergy Endowment Fund through the gift of $1,000 from a farmer in Manitoba, which enabled the diocese to claim some grants made by the English societies. The same kind-hearted person gave $1,000 to St. John's College. The next Synod did not meet till January, 1893, when preparations were made for the first General Synod to be held in Toronto in the autumn of that year. It was a year of synods for the Metropolitan, for his Provincial Synod met in Winnipeg on the 9th of August, at which further preparations were made in order that the approaching General Synod might have full legal sanction. It was a year also of honour and distinction for the Metropolitan of Rupert's Land. In it Her Majesty the Queen was graciously pleased to appoint His Lordship to the office of "Prelate of the most distinguished Order of St. Michael and St. George." The first bishop honoured with this title was George Augustus Selwyn, Bishop of New Zealand, and afterwards of Lichfield. The next was Bishop Perry, of Melbourne, Australia. After him, Bishop Austin, of British Guiana, on whose death the title was bestowed upon the Metropolitan of Rupert's Land.

On September the 13th, the first General Synod of the Church of England in the Dominion of Canada was held in the city of Toronto. It was a goodly sight to see bishops, and leading clergymen and laymen assembled together from all parts of the Dominion, from Nova Scotia to British Columbia. Prominent amongst all, striking in height, size, and appearance, was the great missionary bishop, the Most Reverend Robert Machray, Metropolitan of Rupert's Land. For twenty-eight years he had battled with hard pioneer work, with an attention which never allowed diversion, and a zeal which knew no flagging. He had never taken to himself a wife—the Church needed all his care. With pen, and voice, and energy, with his open purse ever ready to help his struggling work, he was beloved by those who knew him; and those who did not know him saw in him one who was no ordinary man. In a room, among a crowd, one would immediately ask, on seeing him: "Who is that?"

In debate, while important preliminaries were being arranged in the General Synod, he took a prominent part. Questions on which he felt deeply were raised at times, and he spoke so that no one could misunderstand him. When at last all difficulties were adjusted, no one appeared better pleased than the Metropolitan of Rupert's Land.

The enactment that the Metropolitans in Canada should have the title of Archbishop met with hearty approval. And when it was known that his brother bishops had elected the Metropolitan of Rupert's Land chairman of the Upper House, and, therefore, the first Primate of all Canada, it was felt that a worthy choice had been made.

At a great missionary meeting held in St. James' Schoolhouse, Toronto, His Grace the Archbishop of Rupert's Land, and Primate of all Canada, presided. His first act as Primate of all Canada was thus, by a pleasing coincidence, to preside at a meeting on behalf of the cause for which the best part of his life had been spent.

The Archbishop returned to his home in Winnipeg and prosecuted his ordinary duties as of old. There was a deficiency of $3,291.64 in his Home or Diocesan Mission Fund, yet he resolved to supply a clergyman wherever the people in a new district would properly meet a grant. His Grace depended now upon regular aid from Eastern Canada, chiefly through the exertions of the Rev. George Rogers, financial secretary of the diocese.

The financial condition of St. John's College in 1894 had been considerably improved. The debt had been decreased by $15,000 by the sale of land. The General Endowment Fund had also been increased by a bequest from Miss Clouston, in memory of her nephew, the Rev. W. R. Flett, who had been a pupil, scholar, and master of the college. This bequest, in addition to a considerable sum raised in the diocese, enabled the college to claim about seven thousand two hundred dollars in grants from English societies.

To his Synod of last year (1895) His Grace, for the first time apparently, was obliged to speak of an illness which had prevented him from performing some of his duties. These were kindly taken for him by Bishop Young, of Athabasca, who happened to be spending the winter in Winnipeg. The Archbishop's health, however, was soon restored.

He had to lament a deficiency in his Home Mission Fund of $4,249.31, largely due, His Grace remarked, to the receipts from Eastern Canada having fallen under what was expected, and also to some special payments which were made. The receipts from Eastern Canada were acknowledged as $5,239.25, including $657 collected by Canon O'Meara, and over $4,000 by Rev. George Rogers; but this may well be considered small when the great responsibility resting upon the Primate as a diocesan bishop is considered. Outside of the city of Winnipeg his diocese is almost entirely missionary; that is to say, the clergy could not exist were it not for assistance from some common fund. No one can read the charges of the Archbishop, or note his own example and work, without coming to the conclusion that he has done all that a strong, hopeful man could do to induce his own people to support the work growing up around them. But that work grew with such surprising rapidity that, taking into account the peculiar conditions attending a new country, self-help could not possibly keep pace with what had to be done. When he went out to that country as a missionary bishop in 1865, the sound of a human voice was to be heard only here and there, and at long, long intervals apart. His first clergy list practically amounted to 18, distributed over districts as follows :

The present Diocese of Rupert's Land 8, Moosonee 3, Saskatchewan 3, Qu'Appelle with part of Rupert's Land 1, Athabasca 0, Mackenzie River 2, Selkirk 1. There were also two clergymen in England nominally connected with the diocese.

These are all now separate dioceses, with clergy (including the bishops) as follows :

Rupert's Land (Manitoba) 76, Moosonee 8, Saskatchewan (and Calgary) 29, Qu'Appelle 19, Athabasca 6, Mackenzie River 8, Selkirk 4 ; in all, 152.

Such has been the growth of thirty years. His Grace the Lord Archbishop of Rupert's Land and Primate of all Canada has been through all the phases of the rise and growth of the "Great Lone Land." He is still only sixty-five years old, and as assiduous as ever in the performance of his duties.

The Archbishop is well known in Winnipeg and elsewhere in Manitoba, and even beyond it, as a public officer. He has been chairman of the Board of Public Education almost from its commencement, and Chancellor of the University of Manitoba from its foundation. He has written long and exhaustive charges and articles in favour of religious education in the schools, and has proved himself a public educator as well as a spiritual guide to his own flock.

His Grace is now preparing to receive the second General Synod of the Dominion of Canada, which is to meet in Winnipeg in September of this year (1896). In Winnipeg he first presided over his own diocesan Synod; there, too, he first presided over the Provincial Synod of the Northwest; and there, if spared for a short time longer, he will preside over the legislative body of the Church gathered together from all parts of the Dominion of Canada.

St. John's College School (Boys'), Winnipeg.

THE RT. REV. ALEXANDER NEIL BETHUNE, D.D.
Second Bishop of Toronto.
Born, 1800.   Consecrated, 1867.   Died, 1879.

19. THE RIGHT REV. ALEXANDER NEIL BETHUNE, D.D., D.C.L., SECOND BISHOP OF TORONTO.

ALEXANDER NEIL BETHUNE was born at Williamstown, County of Glengarry, in Upper Canada, on August 28th, 1800. He was the fifth son of a Presbyterian ("Old Kirk") minister, who came to Canada from North Carolina with the United Empire Loyalists in 1783. Two of his sons became staunch Episcopalians and honoured dignitaries of the Church, viz., John, who became Dean of Montreal, and Alexander, who became Bishop of Toronto. As a boy young Bethune was sent to school to Rev. Dr. Strachan, at Cornwall; and from that time there commenced an acquaintance between master and pupil destined to continue for many years.

When Dr. Strachan was appointed rector of York (Toronto), in 1812, he opened a grammar school there, and there, in 1891, Mr. A. N. Bethune joined him as his assistant master, and as a student in divinity. His journey from Montreal to Toronto was made by lumber wagon, open boat, steamer, and stage; and when he reached his destination he found it "a little town of about one thousand inhabitants, with but three brick houses in the whole place."*

Mr. Bethune was ordained deacon in 1823, and priest in 1824, by Dr. Jacob Mountain, and was ap-

---

* For the clerical staff at this time in Upper Canada, see p. 82.

pointed incumbent of Grimsby. Here he married Jane Eliza, eldest daughter of the Hon. James Crooks, of West Flamboro. In 1826 Dr. Strachan, then Archdeacon of York, paid him a visit on his way to the Old Country (to take preparatory steps for founding a university for Upper Canada), and left in his charge his second son George.

In 1827 Mr. Bethune was appointed rector of Cobourg, in succession to Rev. W. Macaulay,* who had removed to Hallowell (Picton). In Cobourg Mr. Bethune remained for many years. He took part in all the great public movements which agitated the period, and on which we have already dwelt in the life of Bishop Strachan. In all Dr. Strachan's battles, both as archdeacon and bishop, for the rights of the Church in the "Clergy Reserves" question; in all his struggles for the establishment of educational institutions and their endowments, as well as the endowment of the Church, the Rector of Cobourg was always his faithful abettor and assistant.

As a means of placing the rights of the Church well before the public, or at all events before her own sons and daughters, it was resolved, in 1856, at a meeting of the clergy, to establish a Church newspaper, the management of which was put in the hands of Dr. Bethune, who, in May, 1837, issued a specimen number of *The Church*. The publication proved so far successful that it was enlarged after the completion of the first year, and again at the end of its second volume. Here Dr. Bethune could work in his most

---

* In Mr. Macaulay's time this parish or mission was known as "Hamilton," from the township of that name.

powerful way. He had the pen not only of a ready but of a graceful writer; and, in days when periodicals were not as numerous as they are now, the weekly arrival of *The Church* was eagerly looked for by a large number of readers. It is pleasant to read its columns now. Several bound volumes of it still exist.

When the Diocese of Toronto was formed in 1839, Bishop Strachan appointed his friend and former pupil one of his chaplains; and in 1841 he was entrusted with the important business of training young men for the ministry. The Theological School at Cobourg soon became an important and highly useful institution. Many young men were carefully and conscientiously prepared in it for the ministry, and from time to time took missionary work under the direction of Dr. Bethune. The instructions were carried on in a small brick building which, slightly altered and added to, still stands in Cobourg. It formed, in fact, the nucleus of the divinity school in Trinity University, which was afterwards established at Toronto. Its average attendance of students was fifteen; its whole number of members, from its opening to its close, being forty-five.

When, in 1846, Bishop Strachan resigned the Archdeaconry of York, Dr. Bethune was appointed in his place. Thus was he once more an official assistant to his old master.

At the first episcopal election ever held in Canada, Archdeacon Bethune was the favourite candidate of a large number of the clergy, for it was he alone who (in 1857), as we have already mentioned, contested the bishopric of Huron with Dr. Cronyn.

At the Synod held in August, 1866, the venerable

Bishop, bowed down with the weight of eighty-eight years, was at last obliged to tell his Synod that he could no longer do the work of the diocese single-handed. A Synod was therefore convened for the 19th of September, for the purpose of electing a coadjutor.

The "High Church" party were divided between Archdeacon Whitaker, Provost of Trinity College, who received the largest support, and Dr. Bethune; the "Low Church" voted for Rev. H. J. Grasett, and the moderately inclined for the Rev. T. B. Fuller. After balloting ineffectually for two days, Provost Whitaker in a few graceful words withdrew from the contest, requesting his friends to cast no more votes for him. Dr. Bethune was then elected by fifty-three clergy (necessary forty-seven) and forty-seven lay (necessary forty-six).

Dr. Bethune was consecrated under the title of Bishop of Niagara, on the 25th of January, 1867, in St. James' Cathedral, Toronto, by Bishop Strachan, assisted by Bishop Cronyn of Huron and Bishop Lewis of Ontario.

It was interesting to see the man of sixty-seven kneeling before his old friend and master, now eighty-nine years of age, and receiving the touch of his trembling hand upon his head, the aged pair still associated together in work. First they stood to one another in the relation of teacher and pupil, then of headmaster and assistant, then of bishop and archdeacon, and lastly of bishop and coadjutor. Bishop Bethune was of fragile build, and he looked thin and wan, yet he proved himself possessed of considerable vitality, and addressed himself with energy to the duties of his new office. The diocese was divided into two archdeaconries, named respectively Toronto and Niagara, and occupied by Rev. T. B. Fuller, D.D. (Toronto), and Rev. A. Palmer, M.A., of Guelph (Niagara). A cathedral chapter was also formed with the Rev. H. J. Grasett, B.D., Rector of St. James' Cathedral, Toronto, as Dean. Four canonries and four honorary canonries were also formed. The number of rural deans was also increased to eight. The Episcopal Endowment Fund had by this time reached $41,518.13, and from the interest of this sum the coadjutor bishop was maintained.

After making confirmation tours in several places in the diocese, including a trip to the distant region of Algoma, Bishop Bethune, in August, 1867, proceeded to England and was present at the Lambeth Conference, at which seventy-six prelates were gathered: twenty-three from England and Ireland, six from Scotland, twenty-eight from the colonies and mission fields, and nineteen from the United States.

Bishop Strachan died as his coadjutor was on his way home, and Bishop Bethune arrived just in time to take a last look at the remains of his venerated friend, and to attend his funeral.

Dr. Bethune was now, by the right of succession, the second Bishop of Toronto. The boys' school, which had been commenced in Weston in 1865, was moved to Port Hope in 1868, and was placed in charge of the Bishop's eldest son, the Rev. Charles James Stewart Bethune, M.A.—a name which connected him with the early days of Church history. The diocese was rapidly growing in size and importance.

Bishop Bethune was now close upon the threescore years and ten allotted to man, and he had not the abnormal physical strength, the strong voice and resolute will, that his predecessor had when that advanced period of age was reached. Strong party feeling in the Church began to disturb the peace. Men's minds were stirred to the very depths over questions that were considered on the one hand "high" and the other "low." This feeling began to show itself in the discussions in Synod first on the "patronage question," which was left over from year to year, each year producing the same wearisome debates. It had been the privilege of the Bishop to appoint clergymen to vacant parishes. The laity began to claim this privilege. The clergy by very large majorities resisted it, the laity by small majorities supported it. It was at last arranged in 1871 that the Bishop should have the right to the patronage, but that no appointment should be made without consultation with the churchwardens and lay delegates of the vacant parish. The aged Bishop must have breathed a sigh of relief when this question was ended. Further relief, but of another nature, came to him also in 1873, when the Diocese of Algoma was formed, and also in 1875, when the Diocese of Niagara was set apart. This limited the Diocese of Toronto to the bounds which it still possesses, and left it consisting of the city of Toronto and the counties of Peel, York, Simcoe, Ontario, Durham, Victoria, Northumberland, Peterborough, and Haliburton. Territorially, this was a great relief to the Bishop, but it left him still with a clerical staff of about one hundred, and with eighty-seven parishes and missions.

A "Church Association" was formed in 1873 to inculcate evangelical principles and put some check upon the growth of what was called "sacerdotalism." This Association embraced a few of the clergy of the diocese, and a large number of earnest-minded, wealthy, and influential laymen. From time to time tracts were issued and manuals published, setting forth the principles of the Association, and calling attention to certain practices introduced into some of the churches which it considered subversive of them. A weekly paper was also commenced in 1876, and was called *The Evangelical Churchman*. Trinity College, under Provost Whitaker, was looked upon with such marked disfavour by this Association that a theological college was resolved upon. It began in a very small way in St. James' Schoolhouse in 1877, voluntary instruction being given by some of the sympathizing city clergy to a few young men whose desire was to be prepared for Holy Orders. A college was afterwards secured, and a regular course of instruction established under Rev. James P. Sheraton, B.A.

The Church Association in time established its own Mission Committee, its own Widows and Orphans' Committee, for receiving contributions for the benefit of their sympathizers. All these organizations, however necessary they may have been regarded by those who established them, were very distressing to the Bishop. They affected the funds of the diocese to a very grave extent—the mission fund especially, which was overdrawn each year until a heavy debt was incurred.

The Synods, during these years, were too frequently characterized by acrimonious debates, which often got beyond the control of the chair. The two parties were very closely defined, and regarded one another with no small amount of animosity.

In this state of things the aged Bishop—seventy-eight years old—called the Synod together, in March, 1878, to elect a coadjutor bishop. By this time the diocese had grown to one hundred parishes and missions, and it was a large gathering that assembled for the purpose of electing a coadjutor bishop.

The first ballot showed that a "split" had taken place in the High Church vote, which it was thought would go solidly for the venerable Provost of Trinity College. Twenty-eight clergymen and ten laymen voted for Rev. W. D. MacLagan, of England—now Archbishop of York—and though they soon abandoned this policy it was shortly found that no election could be made. The voting continued till late at night, and extended to the following day.

At two o'clock on the second day, the aged Bishop, much grieved and disappointed, prorogued the Synod with the resolve to continue the work of the diocese as far as his failing strength would allow. His Lordship was permitted to preside over the Synod of 1878, at which he deplored greatly the unhappy divisions in the diocese, and begged the members to seek measures for godly union and concord. In that year he went to England and attended the second Lambeth Conference, but in the following year (February 3rd, 1879) he passed quietly away, leaving the Diocese of Toronto once more vacant.

THE RT. REV. JAMES BUTLER KNITT KELLEY, D.D., D.C.L.
Third Bishop of Newfoundland.
Born, 1832.   Consecrated, 1867.   Resigned, 1877.

20. THE RIGHT REV. JAMES BUTLER KNITT KELLY, D.D., D.C.L., THIRD BISHOP OF NEWFOUND-LAND.

BISHOP KELLY was born in England in 1832. He entered at Clare College, Cambridge, graduating in 1854, was ordained deacon in 1855, and priest in 1856 by the Bishop of Peterborough. He proceeded to M.A. and D.D. in course. In 1855 he was curate of Abington, Northamptonshire. In the following year he was made Chaplain to the Bishop of Sodor and Man, and in 1860 became Vicar of Kirk Michael and Registrar of the Diocese of Sodor and Man, and it may be incidentally mentioned that his position enabled him, to his great pleasure, largely to aid the sainted Keble in his work on the life of the elder saint, Bishop Wilson. He resided at Bishop's Court, and was also diocesan inspector of schools.

On March 18th, 1864, Bishop Feild, of Newfoundland, wrote a most earnest appeal to England for men. "A good clergyman or a kind letter, or both together," he wrote, "will be highly appreciated." In response to this the Rev. Mr. Kelly went at once to Newfoundland, and Bishop Feild found in him a "good clergyman" indeed. He was appointed incumbent of St. John's, Newfoundland, and Archdeacon of that diocese.

Bishop Feild for a long time had been asking for a coadjutor. When he was in England in 1867 he managed to arrange for one, and he himself was permitted to nominate the man of his own choice. He nominated his Archdeacon, who came to England, and was consecrated on August the 25th, 1867, at the Archiepiscopal Chapel at Croydon, by the Archbishop of Canterbury and the Bishops of Rochester and Gibraltar. He was the junior bishop present at the Lambeth Conference that year.

Bishop Feild had sailed until now in his Church ship, with the Homeric name, *The Hawk*, when a new vessel was needed, and Bishop Kelly went to Nova Scotia and superintended her building at Mahone Bay. She was a very perfect model, and was christened *The Star*. On July 21st, 1869, Bishop Kelly started on his first voyage to White Bay and the Labrador stations. It was an anxious time, for *The Star* as yet was an untried ship. She acquitted herself, however, gallantly; and, after affording the means of episcopal visitation to many a dreary spot, and comfort to many a Christian soul, she returned safe and sound on the 16th of October to the harbour at St. John's.

In 1871, when visiting the Bermudas, it was represented to him that several young people in the flagship *Royal Alfred* had been for some time looking for a chance to be confirmed, and he most kindly offered to hold a special service for them, at which eight young officers of the Royal Navy renewed their baptismal vows. Only three months before he had done the same thing for several young Churchmen on board H.M.S. *Pylades*. His words on these occasions were ever "warm, earnest, and affectionate." In May, 1876, he was again in Bermuda, confirming, the Bishop of Newfoundland not being able to attend. On his way he preached in the Bishop's Chapel, Halifax, and won the hearts of those who heard him.

On the 8th of July, 1871, Bishop Kelly arrived at Sydney, C.B., in the *The Star*. On the following day he sailed to visit the harbours and settlements of his charge round Newfoundland. *The Star* presented a beautiful sight under the favouring breeze, with her white sails and tapering masts, surrounded by various ensigns—above all the cross of St. George.

Among other good deeds, Bishop Kelly gave a prize at King's College, Windsor, for Greek Testament. He married, in 1871, Miss Louisa Bliss, daughter of the first Puisne Judge of Nova Scotia. By this marriage Bishop Kelly became brother-in-law to Bishop Binney, whose widow is the eldest sister of Mrs. Kelly.

The new mission ship, *The Star*, was not destined to the long years of service which had characterized her predecessor. During Bishop Kelly's next trip she came to a sudden end. Says the S.P.G. Report for 1871: "The Church ship, with Bishop Kelly on board, was totally wrecked on the coast of Newfoundland." She was insured for barely half her value, and there was great doubt of its being possible to replace her. The attempt, however, was made, and subscriptions amounting to about $5,000 were given. But it was then that Lieutenant Curling came forward with his magnificent offer of his yacht, *The Lavrock*, for missionary work.* The money subscribed was funded, the interest to be used for the maintenance of the

---

* See under Bishop Feild, p. 109.

mission ship. The Coadjutor Bishop lost no time in making use of this fine new ship.

In 1872 he visited in her the distant stations of the diocese. After this Bishop Kelly went to England in the interest of the Episcopal Endowment Fund. He was there on the first "Day of Intercession for Missions," December 20th, 1872. It was a day of importance for Newfoundland, for several men willingly offered themselves for missionary work, and accompanied Bishop Kelly on his return to the diocese in 1873. It was then that Lieutenant Curling, who had given his yacht for God's work, now gave himself, and asked to be sent to some mission which it had been found more than ordinarily difficult to fill.*

Bishop Feild died on June 8th, 1876, at Bermuda. A few months before his death a touching address was presented to him by the people of the cathedral and other churches in St. John's; and in his affectionate reply he spoke warmly of the great benefit conferred upon the diocese by the appointment of Bishop Kelly by the Synod, and expressed his deep satisfaction that he was succeeded by his "faithful, able, and experienced coadjutor."

Bishop Kelly is of fine presence and winning manners, and a most effective preacher. In both Newfoundland and Bermuda this is too well known to need stating. On his visits to Nova Scotia, the people both in city and country, whether "high" or "low," were glad indeed to hear him.

In September, 1876, he inaugurated a subscription for a memorial to his sainted predecessor, by finishing

* "Life of Edward Feild." Rev. H. W. Tucker.

the cathedral which Bishop Feild had so zealously begun. The records which we have before us of his visit to the Labrador coast, starting July, 1870, tell what labours and trials he endured—all the greater as he was by no means so good a sailor as Bishop Feild.

Failing to get a coadjutor appointed, and not being able to keep up the sea voyages necessary to his work, he resigned, July 1st, 1877, and returned to the Old Country, where he became vicar of St. Chad, Kirkby, in the parish of Walton-on-the-Hill, Diocese of Chester, whose Bishop (Dr. Jacobson) found in him an able assistant. On the death of Bishop Jacobson, Dr. Kelly became coadjutor to the Right Rev. Robert Eden, D.D., Bishop of Moray and Ross, and Primus of Scotland; and when that noble prelate died, in 1885, Bishop Kelly succeeded him.

The Star Mission Ship of Newfoundland.

21. THE MOST REVEREND ASHTON OXENDEN, D.D., SECOND BISHOP OF MONTREAL AND SECOND METROPOLITAN OF [EASTERN] CANADA.

WHEN the Most Rev. Dr. Fulford died in Montreal, in 1868, a twofold vacancy was created. The Diocese of Montreal was without a bishop. The Province of Canada (which at that time consisted of the Dioceses of Quebec, Toronto, Montreal, Huron, and Ontario) was without a Metropolitan. The filling of this twofold vacancy had been arranged for. The House of Bishops was to nominate a person or persons to the Synod of Montreal, and the Synod was to elect. Names were to be submitted to the diocese until an election should be secured.

This led to a serious difficulty. The Bishops naturally did not desire a bishop newly chosen from the clergy to be their chief.

The Synod of Montreal assembled in that city on November 10th, 1868. The House of Bishops was present, and consisted of the Bishops of Huron (Dr. Cronyn), Ontario (Dr. Lewis), Quebec (Dr. Williams), and Toronto (Dr. Bethune).* Their Lordships sent down their own names, together with those of the Bishop of Fredericton (Dr. Medley) and the Bishop of Nova Scotia (Dr. Binney). The Synod failed to elect any one of these prelates.

* The Very Rev. Dean Bethune presided over the Synod of Montreal. Thus two aged brothers, sons of a Presbyterian minister of Montreal in its pioneer days, met as Dean and Bishop in a memorable Church event.

THE MOST REV. ASHTON OXENDEN, D.D.

Second Bishop of Montreal and Second Metropolitan of (Eastern) Canada.

Born, 1808. Consecrated, 1869. Resigned, 1878. Died, 1892.

The Bishops then submitted the names of Bishop Hills, of (British) Columbia, Bishop Feild, of Newfoundland, and Bishop H. Cotterill, of Grahamstown, Africa. These names were also rejected by the Synod.

On the following day other names were sent down (all bishops but one—the Dean of Norwich, England), but to no purpose.

The Synod then adjourned without any choice having been made. On reassembling on the 13th of May, 1869, the House of Bishops twice nominated some distinguished clergyman of England, but without effect. Ballots were then taken, again and again, on all the names that had been submitted by the Bishops at the last Synod and the present one, but without result. On the fourth day the wearisome balloting continued, the election settling down at last to a contest between Bishop Cronyn, of Huron, and Rev. Dr. Meyrick, of England, but still without effect, owing to non-concurrence between the clerical and lay votes—the former being in favour of Dr. Meyrick, and the latter of the Bishop of Huron. Finally, as if in despair, a conference between the bishops and the Synod was held, when their Lordships submitted two new names, both clergymen in England: Rev. Ashton Oxenden and Rev. Dr. Monsell. A ballot was then taken, which resulted in the election of Rev. Mr. Oxenden by fifty-seven clerical and forty-four lay votes; whereat there was great rejoicing. It was evident to all that a law so glaringly defective would have to be altered as speedily as possible.

Ashton Oxenden was born at Broome Park, Kent, in 1808. He was the fifth surviving son of the late Sir Henry Oxenden, Bart. In 1831 he graduated at University College, Oxford, and two years later was admitted to the diaconate, and in 1834 to the priesthood, by Archbishop Howley, of Canterbury. After doing some parish work in Barham, near Canterbury, he was appointed rector of the quaint little village of Pluckley, in Kent, which he retained till his election to the Bishopric of Montreal. The only honour that had come to him, in the meantime, was an Honorary Canonry of Canterbury Cathedral.

The name of Ashton Oxenden was a household word in countless Christian homes before it was thus brought prominently before them. His tracts and books reached the working class, and were couched in the simplest possible language, as if written for children. This was their great charm, and they obtained a very wide circulation. The author had lived himself among simple villagers, and he understood how to write what they would understand.

It was owing to this fame that he was elected Bishop of Montreal and Metropolitan of Canada. Mr. Oxenden was consecrated in Westminster Abbey in August, 1869, by Archbishop Tait, of Canterbury, assisted by Bishop Jackson, of London, Bishop Claughton, of Rochester, and Bishop Harold Browne, of Ely.

On his arrival in Montreal he soon made himself acquainted with his diocese. How vast everything must have seemed to him, after his long residence in quiet little Pluckley! But though the diocese was territorially large, he must have been surprised at the small number of parishes in it, and their great distances from one another. They numbered fifty-nine, " having many of them from two to four churches or congregations attached to them." * Of these only eight were self-supporting, the others being to a greater or less extent dependent upon the Church at large for their maintenance. The Metropolitan, as bishop of his own diocese, was always extremely anxious to strengthen the mission stations in his diocese, and to increase their number; and in this, to some extent, he was successful. He was moderate in his Churchmanship, and always counselled forbearance. He would have liked the disuse of the black gown in the pulpit on the one hand, and of the "turning away from the people at Holy Communion on the other." Indeed, he greatly wished to have uniformity of practice, as to the rendering of the services, throughout his whole diocese; but this ideal point was never absolutely reached.

Bishop Oxenden published in 1871, in England, a little book called "My First Year in Canada," from which it appears that many things, prosaic enough here, were matters of curiosity and amusement to one fresh from England. In it he tells of his first intimation of his election to the Bishopric of Montreal. Seated at breakfast one morning in his "sweet Kentish rectory," the postman brought him a letter addressed, "Rev. Ashton Oxenden, Bishop-Elect of Montreal." He was taken much by surprise; but, after consultation with his wife, he saw his way clear to accept the distant call.

In 1871 he presided over the Provincial Synod, exercising with much courtesy and ability his position as Metropolitan of Canada. He presided over the Provincial Synod again in 1872, and also in 1873—

* Bishop's charge to his Synod, 1870.

special meetings that were called for the election of a bishop for the newly constituted Diocese of Algoma.

The episcopate of Bishop Oxenden was marked by the formation of a Sustentation Fund for the diocese, which in 1873 was producing an income of $1,250. It was also marked by the formation of the Montreal Diocesan Theological College. The Metropolitan felt very much the need of young men to fill his vacant missions. Bishop's College, Lennoxville, was his chief source of supply, but this did not yield the numbers he wanted. Yet he hesitated before forming another college, for he did not wish to weaken Lennoxville. However, in the end, he arranged, through the liberality of the Montreal laity, for the establishment of a divinity school, which was looked upon by many as practically the revival, for the Church of England, of the Divinity Faculty of McGill University, and a means of preventing the frustration of the wishes of the founder—Mr. McGill—who left the property for the benefit of the Church of England, and especially with a view to the supply of men for the ministry. But McGill, like King's College, Toronto, was secularized and lost to the Church. Hence Lennoxville was established, as Trinity was in Toronto, a purely Church university.

The Montreal Diocesan Theological College was opened in September, 1873, under the Rev. J. A. Lobley, M.A., the first Principal, an able scholar obtained from England. The Synod Hall was first used in lieu of a proper building. It opened with eleven students.

Dr. Oxenden, as Metropolitan, presided over the Provincial Synod again in 1874, and also in 1877. In 1878 he went to England to attend the Lambeth Conference, and while there he resigned his bishopric. The Dean of Montreal, the Very Reverend Wm. Bond, LL.D., presided at the Montreal Synod of 1878. In that year also Dr. Lobley resigned the principalship of the College, and Rev. Canon Henderson, D.D., T.C.D., was appointed in his place.

The resignation of the Metropolitan was as sudden and unexpected as it was deeply regretted. Various acts of generous sympathy had endeared him to many. He was ever as ready to help the country clergy as those in the more attractive parishes of the city. Called to the episcopate in disturbed if not in troublous times, he lifted the diocese to a higher plane and, by his personal example, awakened alike in clergy and laity a sense of the beauty and power of the religious life.

After his resignation, Bishop Oxenden was appointed Vicar of St. Stephen's, Canterbury, but he soon withdrew from all active work and resided in the south of France, where, occasionally, at Biarritz, he did a little light duty. At Biarritz he died on the twenty-third of February, 1892, at the ripe age of eighty-four.

City of Montreal.

22. RIGHT REV. ISAAC HELLMUTH, D.D., D.C.L., SECOND BISHOP OF HURON.

THE name of Isaac Hellmuth was connected with the Church of England in Canada for a number of years. He was a man of Jewish extraction, and was educated a Jew, but at the age of twenty-four, in 1841, he was led to see that Jesus Christ was the true Messiah, and accordingly became a Christian.

He was a Pole, born in Warsaw, on the 14th of December, 1817, and was educated at Breslau University. In England he became a member of the Anglican Church, and, on his resolve to emigrate to Canada, received from Archbishop Sumner, of Canterbury, and other eminent Churchmen, high and flattering testimonials. The young Pole, the young "converted Jew," with his foreign cast of countenance, round, black eyes, and short, plump form, was regarded as an interesting personage. He came to Canada in 1844, and presented his excellent testimonials to Bishop G. J. Mountain, of Quebec, who gave him Holy Orders—the diaconate and priesthood—in 1846.

Mr. Hellmuth, as a young man of learning, being well skilled in Hebrew, was placed by Bishop Mountain as a Professor in Lennoxville University, and Rector, as well, of St. Peter's Church, Sherbrooke—Lennoxville and Sherbrooke being but a short distance

THE RT. REV. ISAAC HELLMUTH, D.D., D.C.L.
Second Bishop of Huron.
Born, 1817. Consecrated, 1871. Resigned, 1883.

apart. Here Mr. Hellmuth remained for eight years. In his deep searchings into the Christian faith he was led to study with much fervour and strong admiration the doctrines of the German and English Reformers, and became much imbued with evangelical views. This soon involved him in controversy with prominent Churchmen of Canada who could not follow him in his teaching. They were days of strong party feeling.

On receiving the appointment of General Superintendent for the Colonial and Continental Church Society in British America, Mr. Hellmuth gave up his place in the Diocese of Quebec. The controversy between Bishop Cronyn, of Huron, and Provost Whitaker, of Trinity College, Toronto, attracted his attention to the west, and some pamphlets that he had written commended him somewhat to the western Bishop. He accordingly migrated to London the less, where speedy promotion awaited him.

The new Diocese of Huron was rising fast in importance, and men were wanted badly. Dr. Hellmuth, looked upon as a man of eminence, was made by his new Bishop, in 1863, Archdeacon of Huron and first Principal and Divinity Professor of Huron College. His object from the first was to make the see city a great educational centre, and, therefore, two years after his arrival in London, he commenced a college for boys, known as Hellmuth Boys' College. In 1867 he appears as Rector of St. Paul's Cathedral and Dean of Huron, but his parochial and diocesan responsibilities did not curb his passion for establishing schools. Possessed of large private means, he invested them and used them freely in the college and school already mentioned, and in 1869 we find another institution launched on its way, to be known as Hellmuth Ladies' College.

The Dean thus became a prominent man in the diocese, and as Bishop Cronyn's health failed so he rose in importance. When, therefore, the Synod of Huron was called together on the 19th of July, 1871, to elect a coadjutor bishop, his name stood forward as that of the coming man. There was one other name, however, prominently mentioned, and that was the name of the Rev. J. Walker Marsh, the secretary of the Synod. Dr. Hellmuth, however, was elected on the first ballot by 53 clergy (42 necessary) and 78 laymen (66 necessary). Mr. Marsh received 27 clerical and 45 lay votes. The laity vote in this diocese as individuals, and not by parishes.

Dr. Hellmuth was consecrated in London the less on August 24th, 1871, by Bishop Oxenden, Metropolitan, assisted by Bishop Bethune (Toronto), and Bishop Lewis, Ontario. The title of "Bishop of Norfolk" was given Dr. Hellmuth, but this title he bore but a short time, for Bishop Cronyn died in the following September, and the coadjutor became second Bishop of Huron.

In his first charge, which was to the Synod of 1872, Bishop Hellmuth recommended the Canons of the Church of Ireland—by way of preventing anything like ritualism—for use in his diocese. He also strongly condemned "Hymns Ancient and Modern," and spoke in warning tones of the growing evils, as he termed them, of the "Catholic revival." He spoke highly of the Book of Common Prayer, especially the

Thirty-nine Articles, and expressed himself as ready to "banish and drive away" from his diocese "all erroneous and strange doctrine contrary to God's Word."

As to his own diocese, the Bishop pointed out that there was a great dearth of clergy compared with other dioceses. Toronto, with a population of over 600,000, had 139 clergymen; Ontario, with 391,600, had 75 clergy; while Huron, with a population of 782,000, had only 90. This sad state of things he hoped to remedy. "We are living," he observed, "in a day of unprecedented prosperity in every department and branch of industry. Many have become rich who a few years ago had to struggle with difficulties." This prosperity, he argued, should show itself in the advancement of the interests of the Church.

On the day of the opening of this Synod, June 5th, 1872, the corner stone of what was to be a great diocesan cathedral was laid. It was the project of the Bishop himself, and his heart was set upon its completion. Large sums were subscribed for the erection of this cathedral, including $1,000 from the Bishop himself. By 1874 the project had so far advanced that the Synod was able to meet for worship and legislation in a commodious and well-appointed chapter house which had been erected. This was to serve as a pro-cathedral, and regular services were held in it. But while this was going on in the city the Bishop had to report that there were thirty-six townships with 61,000 members of the Church "totally destitute of the means of grace." This pressed heavily upon him. In that year (1874) the Synod of the Diocese of Huron was incorporated by the Provincial Legislature.

Another project was entered into, known as the Western University. In 1877 Bishop Hellmuth greatly desired that a university should be established in connection with Huron College, the property of which had reached the value of about $40,000, with divinity and classical chairs "well and securely endowed." The divinity chair was endowed by Rev. Alfred Peache, of England, by the munificent gift of $25,000. At that time the Bishop computed the population of the diocese to be about 700,000, and comprised 13 counties, 148 townships of 12,000 square miles, with numerous flourishing towns and villages.

In 1878 Bishop Hellmuth held "the largest ordination that ever took place in the Canadian Church."* Nine were ordained deacons and seven advanced to the priesthood. In that year also the Bishop attended the Lambeth Conference in England, and visited, on a confirmation tour for the Bishop of London, Norway, Sweden, and Denmark. He returned to England again in 1880 to obtain subscriptions for the "Western University." In his absence the diocese was administered by the Right Rev. Dr. Alford, sometime Bishop of Victoria and Hong-Kong. The diocese continued to be characterized by marks of prosperity. The S.P.G. withdrew its last shilling of aid in 1881, and "Huron, the Garden of Canada, no longer needed assistance from the mother country."

To the Bishop's great satisfaction, the Western University was opened on the 5th of October, 1881, and in connection with it a medical faculty was formed.

But, in the midst of all these projects, the Boys'

---

* Huron "Journal of Synod," 1879, p. 25.

School, the Girls' School, the Divinity College, the Western University, the Diocesan Cathedral—which, by the way, had never advanced beyond the opening of the chapter house in 1872—in the midst of all, Bishop Hellmuth suddenly resigned the diocese in 1883 and took up his residence in England. Here he was appointed Suffragan Bishop of the Diocese of Ripon, but on the death of the Bishop (Dr. Robert Bickersteth) the office of suffragan ceased, and Bishop Hellmuth was subsequently appointed Rector of Bridlington, Yorkshire.

Among the literary works of Bishop Hellmuth may be mentioned " The Authenticity of the Pentateuch," and " The Divine Dispensation." His crowning work, however, is a critical commentary on the Hebrew Scriptures.

The Bishop has been twice married, first to Catharine, daughter of General Evans, of the British army, by whom he had two sons and one daughter. The daughter married Captain Glancy of the Royal Engineers. The second son is now dead, but the elder son, Mr. Isidore Hellmuth, a graduate with honours at Cambridge, is at the present time a barrister in London, Ontario. The Bishop married again a lady of high standing in England.

23. Right Rev. John Horden, D.D., First Bishop of Moosonee.

JOHN HORDEN was an Englishman, and was born of humble parents at Exeter, in 1828. His father is said to have been a printer, but he and his mother were excellent Christian people, who brought up their boy "in the nurture and admonition of the Lord." At seven years of age he was entered at St. John's School, Exeter, a charity of long foundation. Here, under religious influences, those influences which English schools so often give, and which here, alas, they do not, John Horden resolved, when quite a child, that he would be a missionary. In those days the same impulse to missionary work was not given in England as is given now, yet this fine English lad never forgot his childish resolution, though the chance for carrying it into effect seemed long delayed.

He had to go to work, and was therefore apprenticed to a trade, in which he learned that ready use of his hands which in after life stood him in good stead in the holy calling which came to him. In 1850 he offered himself to the Church Missionary Society, and was accepted, to be sent to the foreign field when opportunity should offer.

This was not long delayed. On the 10th of May, 1851, the expectant missionary received a letter from the secretary of the C.M.S., telling him that he had

THE RT. REV. JOHN HORDEN, D.D.
First Bishop of Moosonee.
Born, 1828.   Consecrated, 1872.   Died, 1893.

been appointed to Moose Factory, on James' Bay, the southern point of Hudson's Bay in British North America. His work was to be amongst the Indians there. It was a dreary post, where no white people were, except the officers of the Hudson's Bay Company. He had but a few weeks to decide, and, moreover, the C.M.S. required that he should go as a married man. He at once resolved to go. Miss Elizabeth Oke had already given him her heart, and, on application, hasty though it was, gave her hand, too. On the 8th of June (1851) the young couple were on the ship and on their way to the new world of icebergs, exile, and Indians. But the hopes of a young man of twenty-three are not easily chilled.

On the 26th of July they had reached Hudson's Bay. Before them to the right lay a barren, bleak, but lofty and majestic shore; to the left an immense field of ice, extending many miles. The blocks of ice, floating about in all directions, piled in upon them from right and left, and for a whole week—in the middle of August—they were locked in their cold embrace, unable to move.

On the 26th of August, however, the missionary and his bride were safely landed at Moose Fort. The fort is situated on a large island, and is surrounded by the wigwams of the Indians, with here and there a house and the old factory and its stores, while in the distance stood "a neat little church, with a suitable tower." The Wesleyan Methodists had had a mission here, but had abandoned it. Mr. Horden came into undisputed possession. No other denomination of Christians disturbed him.

Mr. Horden set to work at once. Within a few hours of his arrival he had visited some three hundred people—all that were on the island. On the following day he began to learn the Cree language, and in eight months, to the great joy of the Indians, he was able to preach to them without an interpreter. It was a language, too, he said himself, harder than Latin and Greek. At first, of course, he made the usual mistakes of one trying a new language. Somewhat to the amusement of his Indians, he told them once that Eve was made out of one of Adam's pipes !

He had much to teach these people. Their customs were barbarous and cruel. Old people were strangled by their children when they wanted them no longer to live.

In the summer—the short summer—of 1852, the missionary was gladdened by the arrival of good Bishop Anderson, who had travelled fifteen hundred miles over lake and river to welcome the new addition to his staff. To his surprise he found him already at work, teaching the Indians in their own language, and so beloved by them that he could not remove him as he had thought of doing, that he might prepare for the ministry. Therefore, like a good and sensible Bishop, having duly examined the excellent young man before him, he made him a deacon in the presence of his own people, and, before he left, ordained him a priest also. Thus was he honoured among those he was serving.

From that time Mr. Horden began a great missionary career. In winter he travelled by dog-sleighs or on snow-shoes, clad in a pilot coat with scarf and heavy mittens and a flannel and fur cap. He soon learned the distressing condition of the Indians owing to lack of food. One man lived through a winter on his own children! There were six little ones; he killed and ate them all. This was a heathen Indian. Many heroic battles against hunger by Christian Indians are afterwards described, sometimes even to death, without such revolting expedients being resorted to.

Dog Trains in the North.

Mr. Horden was a great linguist. Besides the Cree language he learned a little Norwegian, for there were some of that tongue about the fort. He learned Eskimo and Ojibbeway, and studied also Hebrew, in order that he might make better translations of the Old Testament into his various new languages.

When he had translated the Gospels into the sign or syllabic language, he sent them to England to be printed. As there was no one to correct the proof-sheets in England, the C.M.S. sent him a printing press and outfit, and told him to print it himself! Of this art he knew nothing, but he determined to learn. He soon had the press put together and his type sorted. Then laboriously he set up part of his work, and with some anxiety put it on the press. The

Indians had seen him go day after day to his office, and return with marks of anxiety upon his face. They feared he was losing his reason, and for the insane they have a great awe. But suddenly they were rejoiced when their missionary rushed out with his face radiant and his hands full of the precious leaves, which he scattered to the people and said, " See here, see here what God has done for you !" Mr. Horden had added to his list of trades and accomplishments that of printer. The book proved to be a great success.

By the year 1864 it was estimated that Mr. Horden had baptized about 1,800 Indians, and in that year he resolved to pay a visit to England. Three of his children were old enough to go to school, and he and his wife were to leave for England on the arrival of the ship. But the ship came not. She had been wrecked within the bay, and nearly everything but the letters was lost. In 1865 they tried again, and after encountering great dangers arrived safely at Exeter. In 1867 Mr. and Mrs. Horden were back at their work again. They returned by steamer to Montreal, and then took a canoe journey through the wilderness of twelve hundred miles. It was trying for them. Three children were left behind—when were they to see them again? The long separation of father and mother from their children is not the least of the many trials of a missionary's life. Two little ones were with them, but it was difficult to care for them well on so hard a journey. Mr. Horden brought a harmonium with him from England for his church, and, with characteristic energy, learned to play it.

We have not space to describe his frequent journeyings and unwearied labours as he went from post to post and taught the people committed to his care. But at length his toil was rewarded by a call to the episcopate, and in connection with this he went to England in 1872. By that time he had built five churches in different parts of his wide field. He aided largely in the erection of these churches by his own manual labour, his early training as an artisan being, in that particular, of great use to him. He also had taught the Indians to work and to give, so that the churches were really the product of their own energy and self-denial. Heathenism had become almost extinct. Twelve native teachers, trained by him, were ministering to their brethren; and the number of declared Christians in his mission was estimated at 1,625.*

Dr. Horden (for the Archbishop of Canterbury had conferred upon him the degree of D.D.) was consecrated in Westminster Abbey, on December 15th, 1872, by the Archbishop of Canterbury (Dr. Tait), assisted by the Bishop of London (Dr. Jackson) and other English prelates; also his old diocesan, Bishop Anderson, whose hands had previously been laid on his head in the wilderness to give him the Holy Orders of the diaconate and priesthood. How different the scene—from the little wooden church at Moose Fort to the stately and magnificent building where the two missionaries again meet for the highest honour that can be given to man, by the laying on of hands!

The new diocese was to be called Moosonee. It embraced, as it still does, the shores of Hudson's Bay,

* "Splendid Lives Series: John Horden." By A. R. Buckland, M.A.

a strip of land running up the eastward and westward sides of it, indefinitely to the north, and extending southward to the Canadian Pacific Railway. Territorially it is the largest diocese in the world.

Besides the small English-speaking communities scattered throughout the diocese, there were in it four different and distinct peoples, inhabiting different localities and speaking different languages, the Crees, Ojibbeways, Eskimos, and Chipewyans.

Bishop's Court, Schoolhouse, etc., Moosonee.

Bishop Horden left England in May, 1873, and returned to Moose by Montreal as before, battling with hardships, scanty fare, and mosquitoes as he went. His first ordination was that of two native teachers whom he had trained himself. He placed them among the Ojibbeway Indians.

In 1885 the Bishop attended the first Provincial Synod held in Rupert's Land. Two new dioceses had been formed, so that there were now four in all— Rupert's Land, Moosonee, Saskatchewan, and Athabasca. Bishop Horden helped to form the first House of Bishops for the Northwest.

Returning to his work he pursued his journeys with all his old-time enthusiasm and energy, his chief home employment being the translation of Scripture,

Prayer Book, hymns, etc., into the languages of his people. He had but a small staff. The Rev. J. H. Keen worked at Moose and Rupert's House. Rev. Mr. (afterwards Archdeacon) Winter was at York Factory, and in 1878 the Bishop ordained Mr. Peck, who had been labouring among the Eskimo.

The second Provincial Synod of Rupert's Land was opened in Winnipeg on August the 13th, 1879. Bishop Horden preached the opening sermon. It was the discourse of a good, spiritually-minded man. He showed great solicitude for the red man, especially as to his probable future.

When Bishop Horden was at Winnipeg, he was really on his way to visit the western portion of his

Cree Church at York Factory.

own diocese, the leading station of which was York Factory, which he reached after a long and desolate journey. It is situated at the mouth of the Nelson river. From thence he pushed northward, in the month of February, along the western shore of Hudson's Bay to Fort Churchill, the most northerly spot of the diocese where man is to be found. In a temperature varying from twenty-eight to forty degrees below zero, often against a cutting wind, he pushed on with a guide and attendants in his cariole, drawn by dogs. At night they camped out and slept in the open air. Clearing the snow from the ground, raising a wall of pine trees four feet high as a protection against the wind, building a large fire in front of it, carpeting the space between with pine brush, cooking and taking supper, listening perhaps to a story from some hunter in the party, joining in a short service of praise and thanksgiving, lying down upon the pine brush carpet as a bed, and sleeping soundly —such was the programme at night.

Churchill is one of the coldest spots on earth, having eight months of continuous winter and only six weeks of real summer. The wife of the agent there was often years without seeing the face of a civilized woman. Here, however, the Bishop was enabled to place a missionary, whose labours in time were so greatly blessed that nearly all the residents were to be found in attendance upon the Holy Communion.

The Bishop returned to York Factory, and from there sailed for England, which, in reality, was the most expeditious way by which he might return to Moose Fort. He returned by way of Montreal and Mattawa in 1882. Cheers, and flag, and bell announced his arrival.

The scarcity of food was a terrible spectre in Moosonee. Every dependence had to be placed upon the arrival once a year of the Hudson's Bay ship. In 1883 this ship did not arrive till towards the close of September. Had she not come it would have meant a winter of misery for all, and death to many. The Bishop suffered from anxiety till the good ship came, and then he procured money for an extra supply, so that, should the ship ever fail them, they might have enough to sustain life. This custom has been continued ever since.

We are sorely tempted here to give some of the Bishop's own picturesque descriptions of his journeys and of the grand scenes of nature by which he was surrounded, the expeditions over the snow, the Eskimo dog teams, the breaking up of the ice, attended almost by the terrors of an earthquake, followed by a mighty rush of waters ready to sweep away everything before it, the people being warned by the alarm bell, and having sometimes to take refuge in the Hudson's Bay Factory, that ever-constant friend of the white man and the Indian alike, then the coming of summer, the trips by canoe—but space forbids.

Since 1882 Mrs. Horden had been in England. After six years of separation the Bishop, in 1888, resolved to pay another visit to his native land. After a long and tedious canoe journey, the privations of which he now began to feel keenly, he reached Montreal, and was soon again in England. He was now sixty years old, and at the anniversary meeting of the C.M.S., held in 1889, in Exeter Hall, the venerable missionary was a conspicuous figure. He was loudly

cheered. In a few days he said good-by to England
—his last good-by—and returned by Montreal again
to his old work. But he was not what he had been. He
still journeyed to distant places, but he could no longer
"sleep in the open air, with the thermometer forty
degrees below zero." Like Moses, he must seek for
the Joshua that was to succeed him. He had met
the Rev. J. A. Newnham, of Montreal, and recommended him to the C.M.S. for that position.

Mr. Newnham reached Moose Fort in 1891 to
work for a while as a missionary with the Bishop in
preparation for his future work. Bishop Horden contemplated returning to England for a few years' rest
before his final call should come.

But his precious translations were not yet finished.
On these he worked steadily, till on the 21st of
November (1892) he was stricken down with rheumatism, and unable to work any more. He died somewhat unexpectedly on the morning of January 12th,
1893. His daughter, Mrs. Broughton, was present
to close his eyes. For a time he lay in state in the
little church that had been his cathedral, and all,
young and old, took a last lingering look at the face
of him whom they loved, before he was laid to rest
in his own churchyard, among a people whose missionary, pastor, and friend he had been for over forty
years. In England a monument now stands in Exeter
Cathedral to his memory, and also one in the school
which he attended as a boy, and under this are the
appropriate words:

"Faithful unto death."

THE RT. REV. FREDERICK DAWSON FAUQUIER, D.C.L.
First Bishop of Algoma.
Born, 1817. Consecrated, 1873. Died, 1881.

24. Right Reverend Frederick Dawson Fauquier, D.C.L., First Bishop of Algoma.

FREDERICK DAWSON FAUQUIER was born at Malta in June, 1817. He came to "Upper Canada" in 1836, and commenced life as a farmer near Woodstock; but his superior education, gentlemanly bearing, and consistently religious life recommended him as a young man well suited for the sacred ministry. The country was then young, and men were sorely needed to fill the clerical ranks. At that time the Rev. Dr. Bethune had his theological school at Cobourg, and here Mr. Fauquier studied his divinity. In 1845, in his 28th year, he was made a deacon by Bishop Strachan, who also in the following year priested him. He was placed in charge of South Zorra, in the County of Oxford, and there he quietly and faithfully laboured year in and year out, his congregations increasing and improving as the population grew apace and the land yielded wealth to those who tilled it.

Mr. Fauquier was present at the formation of the Diocese of Huron, in which district of country his lot had been cast. He was a warm supporter of Archdeacon Bethune, his quondam instructor, and would have been glad to see him bishop; but when the suffrages of his brethren said otherwise, he became a faithful priest to Dr. Cronyn, his new diocesan.

He was a man of quiet and gentle disposition, and

one whose sweet piety made itself felt. Though differing from the views of most of his colleagues in Huron Diocese, he was respected by all, and in 1865 he was chosen as one of the delegates to the Provincial Synod, and also for the session which was held in 1871, and was present at a special meeting called in the following year for the purpose of electing a missionary bishop to oversee the great stretch of northern country known as Algoma.

This was rather a memorable session. It lasted four days, though called together for the one definite object of framing a canon for the establishment of missionary bishoprics, and for the election of a missionary bishop. At last everything was ready. The Upper House was to send down a name or names for selection by the Lower House. On the morning of the fourth day (December 14th, 1872) the Bishops, that is to say, Dr. Oxenden, Montreal (Metropolitan); Dr. Lewis, of Ontario; Dr. Williams, of Quebec; and Dr. Hellmuth, of Huron, sent down the name of Rev. F. D. Fauquier. On the first ballot it became very evident that it would probably be a difficult matter to choose any one, for the clergy voted "Yes" by 31 (necessary 25), and the laity "no" by 26 (necessary 18). Other names were sent down, but to no purpose. After the eighth ballot a conference was held, and it was agreed to unite upon the name of Rev. J. P. DuMoulin, who accordingly was elected on the ninth ballot by 27 clerical votes (necessary 23), and 33 lay (necessary 19).

Shortly after the Synod separated, however, Mr. DuMoulin withdrew from the offered post.

The Provincial Synod, therefore, had to assemble

again in the following year (1872). The Bishops sent down the name of Rev. Charles Hamilton, of Quebec, who, however, stated that under no circumstances could he undertake the office. By this time the Rev. Mr. Fauquier had been made an Archdeacon in his own diocese, and the Upper House returned to his name as to their first love. It was sent down for election. The clergy accepted it by a handsome majority, but the laity by four votes refused it. On the third ballot, however, they, by four votes, accepted it. Archdeacon Fauquier was therefore declared elected. With such difficulty was it—owing, alas, to party feeling—that the first missionary bishop of Algoma was secured.

The diocese over which he was to preside is connected in the first instance with the aborigines—the Indians of this country.

When the Hon. and Right Rev. Dr. Stewart was Bishop of Quebec, with jurisdiction over "Upper Canada," a society was formed in York (Toronto) for "Converting and civilizing the Indians and propagating the Gospel among destitute settlers in Upper Canada." It was formed in the year 1830, at a time when there were many Indians in Ontario still in their heathen state. This society sent a layman, a Mr. J. D. Cameron, to Sault Ste. Marie, which was then a station of the Hudson's Bay Company, to be a teacher among the Indians ; but this gentleman proving unsatisfactory—having, in fact, himself left the Church—the Society sent Mr. William McMurray, in 1832, to take charge of the mission. Mr. McMurray had the good will and support also of Sir John Colborne, the Lieutenant-Governor of Upper Canada, who was deeply interested in the conversion and care of the poor Indians—once the lords of the soil, now being driven far away to the west, where the forests alone were willing to shelter them. In 1838 Rev. Mr. McMurray (for he was ordained by Bishop Stewart in 1833) retired from this mission, having built a log church there, and was succeeded by Rev. F. A. O'Meara, an enthusiastic and unwearying worker among the Indians. Mr. O'Meara afterwards, at Manitoulin Island, in the Georgian Bay, spent many years of isolation among them. Other missionaries followed—Rev. G. A. Anderson, Rev. James Chance, Rev. Peter Jacobs—the last named being stationed at Manitowaning.

Bishop Strachan, in 1842, paid a visit to these regions, and officiated at Sault Ste. Marie. Far-seeing as he always was, he stated that a bishopric ought to be established there, to be known as the Diocese of St. Mary.

The Rev. J. F. Sims appears as a missionary at Manitoulin in 1865, Mr. Chance being still at Garden River, and Rev. J. Carry at Sault Ste. Marie. In 1867 the name of Rev. H. B. Wray is added as being stationed at "Muskoka"—a large district destined to be well known in Canadian history. Sault Ste. Marie lay vacant for several years, and in 1870 was joined to Garden River under Mr. Chance. In that year also Manitoulin Island was placed in charge of Rev. Rowland Hill—Rev. Mr. Sims having lost his life by falling from his boat in calm weather. He was drowned in the presence of his wife and child. Muskoka, having lost Mr. Wray, was placed in charge of Rev. Thomas Ball. Parry Sound also, in 1870, was provided with a clergyman, Rev. Robert Mosley. In 1871 a clergyman, Rev. W. Newton, Ph.D., was stationed at Rosseau, in the District of Muskoka; Rev. E. F. Wilson was placed in charge of Garden River and Sault Ste. Marie; and in 1872 Rev. C. B. Dundas was

Hudson's Bay Factory, Fort William.

placed at "Prince Arthur's Landing"—now called Port Arthur—on Thunder Bay, Lake Superior The Rev. J. W. Rolph was at Sault Ste. Marie. Close to this place is Fort William, an old station of the Hudson's Bay Company.

Such was the state of things when Archdeacon Fauquier was elected bishop of the great straggling territory henceforth to be known as the Diocese of Algoma. The consecration took place in Montreal on October 28th, 1873, by the Metropolitan (Bishop Oxenden), assisted by Bishop Lewis (of Ontario), Bishop Williams (of Quebec), and other prelates.

By the first steamboat, after his consecration, the

new Bishop left Collingwood, and after a rough passage arrived at Sault Ste. Marie on the 6th of November. He visited Garden River, where he was addressed by the Indian chief, who gave His Lordship a warm welcome. Returning to Collingwood on November 13th, the Bishop proceeded at once to England, where he arranged with the S.P.C.K. and the Colonial and Continental Church Society for grants in aid of his work. A lady had sent out from England to the Metropolitan of Canada over $2,000, to be applied to the erection of a see house at Sault Ste. Marie. This lady presented the Bishop, when in England, with the further sum of $4,500 for the same object.

Returning to England in May, 1874, the Bishop again visited the Sault, and also the Muskoka, Parry Sound, and Algoma districts. In his report to the Provincial Synod of that year, he pointed out the self-denial and hardships of the few clergy under his charge, and hoped that their isolation might arouse the kindly sympathies of the Canadian Church on their behalf.

By 1877 the clerical staff had increased to nine, and sixteen lay readers had been appointed, who began to prepare the way for new missions. The churches numbered eleven, and were all free from debt. The Bishop taught his people to put up buildings, however lowly, which should serve as churches—buildings to be used for no other purposes than the worship of God. Rev. E. F. Wilson had erected at Garden River the famous Shingwauk Home, to be an industrial school for Indian boys.

The Bishop, however, began to feel sorely the need of funds. The Provincial Synod, in setting off Algoma as a missionary diocese, had made no provision beyond the stipend of the Bishop, who, therefore, found it incumbent upon him to collect money for his diocese, wherever it might be procured. As early as 1877 the Bishop requested the Synod to make some definite arrangement to relieve him of this irksome duty, but no steps to do so were taken by it.

The episcopal visitations in Algoma involved long, tedious, and sometimes perilous journeys, yet Bishop Fauquier was most assiduous in this as well as in all his other duties. His visits to Muskoka were paid usually in the winter. Day by day he penetrated the great wilds, seeking for new places, sometimes tramping wearily through the snow and sleeping in settlers' huts amidst great discomfort and cold. In summer his custom was to visit the islands in the great Georgian bay and the stations along Lake Superior. He sailed from day to day in an open boat, accompanied by a missionary, sleeping under canvas at night, sometimes in clothes never quite dry. Such was his work. Yet this was more pleasant to him than visiting wealthy congregations to beg from them money for the support of his work. It was only the urgency of the case that forced him to do it. The white population kept increasing beyond his ability to supply the clergymen to minister to them. And this was a grief to the Bishop.

The constant journeying and anxiety as to his work soon told upon Bishop Fauquier. In 1881 he began to show signs of failing strength, yet he braced himself for his work, and pulled hard against the stream. Before the year closed, however, he was bidden to go up higher. On the 7th of December, at the age of sixty-four, he died suddenly in Toronto of heart disease.

He had been a faithful bishop. He found the diocese with seven clergy, nine churches, and no parsonages. He left it with thirteen clergymen, thirty-four churches, and seven parsonages, besides the handsome see house at Sault Ste. Marie. He found it with no homes for Indian children. He left it with two handsome buildings at Garden River, the Shingwauk, for boys, opened on August 2nd, 1875, and the Wawanosh, for girls, opened on August 19th, 1879.

About a mile from Sault Ste. Marie there stands a handsome chapel, built of stone set in wood. It is a chapel for the Indian homes, and was commenced shortly before the death of Bishop Fauquier, and after he was laid to rest it was completed as his own memorial chapel. Such it is called—"The Bishop Fauquier Memorial Chapel." It is a monument of the sweet and quiet life which first built up the missionary diocese of Algoma.

His remains, with those of Mrs. Fauquier, his faithful helper, who had died but one month before him, were transferred, in accordance with his known wish, to the little Indian cemetery at Sault Ste. Marie, and on the 22nd of May, 1892, were laid to rest among those whom he had loved, and in whose service he had laid down his life.

THE RT. REV. JOHN McLEAN, D.D., D.C.L.
First Bishop of Saskatchewan.
Born, 1828. Consecrated, 1874. Died, 1886.

25. Right Rev. John McLean, D.D., D.C.L., First Bishop of Saskatchewan.

SCOTLAND gives Canada its next bishop. John McLean was born at Portsay, Banffshire, in 1828.
He graduated at the University of Aberdeen in 1851, receiving the degree of M.A. He came to Canada, and was among the earliest candidates for the ministry ordained by Dr. Cronyn, bishop of what was then the newly formed Diocese of Huron. He was ordained both deacon and priest in 1858, at thirty years of age, and was appointed assistant curate of St. James' Cathedral, Toronto, and afterwards curate of St. Paul's Cathedral, London. He began at a very early period of his ministry to show much energy and vigour of character. He was resolute and sturdy in everything that he did. This showed itself in his preaching, which was terse and pointed, hurled forth with stentorian voice and couched in tones honestly imported from old Scotia. His very walk was that of a man of energy. Somewhat short of stature, but of good physique and robust form, he moved forward always as if on business.

Bishop Machray, of Rupert's Land, who himself was an Aberdeen man, and had been an intimate friend of John McLean's from their university days, began to be in want of a right-hand man—some one to help him in his diocese, which for extent of territory was second to none on earth—and Mr. McLean, in 1866, went to him to Winnipeg, which was then a little village of about three hundred inhabitants. Here he was made Rector of St. John's Cathedral, Warden and Divinity Professor of St. John's College, Archdeacon of Assiniboia, and Examining Chaplain to the Bishop.

In 1871 the universities of Trinity College, Toronto, and Bishop's College, Lennoxville, conferred upon Archdeacon McLean the honorary degree of D.C.L. He received also the degree of D.D. from Kenyon College, Ohio.

In the life of Bishop Machray we have already referred to the history of the early days of St. John's College, Winnipeg, and of the Church work connected with it. In all that work, the raising of money for the college, the creating of sympathy for it, the training of students, the management of its business affairs—as well as the necessary duties connected with the cathedral and the diocese—the Bishop had an able co-worker in his warden and archdeacon. When absent from the diocese, the Bishop found in him an efficient commissary, for he not only attended to the necessary routine connected with that office, but he paid visits, when practicable, to some of the parishes and missions.

After eight years of this work, the C.M.S.—largely through the representations of Bishop Machray—resolved to assist in the formation of two new dioceses, one in the Saskatchewan district, and the other in Athabasca and the extreme north of Canada. For bishop of the Saskatchewan district, Archdeacon McLean was recommended to the C.M.S., and accepted. He was consecrated in England, at Lambeth, on the 3rd day of May, 1874, by the Archbishop of Canterbury (Dr.

Tait), the Bishop of London (Dr. Jackson), St. Asaph (Dr. J. Hughes), Algoma (Dr. Fauquier), and Bishop Anderson, the retired Bishop of Rupert's Land.

Referring to this consecration, the Archbishop of Canterbury, at the annual meeting of the C.M.S., said: " This morning I officiated at the consecration of a bishop for Victoria (Hong-Kong, Dr. Burdon), for Central Africa (Dr. Steere), and one for a new diocese of British North America, the name of which I never attempt to pronounce in public."

This unpronounceable diocese embraced the territories of Saskatchewan, Assiniboia, and Alberta, in all of which were a large number of wandering Indians.

On the morning of January 28th, 1875, Bishop McLean set out from Red River for his new home, leaving his wife and family to go out in the following summer. It was quite a unique journey. The cariole in which he travelled was a light oak sled, with parchment sides, drawn by four trained dogs. The luggage and provisions were drawn on two sleds also by dogs. Three Indians accompanied him, one to lead the way and tread down the snow with his snow-shoes to make a path for the dogs, and one to run by the side of each team. He held a series of confirmations and services all along the route. Thus he journeyed for more than a thousand miles over trackless wastes of snow, sometimes on the lakes, at others along the course of rivers, and again through the woods. In this primary tour the Bishop visited Nepowewin Mission, a field occupied some years previously by the Church Missionary Society, and served by a native missionary, Rev. Luke Caldwell, who died shortly after; Prince Albert, having a popula-

tion of about 500, but no church building; and White
Fish Lake, afterwards Asissippi, sixty miles north of
Carlton House, in charge of John Hines, a catechist,
assisted by George McKay, a native of the country.

Bishop McLean was a great believer in endowments, and had a peculiar gift in the way of raising
money. Before he left England, at the time of his
consecration, he had collected £6,200, or nearly $31,000,
and on his return there in 1878 he increased that to
nearly $50,000.

The Bishop began his work with one priest, a
native deacon, and a catechist. Such was his staff. It
was chiefly at first an Indian diocese. It was a vast
area containing about thirty thousand heathen Indians,
with a few small settlements of white people. There
were no endowments, no churches. As far as the
Church of England was concerned, everything had to
be begun with a bishop, a priest, and a deacon.

The Bishop saw that he must have a trained band
of workers among the Indians, and these he thought
ought to be natives of the country, familiar with the
language and modes of thought of the people.

He at once formed a divinity class, and sent out,
after a few months' instruction, three persons on probation in different parts of the field. But he saw that
no real good could be done without the aid of a regular
and permanent diocesan institution, and this led to
the establishment of Emmanuel College. It was really
a training college for native helpers, where the pupils
would be taught English and theology, as well as their
own language reduced to grammatical form. In answer
to the Bishop's urgent appeals in England and Canada,

money enough was secured to commence the erection of a building in 1879. The work began with the Bishop himself as warden and professor of divinity and two tutors to assist him. A collegiate school for boys (Indian) was afterwards formed in connection with it, and instructions given in English, Latin, Greek, and Mathematics. The Bishop's right-hand man was the Rev. J. A. Mackay, who was a successful teacher in the Cree language.

By the year 1882 the Bishop had raised nearly $20,000 for Emmanuel College, and over $8,000 for general purposes. He had travelled many hundreds of miles, in winter by dog-sleighs, in summer in open boat on the lakes and rivers, going in all directions, confirming and strengthening his infant churches as by degrees they sprang up.

The Cathedral, Prince Albert, Saskatchewan.

On August 31st, 1882, he called together his first Synod. It was held at Prince Albert, and at it he was able to say that his clerical staff had reached the number of sixteen. A few months after this Synod, Assiniboia was formed into a diocese and relieved the Bishop of a large district; but at the same time some additional northern territory was given him, including the C.M.S. stations of the Pas, Cumberland House, Grand Rapids, and Moose Lake.

In 1883 the Bishop journeyed through the District of Alberta, visiting the new C.M.S. mission to the Blackfoot Indians, also Fort Macleod, the Indian missions on the Blood and Piegan Reserves, Calgary, where a missionary was sorely needed; Pincher Creek, where the sum of $500 was subscribed towards building a church; and Edmonton, where arrangements were made for the support of a clergyman.

Again the Bishop visited England, returning in 1874. He had procured large grants of money, which raised the Episcopal Endowment Fund to $75,000, and Emmanuel College Fund to $10,000. The Bishop was befriended in his work by four of the great English societies: the C.M.S., the S.P.G., the S.P.C.K., and the C. and C. Church Society. He had many agents in Eastern Canada also sending him money. He boldly encountered men in their homes and offices, and preached to them the necessity of giving to the support of the Gospel, and in this way got good returns for his diocese.

The work of the Bishop was unhappily interrupted for a time by the rebellion of 1885 under Louis Riel. It was then that he felt proud of his Christian Indians, all of whom remained loyal to the British Crown. Those of the Indians that were rebels were heathen.

Peace restored, the faithful Bishop was soon again at work. He visited Ontario in the autumn of 1885, and everywhere was received with fresh tokens of sympathy and regard as he recounted in his own graphic, fervent style the story of Saskatchewan's late trials, discouragements, conflicts, and deliverance.

At the Bishop's last Synod, which was held on the third of August, 1886, he reported the total number of clergy to be twenty-two, supported as follows : Eleven by the C.M.S., as missionaries to the Indians ; seven by the S.P.G., six being for settlers and one for Indians ; one by the Canadian Church, half his salary being from the Domestic and Foreign Missionary Society, and half being supplied by St. James' Cathedral, Toronto ; one by private contributions from England for the Indians ; and one by Government, at Battleford Training School. Besides these twenty-two clergy were seven catechists in charge of mission stations—three supported by the S.P.G. and four by the C.M.S.—making in all twenty-nine missionaries. He announced a gratifying increase to the Clergy Endowment Fund, which was now in a good condition and favourably invested. The following missions had become almost self-supporting, viz. : Fort Macleod, Calgary, Battleford, and Prince Albert. A large number of new churches had been recently erected, principally at Fort Macleod, Pincher Creek, Calgary, Battleford, and a second one at Prince Albert ; and the S.P.C.K. had been helpful to them all. Emmanuel College, with its two hundred acres of excellent farming land attached, was to be made more useful in affording for the pupils practical outdoor training in farming and gardening, in addition to that of the class room. The C.M.S. report of the period gives this additional statement of diocesan statistics: Native Christians estimated at about 3,000, communicants 411, schools 13, scholars 458. The schools in the diocese are mainly supported by Government, but the thirteen just mentioned are attended by native scholars—the converts of the Society.

Almost immediately after the close of the Synod the Bishop set out on a long tour westward, taking with him his son, a lad of fifteen years. When at Edmonton he was taken ill and turned homeward. He had gone but a little way when his horses took fright, and he was thrown from his wagon and seriously injured. He was obliged to return to Edmonton, and here with no comfort near, no nurse except his son, he lay in pain, and often delirious, for three weeks. He felt himself a dying man, and he longed to see his wife and children. He was too weak to bear the fatigue of a land journey, and he determined to venture a journey by the river. It was now autumn; the frosts were increasing each night, the river would soon be frozen, no time therefore was to be lost. He caused a small skiff to be got ready; a canvas covering was placed over one end, and under this poor shelter he lay for twenty-one days and nights. At last, on the 2nd day of November, 1886, he reached home, saying, "This journey has given me my death-blow," and on November the 7th he entered into rest. One of the noblest and best heroes of the great Northwest, a friend alike of the white man and the Indian, he lived and died at his post.

THE RT. REV. WILLIAM CARPENTER BOMPAS, D D.

First Bishop of Selkirk (also First Bishop of Athabasca and First Bishop of Mackenzie River).

Born, 1835.   Consecrated, 1874.
First Bishop of Athabasca, 1874.   First Bishop of Mackenzie River, 1884.
First Bishop of Selkirk, 1890.

26. THE RIGHT REV. WILLIAM CARPENTER BOMPAS,
    D.D., BISHOP OF SELKIRK.

William Carpenter Bompas is an Englishman, and was born in London in the year 1835. He received the diaconate at the hands of the Right Rev. John Jackson, Bishop of Lincoln. Six years afterwards (in 1865) the newly consecrated Bishop of Rupert's Land, Dr. Machray, acting for the Bishop of London (Dr. Tait), ordained Mr. Bompas to the priesthood. This was in consequence, no doubt, of Mr. Bompas having offered himself to the C.M.S. for missionary work in North America. The destination assigned him was the Mackenzie River, and the Yukon district, where, since 1858, Rev. Mr. Hunter and Rev. W. W. Kirkby, and afterwards Rev. R. Macdonald, had done hard and rigorous missionary work.

When Mr. Bompas resolved to join this mission, Mr. Kirkby was at Fort Simpson, and Mr. Macdonald at Fort Yukon, with a dreary waste of eight hundred miles between them. A handsome church, dwelling-house, and school were erected by Mr. Kirkby at Fort Simpson, largely by his own hard manual labour.

Mr. Bompas left London on the 30th of June, 1865, immediately after Bishop Machray had ordained him to the priesthood, and reached Cumberland House, on the north bank of the Saskatchewan, on the 28th of August, journeying in a large canoe, paddled by a crew, across Cumberland lake, along Sturgeon river, and across Beaver lake. From Frog Portage, hoisting a sail, they moved on along Rapid river, and reached Portage la Roche on the 12th of October. After eight days' paddling they arrived at Fort Chipewyan, on Lake Athabasca, from which place three Indian lads paddled Mr. Bompas down Slave river to Slave lake, ice forming on their paddles as they went. On the ninth day the water had frozen so hard that they had to abandon the canoe and baggage and push on as best they could on foot; and, after two days' scrambling through brushwood and thickets, they reached a Hudson's Bay post called Fort Resolution. Here Mr. Bompas remained three weeks, till the ice on Slave lake became sufficiently firm to enable him to resume his journey by dog-sleigh and snow-shoes. In this way he pushed on to Fort Simpson, and arrived on the morning of Christmas day. The delight of Mr. Kirkby on his unexpected arrival may be imagined. Such a thing as a visitor reaching them in winter was unheard of. It was, indeed, a merry Christmas to him. For six years he had lived practically a life of exile. Little did he dream that a clergyman all the way from "dear old England" would preach for him on Christmas day, as Mr. Bompas did. His text was well chosen: "Behold, I bring you glad tidings of great joy."

Here Mr. Bompas remained till Easter, studying the language of the natives. He then went to Great Bear Lake and began that career for which he has been so noted, of making himself as nearly as possible one with the Indians, that he might win them to Christ.

He lived in their tents, and found that their mode of life quite agreed with him. But he journeyed about, also, to different posts. In two years he had travelled 1,300 miles on foot, preaching the Gospel to 1,500 Indians belonging to four different tribes.

In 1868 he paid a visit to the lonely Fort Yukon, where Mr. Macdonald, who had been labouring there alone for seven years, greeted him with a welcome the warmth and gladness of which may be well imagined. Here, in 1870, Mr. Bompas formed his first acquaintance with the Eskimo. He went down the Mackenzie river in April on snow-shoes, and found them, as he describes them, an interesting people, but plunged in the darkness of heathenism. They inhabit the coast of the Arctic sea at the north of the great river Mackenzie. In winter they live in their ice houses, in summer in tents made of deer skin, and in the autumn in wooden huts partly underground, and covered with earth. The chief home of the Eskimo is on the ice, and yet they live almost entirely without fire. Their miserable little smoking lamps give all the heat they need. Too much heat would melt their houses.

Here, in these filthy abodes, this self-denying missionary lived and taught these creatures of the Polar regions. Living in a country of a long uninterrupted night, or else of a short, hot, blazing summer—he taught them as best he could the unsearchable riches of Christ.

In 1874 the C.M.S. recalled Mr. Bompas to England to invest him with the powers of the episcopate. He was consecrated " Bishop of Athabasca " on the 3rd of May, in St. Mary's Church, Lambeth, by Archbishop Tait, of Canterbury, assisted by the Bishop of London (Dr. Jackson) and the Bishop of St. Asaph (Dr. Hughes). The newly-consecrated Bishop married in England the lady whom, it is said, he had wanted to marry nine years before. But for long intervals during their married life Mrs. Bompas, owing to the rigorous field of labour where her husband had to work, and his enforced migratory life, lived in England.

The Bishop returned immediately to his work, taking with him Mr. A. C. Shaw, who was ordained at Winnipeg *en route*, and stationed at Fort Vermilion on Peace river. In November he held his first confirmation, admitting Indian converts to the sacred rite. He also in the same month advanced to the priesthood Mr. W. D. Reeve, who was in charge of Fort Simpson, Mr. Kirkby having gone elsewhere, and in the following year took the important step of ordaining Mr. A. Garrioch, one of the native lay agents, to the ministry.

The Bishop held his first synod at Fort Simpson, on September the 4th, 1876. Archdeacon Macdonald was there from the Yukon, and he, with Mr. Reeve and the Bishop, and four or five European and native laymen, constituted the synod. Rev. A. Garrioch and Rev. Mr. Shaw were hundreds of miles away at the time.

In thirteen months the Bishop had traversed the extreme breadth of the diocese, from the Yukon in the far northwest to the borders of Rupert's Land in the southeast, a distance of about two thousand miles. As if his own vast region was not enough for the energies of one man, he was ever ready to help in work that lay beyond it. Bishop Hills, of Columbia, requested him to visit Metlakatla, which lay beyond the Rocky Mountains. Though he left in August, it was drawing near to the close of November before he reached his destination. Towards the end, as he was crossing the Rocky Mountains, he and his party had a desperate race with winter, but, as he describes it himself, they descended the western slopes, " leaving grim winter frowning down upon them from the heights behind."

In 1880 the heart of Bishop Bompas was gladdened by a gift, made by an unknown friend of the C.M.S. in England, of £1,000 to establish a mission among the Eskimo of the Mackenzie. To this charge the Rev. J. H. Canham was appointed. Thus a good work was done among the heathen Indians, and many converts were made for Christ. The hardships encountered in doing work of this kind may well be imagined. In 1883 the Bishop visited Rampart House, the last post of the Hudson's Bay Company in the far north. Here, within the Arctic Circle, near the borders of Alaska, lived and died the Rev. V. C. Sim. He died in 1885 from exposure and the want of good and sufficient food. When the Bishop visited him, he was quite well and strong, working most successfully among the Soucheux Indians, of whom at that time two thousand were Christians. But the missionary fell at last, to the great grief of the Bishop.

To remain constant at work of this kind, without flitting to more genial fields of labour, involves much perseverance and reliance upon God. Bishop Bompas is one whom nothing could tempt from his post of duty. He did not attend the Provincial Synods at Winnipeg, for he felt that his presence was required at home. And when, in 1884, his diocese was subdivided, instead of retaining Athabasca, the more southern and fairer field of the two, he chose for himself the frozen north still, and was appointed Bishop of Mackenzie River, the Rev. Richard Young being placed over Athabasca.

Two fresh missionaries arrived to assist Bishop Bompas in 1886, the Rev. C. G. Wallis and Mr. J. W. Ellington. Archdeacon Macdonald, also, who had been away on sick leave, returned to his work. Mr. Ellington and Mr. D. Kirkby (son of Archdeacon Kirkby) were ordained by the Bishop in August, and on the 21st of September (1886) a synod was held, at which the Bishop and five clergymen were present.

In 1888 the Rev. W. Spendlove, Registrar of Mackenzie River Diocese, made an appeal on its behalf to the people of Canada. In his appeal he said that in the diocese there were ten missionaries, several of whom had wives helping them, entirely supported by the C.M.S., and he adds:

"For twenty-two years Bishop Bompas, a man of learning and holiness, has laboured here, and with only one short visit to England has made it his home, or, rather, his residence. Home he has none, on earth. Many thousand miles on snow-shoes, and in canoe, and boat, he has travelled, facing every danger, fearing no foe, untiring, yea, increasing in his labours. He has carried the Gospel throughout the length and breadth of those vast solitudes, literally to the uttermost parts of the earth. Hardy, self-denying, yet humble, he ranks high among the apostolical missionary bishops for zeal and devotion to Christ in the Church of God."

In 1890 a further division was made of the great northern diocese by setting off the lonely Yukon territory, upon the borders of Alaska, under the name of the Diocese of Selkirk. Bishop Bompas again showed his extraordinary powers of self-denial and perseverance, by going himself to the new and most inhospitable region, and leaving the better favoured territory to a younger man—Bishop Reeve. The work is entirely of a missionary character, as, with the exception of a few traders and gold miners, all the people are Indians, many of whom have been brought to the truth through the devoted labours of Archdeacon Macdonald. Three or four clergymen alone form his staff.

The name "Selkirk" is taken from a fort or trading post of that name, now abandoned, called after Lord Selkirk, the founder of the Red River colony. Bishop Bompas has thus driven himself into further exile. Supplies and mail are only to be had at very long intervals, and freight charges, owing to the long distances, are enormous.

Yet the good Bishop has never complained. Indeed, in his own book, "History of the Diocese of Mackenzie River" (S.P.C.K.), he converts his hardships into blessings. The climate is healthy, the long evenings afford opportunity for study, and in winter the missionary work is light !

The Bishop is an enthusiastic Bible student, and, being familiar with Hebrew and Syriac, makes his own researches into the meanings of passages that require investigation. He has also written many verses, and these always breathe the sweetest piety and trust in God.

Though but sixty-one years of age, he appears, as he stands by his log see house and large storeroom, where his supplies of food are kept—a year's amount

See House and Storeroom of Bishop Bompas.

on hand being always necessary—a venerable patriarch. He knows but little of the outside world. His faithful wife is with him. Now and then he sees one of his devoted missionaries. He takes his long, tedious journeys, and talks and prays with his Indians, and so, in the very region of the Arctic Circle, he toils and prays, with the one great object of his life still resting upon him, the conversion of the sons of men to the living Christ, the eternal Son of God.

THE RT. REV. THOMAS BROCK FULLER, D.D., D.C.L.
First Bishop of Niagara.
Born, 1810.   Consecrated, 1875.   Died, 1884.

27. THE RIGHT REV. THOMAS BROCK FULLER, D.D., D.C.L., FIRST BISHOP OF NIAGARA.

THOMAS BROCK FULLER was born on the 16th of July, 1810, in the Garrison, Kingston (Ontario), where his father, Major Thomas Fuller, of the 41st Regiment, was stationed at the time. He was of Irish origin, and on his mother's side was descended from Archbishop Loftus, one of the founders of Trinity College, Dublin.* On his father's side he was of the lineage of "Worthy Master Fuller," the Church historian. The gallant Sir Isaac Brock, after whom he was named, was his godfather. Deprived of both his parents when quite young, he was adopted by his aunt, Mrs. Leeming, wife of Rev. W. Leeming, Rector of Chippawa and Stamford. His early education was received at the Grammar Schools of Hamilton and York. He studied divinity at Chambly, and was admitted to the diaconate by Right Rev. Dr. Stewart, second Bishop of Quebec, in 1833, in the Quebec Cathedral. After serving a short time as curate at Montreal, where he went through a terrible experience in ministering to the sick and dying during a visitation of cholera, he was ordained priest at Toronto by Bishop Stewart. A few months after this he married Cynthia, eldest daughter of the late Samuel Street, Esq., of

* "Useful Lives." By Venerable Archdeacon Dixon.

Clarkhill, near the Falls of Niagara. In 1836 he was sent as a missionary to Chatham, in the far west of "Upper Canada," now in the Diocese of Huron. For four years he laboured alone in the two counties of Lambton and Kent, establishing several stations, which afterwards became important parishes.

Mr. Fuller was a shrewd observer of events as they passed by. He noticed the weak state of the Church, and set himself to enquire into its prospects for the future. In 1836 he published anonymously a pamphlet on "The State and Prospects of the Church in Canada." It foretold the speedy withdrawal of all State aid and the secularization of the clergy reserves, and suggested that immediate steps should be taken for systematized self-help, by forming synods, and carrying forward plans for evoking spontaneous liberality on the part of Church people. These suggestions very soon afterwards, from dire necessity, took practical shape.

Owing to his wife's wealth, Mr. Fuller was enabled to live independently of support from the people. In 1840 he was appointed to the rectory of Thorold, which, it is said, he served gratuitously for twenty-one years, establishing new stations in various directions in the vicinity of the Welland Canal.

In 1861 he was appointed Rector of St. George's Church, Toronto, and shortly afterwards he presented his old people at Thorold with $11,000, which he had advanced towards the erection of their beautiful church. He remained Rector of St. George's for fourteen years, and enjoyed the steady improvement which a growing city helped him to make in his parish.

He had a good practical knowledge of men and

things. Bishop Strachan found him useful in the diocese, and in 1869 appointed him Archdeacon of Niagara. At the episcopal election held in Toronto in September, 1866, to appoint a coadjutor for Bishop Strachan, Dr. Fuller had many firm supporters, as we have seen, during the whole nine ballots.

Archdeacon Fuller had always a great desire to see the Niagara district formed into a separate diocese. It was his wife's home, and had been his own for many years. It possessed many attractions, the climate being much milder than other parts of Canada, so much so that tender fruits, such as grapes and peaches, grew in enormous quantities; its scenery was magnificent, especially in the vicinity of the great cataract, the spray of which could be seen from a great distance and its roar of foaming waters heard for many miles. Ecclesiastically, it was connected with some of the earliest scenes in the history of Upper Canada. Old Fort Niagara still stands to remind the passer-by of the days of early strife, when the colony itself was still a wilderness. Here, at Niagara-on-the-Lake, then called Newark, the first Parliament of Upper Canada was held by Governor Simcoe in September, 1792, in a small frame house built for the purpose. Here lived one of the earliest clergymen of the province, Rev. Robert Addison, who received the support and encouragement of Col. Butler and his rangers. The burying ground of the old St. Mark's Church still has tombstones scarred by wanton soldiers in the war of 1812. Brock's monument overlooks the scene of the great battle which saved Canada to the British Crown, and made historic the vicinity of Queenston Heights.

Grimsby, too, in the midst of a beautiful fruit country, possessed a church since the beginning of the century; and Ancaster, close to the lovely Dundas valley, had church services established as early as the year 1818. Chippawa, almost within sound of the great foaming waters, had services early established there, and through the munificence of T. C. Street, Esq., was endowed to the extent of $12,000. The whole district, including the large County of Wellington, had become thickly populated and prosperous. Three of the early towns had become cities, viz., Hamilton, St. Catharines, and Guelph. Parishes had multiplied everywhere, until they seemed fairly to demand that they should be formed into a separate diocese.

Then it was that Mrs. Fuller and her sister, Mrs. O. T. Macklem, offered $15,000 towards the commencement of an endowment for a new diocese, which they desired should be called by the name "Niagara," the name that had been familiar to them from childhood. This led to other subscriptions—mostly, it would seem, "promises to pay," but sufficient to warrant, as it was thought, the formation of a new diocese.

The House of Bishops was satisfied with the assurances given regarding the endowment of the see, and the diocese was formed, consisting of six counties, viz., Haldimand and Welland, on Lake Erie; Lincoln, on the Niagara River; Wentworth and Halton, on Lake Ontario; and Wellington, lying inland, and west of Halton. These contained a Church population of nearly fifty thousand souls, and, in all, fifty-six clergymen.

Archdeacon Fuller, of course, had been very active

in the formation of this new diocese, and it was a foregone conclusion that he would be the first Bishop. At the election which was held in Hamilton on the 17th of March, 1875, he received 32 clerical and 33 lay votes, the numbers necessary being 26 and 23 respectively. Dr. Fuller was consecrated on the 1st of May, 1875, in St. Thomas' Church, Hamilton, by the Most Rev. the Metropolitan (Dr. Oxenden), assisted by Bishop Bethune, of Toronto, and Bishop Hellmuth, of Huron.

The new Bishop commenced his episcopate at the age of sixty-four. Though suffering from an inward disease, which whitened his face and lips, and rendered him at times somewhat infirm, he addressed himself to his new duties with great vigour. Taking up his residence in Hamilton, he made Christ Church his cathedral, and appointed the rector, Mr. Geddes, dean. The Synod of the new diocese met on May 26th, 1875, and a constitution was formed. The parishes were, in all, forty-seven.

The Episcopal Endowment Fund from the first was not in a satisfactory condition. The first year it yielded an income of $449.76, which was paid to the Bishop. This afterwards rose to $1,788.46, but dropped again to $1,259.33. Had not the Bishop been a man of private means, the condition of the diocese would have been deplorable. But little success attended the efforts of those who endeavoured to collect the subscriptions originally promised.

Bishop Fuller always addressed his synods at length upon subjects of interest to the Church. As a chairman he governed with a firm but fair hand. He attended the Lambeth Conference in 1878. He addressed his Synod for the last time in 1884, by which time he had become very feeble. His strength evidently was fast going from him. He died in Hamilton on the 17th of December, 1884, in the seventy-fifth year of his age.

The Church made steady progress during his episcopate, the parishes having increased from forty-seven to fifty-one, and many of the missions having become self-supporting. The funds, too, except the Episcopal Endowment Fund, were in a satisfactory condition. The Mission Fund was paying grants to the extent of about $4,000 a year. The Widows and Orphans' Fund amounted to $6,894, the Clergy Trust Fund to $154,133.12, the Rectory Lands Fund to $95,558.86, and the Episcopal Endowment Fund to $25,988.21. There was also a Sustentation Fund amounting to about $500.

By his will the Bishop left $4,000 for certain country missions in his diocese, $500 for the continued publication of some of his tracts and pamphlets, and $500 for the Poor Fund of his old parish of Thorold.

Old Fort, Niagara-on-the-Lake.

THE RT. REV. LLEWELLYN JONES, D.D.
Fourth Bishop of Newfoundland.
Born, 1840. Consecrated, 1878.

28. THE RIGHT REVEREND LLEWELLYN JONES, D.D., FOURTH BISHOP OF NEWFOUNDLAND.

ON the resignation of Bishop Kelly in 1877, the Synod of Newfoundland relegated the choice of a bishop to the Archbishop of Canterbury (Dr. Tait), the Bishop of London (Dr. Jackson), and Rev. Prebendary W. T. Bullock. They selected the Rev. Llewellyn Jones, Rector of Little Hereford.

The clergyman thus chosen was born in Liverpool on the 11th of October, 1840, and was partly educated at the Collegiate Institution in the same city. After further instruction at Harrow, Mr. Jones graduated at Trinity College, Cambridge, and studied divinity at the Wells Theological College. He was ordained both deacon and priest by the Right Rev. Dr. Philpott, Bishop of Worcester. After serving as curate for ten years at Bromsgrove, he was appointed in 1874 to the rectory of Little Hereford, with Ashford Carbonell, where he was when, in 1878, the call came to him to be Bishop of Newfoundland.

He was consecrated by Royal mandate on the 1st of May, 1878, in St. Paul's, by Archbishop Tait, and the Bishops of London (Jackson) and Hereford (Atlay).

The Bishop proceeded at once to his new post of duty, arriving at St. John's on the 4th of June. The Rev. J. M. Wood (who had administered the diocese in the interregnum) and all the clergy gladly welcomed him as their diocesan.

Before fifteen months had elapsed, Bishop Jones had made himself acquainted with almost every corner of his immense diocese. The people of Bermuda, six hundred miles away, were glad to welcome him as their bishop when, in 1880, he paid them an official visit. He found the Church ship, the *Lavrock*, of great use in paying his regular visitations.

In 1881 the Bishop married Elizabeth Alice, second daughter of Sir A. G. Archibald, K.C.M.G., then Lieutenant-Governor of Nova Scotia. In 1882 he was able to supply a clergyman for Battle Harbour, on the Labrador coast, which had been vacant for four years; also one for Forteau's-cum-Flower's Cove, in the Strait of Belle Isle, vacant for seven years.

Bishop Jones, as was natural, took a great interest in the fine cathedral which Bishop Feild had been able partially to erect, and addressed himself to the important task of completing it. In 1883 this work was reported as progressing favourably, the transept walls and tower being built up at a cost of about $95,000. About a thousand tons of freestone were placed in position during the year. But it was reported that about sixty thousand dollars would be needed to fit the cathedral even temporarily for public worship.

Thus the mind of the Bishop was harassed for funds. When he looked beyond St. John's, all thought of his cathedral was suspended on account of the struggling missionaries, fighting continually against danger and want. Of the fifty-five clergymen working at their posts, thirty-nine were missionaries of the S.P.G., without whose aid work in Newfoundland could not be carried on. It is almost entirely a mission field. The missions rarely are able to grow into self-supporting parishes, owing to the poverty of the people. The devotion of the missionaries of Newfoundland is remarkable and unsurpassed anywhere on earth.

In 1888 the Bishop made his visitation cruise in a schooner called *The Sapper*, belonging to the Rev. J. J. Curling, who, it will be remembered, gave his beautiful yacht, the *Lavrock*, as a mission ship for the diocese, and then gave himself as a missionary.

But all the splendid instances of devotion, heroism, and liberality did not shield Newfoundland from disaster. In 1892 a destructive fire swept over the unfortunate city of St. John's, and in its terrible course seized the grand cathedral, which in its inception had been the joy of Bishop Feild, and in its progress towards completion the pride of the present diocesan. The inexorable foe devoured also in its course the Bishop's house, the residences of the city clergy, the Synod Hall, the Orphanage, and the schools. Even the Church ship was also partially destroyed. Apart from the loss to the Church, ten thousand people of St. John's were left homeless, and had lost everything that they possessed. It was a city of about thirty-one thousand inhabitants, but the buildings were chiefly of wood. The fire occurred on the 8th of July, 1892, when everything was dry and hot—and the result was a great public disaster. Five clergymen were burnt out, besides the Bishop—Messrs. Pilot, Harvey, Thompson, Dunfield, and Hancock—and everything was lost. One pathetically exclaimed: "*Omnia mea mecum porto.*" The Bishop lost all but a collar and a pair of socks!

As for the cathedral, it was insured, but only for

a small amount, and in such a way that the money could not be used except to pay outstanding debts. It stood, roofless, floorless, windowless—its walls charred and cracked, and no money to help it.

The Bishop at once made an appeal for help all over the world. A great task lay before him, but from it he did not flinch. The faithful S.P.G. made appeals, and not in vain. Before the middle of September (1822) £4,400 (over $21,000) had been received. "After the fire a still small voice." A temporary building of wood was erected in 1893, close to the cathedral, to accommodate the congregation accustomed to assemble in the one grand edifice; and the work of restoration was immediately commenced on the choir and transepts, with a view to making them habitable as soon as possible. The *Lavrock* also was repaired, and the Bishop made a wide and stormy circuit in her. Though forty years old, and often roughly handled, she yet knew how to behave well in a storm.

But just as things began to look up a little another great disaster fell upon Newfoundland, in the complete financial collapse of the colony. The Commercial and Union Banks suspended payments, and even the Government Savings Bank was unable to pay the full amounts of the deposits entrusted to it. There was no specie in the country. Paper money only was in use, and now this was of no value. Clergymen's stipends, small as they were, could not be paid. They were in want of the bare necessaries of life. From dire necessity Bishop Jones petitioned the first and dearest friend of the clergy, the venerable S.P.G., on the 10th of December, 1894, to remember them in their distress. Such was the Christmas time of 1894 for unfortunate Newfoundland.

The Bishop's appeal was not in vain. The S.P.G. allowed the quarterly instalment to be drawn in advance, and sent out in actual gold and silver about five thousand dollars. A special relief fund was also immediately opened, and the money that came in for it was transmitted monthly to the Bishop.

Money, however, is not altogether wanting for Church purposes in Newfoundland. The *Diocesan Magazine* for April, 1896, contains the names of numerous subscribers towards the re-erection of the Synod buildings. At the head of the list is the Bishop, with a subscription (paid) of fifty dollars. It is followed by over two hundred and thirty names, representing $2,570.60, of which $1,734.60 has been paid.

Such is the work in which the present Bishop of Newfoundland is engaged. Few bishops probably throughout the world have harder or more harassing work than that which falls to his lot. Yet he does it, and does it well. He has already done eighteen years of this hard work, and seems prepared for many years yet to come. As a preacher the Bishop is deliberate and striking in manner, and his discourses are full of originality and force. His custom now is to spend the winter in Bermuda, amidst the warmth of the tropics ; and the summer months in and about Newfoundland. But wherever he goes he wins the esteem and veneration of a united flock.

29. The Right Rev. Wm. Bennett Bond, LL.D., Third Bishop of Montreal.

WILLIAM BENNETT BOND was born at Truro, County of Cornwall, England, in the year 1815. He was educated partly there and partly in London. At an early age he emigrated to Newfoundland, and after engaging there in some secular pursuits began to study for the sacred ministry. In 1840 he removed to Quebec, where he was enabled to complete his studies, and in that year was admitted a deacon by the Right Rev. G. J. Mountain, who, also, in the following year (1841), ordained him priest in Montreal. Immediately after his ordination he returned to Newfoundland, and was married to Miss Eliza Langley, whom he brought back with him to Montreal.

He began his ministerial career as a travelling missionary in the Eastern Townships, with Lachine as his headquarters. In addition to his clerical duties, he worked at establishing schools in connection with the Newfoundland School Society.*

In 1848 Mr. Bond was appointed assistant minister to Rev. Dr. Leach, Rector of St. George's Church, Montreal. With this Church, which soon grew to be one of the finest in Canada, Mr. Bond was destined to have a long connection. Its first situation was on

* "Canadian Portrait Gallery."

THE RT. REV. WILLIAM BENNETT BOND, D.D.
Third Bishop of Montreal.
Born, 1815.   Consecrated, 1879.

Notre Dame Street, near McGill Street. On the resignation of Dr. Leach, in November, 1862, Mr. Bond was appointed rector. He and his church became a great influence for good in Montreal. Sound judgment marked his career from the first. He was a splendid organizer, and a model parish priest. Tall and massive in appearance, it was not hard for him to assume the position of command, especially as that command was always tempered with love. Mr. Bond, knowing the power of popular preaching, secured, in 1863, the Rev. Edward Sullivan, then a young priest of Huron Diocese, and fresh from Ireland, as his assistant.

In 1866 Mr. Bond was appointed a Canon of Christ Church Cathedral, Montreal, and in 1868 Mr. Sullivan left him for the rectorship of Trinity Church, Chicago. Another young Irishman from Huron Diocese, the Rev. James Carmichael, a stirring and eloquent preacher, was appointed to succeed him. Shortly after this, in 1869, Bishop Fulford, having passed away, the Rev. Ashton Oxenden became Bishop of Montreal, and found Canon Bond a most useful and valuable adviser. About this time (in 1870) the old St. George's Church was abandoned for the present commodious and handsome building on Dominion Square, one of the finest sites in Montreal. In 1871 the Bishop advanced Canon Bond to the rank of Archdeacon. He had also become Rural Dean, and in 1874 was further promoted to the office of Dean, though not connected in any way with the cathedral. The new office caused him to rank next to the Bishop.

In 1878 the Rev. James Carmichael, who had been

Dean Bond's valued assistant for several years, removed to Hamilton, in the Diocese of Niagara, to be Rector of the Church of the Ascension there. And in that same year Bishop Oxenden resigned the Bishopric of Montreal, and returned to England.

The Synod of Montreal met on the 16th day of October (1878) to elect a bishop. The first ballot resulted in the election of Dean Bond by 53 clerical votes (43 necessary), and 49 lay (40 necessary). Bishop Machray (Rupert's Land) received 26 and 13 votes.

Thus had Dean Bond risen to the highest post the clergy and laity of Montreal could bestow upon him.

He was consecrated on the 25th of January, 1879, in St. George's Church, by the Bishop of Fredericton (Dr. Medley), assisted by the Bishops of Nova Scotia (Dr. Binney), Quebec (Dr. Williams), and others. The Rev. Edward (now Dr.) Sullivan was then called from Chicago, and became Rector of St. George's.

Bishop Bond threw himself at once into the work of his new office with all that thorough care and sound judgment which had ever been his marked characteristics. He at once identified himself with the trials and hardships of the country clergy, and used all his powerful influence in the wealthy city of Montreal to secure for them, if possible, better support and brighter prospects. His mission fund was soon relieved of debt. There were, at the time, eighty parishes and missions in the diocese, eleven in the city of Montreal, and sixty-nine in the rural districts. Nine in the city and twenty-one in the country were self-sustaining. Eight received grants from the S.P.G., and five received aid from the Clergy Trust Fund of Montreal. None of the city churches of Montreal, except St. Thomas', had any endowment, and five of them were heavily encumbered with debt. The Bishop took a lively interest in the Theological College which Bishop Oxenden had started, and which was affiliated with McGill University.

In 1882 Dr. Sullivan was elected Bishop of Algoma, and Rev. Canon Carmichael called back from Hamilton to be Rector of St. George's. Thus Bishop Bond said good-by to one old, well-tried assistant, and welcomed another back as his adviser and friend.

The Rector of the Cathedral at this time was the Rev. M. S. Baldwin, who, as such, was Rector of Montreal. The Bishop now appointed him Dean of the diocese. In that year (1882) the Bishop was able to announce to his Synod that Mr. Adams, of Adamsville, had built a handsome brick church at his own cost for the people of that place, and that Trinity Church, Montreal, which had been under the auctioneer's hammer, had been saved to the Church through the liberality of Mr. A. F. Gault and some other noble-hearted laymen of Montreal; also that Mr. Gault had presented the Theological College with a large handsome building, a very valuable property on Dorchester Street. The college, since the rule of Bishop Bond commenced, had been under the charge of the present Principal, Rev. Canon Henderson, a kind, conciliatory man, who has done much to make the college popular.

In 1883 the Bishop was left, by the will of the late Major Mills, $30,000. Of this he gave ten thousand to the Sustentation or Mission Fund, ten thousand to the Endowment Fund of the Theological College, and the balance, about nine thousand dollars, to the Superannuation Fund. Thus can the wealthy make glad those who are working to build up the Church of God!

Bishop Bond always took great interest in the Sabrevois mission work. In his diocese were many French-speaking people; and the attempt to minister to such in their own tongue, and through the medium of the Anglican Prayer Book adapted to their case, received the Bishop's warmest approval and support. The Sabrevois College educates young men to minister to the French. The Ladies' College at Dunham—an institution which partook of a diocesan nature—was fostered continually by the influence of the Bishop.

In 1883 Bishop Bond said good-by to one of his most influential clergymen, Dean Baldwin, who was elected Bishop of Huron. Bishop Bond at once elevated his old friend and co-worker, Canon Carmichael, to be Dean of Montreal.

The Bishop was an indefatigable worker and visitor in his diocese, and every parish and mission in it was well known to him. Every year he visited each place with business-like regularity. He went not merely as a confirming officer, but as the overseer of his diocese. He took regular journeys, and required the clergy to prepare candidates for confirmation, if they had any. If they had none, he visited them all the same. In this way he identified himself with the work of the whole diocese as it went on, year by year. He did not attend the Lambeth Conference in 1888, because he felt that his diocese needed him at home.

In 1892 the Bishop announced that a wealthy

lady, Mrs. Phillips, had left to the diocese $20,000, to be divided equally between the Sustentation (or Mission) Fund and the Theological College. The good example of remembering the Church in the last will and testament of the wealthy has been shown more in Montreal, perhaps, than in any other part of Canada. The Synod of that year (1892) was held in January, instead of June, a custom which has been continued ever since.

In 1893 Bishop Bond was prostrated with a heavy illness, which very nearly took him away. Prayers were offered in the churches for him, and he was mercifully given back to the diocese. He met his Synod in January, 1894, and spoke hopefully of being able to resume his work as of old, except as regards public speaking, which, for a time, his physicians insisted he should abstain from. In the following year (1895) he was still able to pursue his visitations in the diocese ; but he received some aid from the newly-appointed Bishop of Moosonee, Right Rev. J. A. Newnham, for many years one of his clergy.

To the Synod held in January of the present year (1896) the Bishop was able to announce that, through the munificence of Mr. A. F. Gault, the Theological College was to have an entirely new building, thoroughly equipped for collegiate purposes, with chapel and principal's residence complete. Of Mr. Gault, he said: " I offer him the thanks and blessing of his aged Bishop, and I fervently pray that the good God and Father of all may ratify these prayers and make them valuable to the comfort and peace of his own soul."

Through the will of the late Henry Ogden

Andrews, two useful charities are to be established in connection with the Church in Montreal, one for emigrants and kindred uses, and the other for aged ladies in reduced circumstances.

Such instances of beneficence are worthy of imitation throughout the whole Dominion. The Bishop of Montreal is able to state that steady progress has been made in every and all branches of Church industry. No doubt His Lordship's own faithful and patient work has had much to do with this happy state of things.

A. F. Gault, Esq., Montreal.

And this work he continues unabated. Though eighty-one years of age, he held last year eighty-seven confirmation services (the largest number of confirmation visits during his episcopate), and visited one hundred and five parishes and outposts. While pre-eminently a man of prayer, his motto evidently throughout has been "*laborare est orare.*"

THE RT. REV. ARTHUR SWEATMAN, D.D.
Third Bishop of Toronto.
Born, 1834.   Consecrated, 1879.

30. THE RIGHT REVEREND ARTHUR SWEATMAN, D.D., D.C.L., THIRD BISHOP OF TORONTO.

BISHOP BETHUNE, the second Bishop of Toronto, died on the 3rd of February, 1879; and on Thursday, the 27th of the same month, the Synod met to elect a new diocesan. It was a memorable occasion. The diocese had become terribly divided through party strife. The Church Association, as described under the life of Bishop Bethune, had become a powerful organization, supported chiefly by laymen. The great bulk of the clergy were attached to Archdeacon Whitaker, Provost of Trinity College, and, if left to themselves, would have chosen him at once for their bishop; but a majority of the lay delegates in Synod were opposed to him. They selected for their candidate the Rev. Dr. Sullivan, then on his way from Chicago to accept the rectory of St. George's Church, Montreal. This state of things made it evident from the start that the election of a bishop would be a very difficult matter. The first ballot resulted in 80 clerical votes (54 necessary) for Archdeacon Whitaker and 39 lay votes (50 necessary). Dr. Sullivan received 25 clerical and 54 lay votes.

After balloting for a whole week, with much the same result, an agreement was made that a clergyman acceptable to the Evangelical party should be elected bishop, on condition that the Church Association should be disbanded. The Venerable Archdeacon Sweatman, of Huron Diocese, was then elected, eighty-eight clergymen out of ninety-six, and ninety-three parishes out of ninety-four, voting for him.

Arthur Sweatman was born in London, England, in 1834. He is a son of the late Dr. John Sweatman, of Middlesex Hospital, an eminent London physician. His primary education was obtained in private schools. He spent several years as a student of London University College, and in 1859 graduated from Christ's College, Cambridge, with mathematical honours, as Senior Optime. He was ordained by Bishop Tait, of London, and became curate of the Church of the Holy Trinity, Islington. While there he founded the Islington Youths' Institute, an evening club for boys, which has since become well known. Mr. Sweatman came out to Canada in 1865, to be first Headmaster of the London Collegiate Institute. He returned to England in 1868, and married Miss Garland, of Islington. In 1871 he became Mathematical and Science Master in Upper Canada College, Toronto. In 1872 he was appointed Rector of Grace Church, Brantford, and Examining Chaplain to the Bishop of Huron. From 1873 to 1879, he acted as Clerical Secretary to the Synod of Huron, and Secretary to the House of Bishops. In 1874 he became Headmaster of Hellmuth College. He was appointed assistant Rector of Woodstock and Archdeacon of Brant in 1876, and was Bishop's Commissary in 1878 and 1879.

Dr. Sweatman was consecrated in St. James' Cathedral, Toronto, on the 1st of May, 1879, by Right Rev. Dr. Williams, Bishop of Quebec, assisted by other Canadian bishops. In the same year he received the degree of D.D. from Cambridge.

The first Synod under his presidency was held on Tuesday, June 10th, 1879. His charge was a full and able exposition of his own Church views, which were those of moderation. The dust soon cleared away from the great contest that had taken place. The Church Association was disbanded, and a fair start of a somewhat new state of things was made.

The Mission Fund, which had been heavily in debt, was speedily relieved of it by plans devised and recommended by the Bishop himself.

In June, 1881, the Venerable Archdeacon Whitaker, who for nearly thirty years had been Provost of Trinity College, resigned and returned to England. The Bishop was sent to England that summer to obtain a successor to him, and secured the Rev. C. W. E. Body, a man with a brilliant scholastic record.

The first Dean of Toronto, the Very Rev. Dr. Grasett, died in 1883, about the time when Bishop Sweatman was endeavouring to have an entirely new cathedral built for Toronto, which should not in any way be connected with parish work. The first Bishop of Toronto (Dr. Strachan) bequeathed four hundred acres of land to assist in setting up, if possible, a complete cathedral establishment for Toronto. The Synod of 1872 contemplated carrying this out as a memorial to Bishop Strachan, by selling the land and building a new cathedral, but nothing ever came of it till Bishop Sweatman revived the matter and earnestly pleaded for it. The Synod endorsed the Bishop's wishes, and, through the Executive Committee, secured about four acres and a half of land outside the city limits, in what was called "Seaton Village."

The city of Toronto, as time went on, began to grow very rapidly. The click of the workman's hammer was heard in every direction, and large rows of splendid buildings sprang up like magic everywhere. The distant territory of "Seaton Village" was incorporated within the city limits, and soon began to wear a city aspect. The Bishop had not intended to commence the building of the new cathedral till such time as the establishment should be set up and a fair way clearly seen for meeting the financial obligations that it would involve. But the building fever at this time was strong in Toronto. The dangerous period of a "boom in land" had set in. The unoccupied ground contiguous to the site of the proposed "Cathedral of St. Alban the Martyr" was called "St. Alban's Park."

The trustees of this property, in order, no doubt, to enhance its value, offered (in 1885) to give $2,000 towards the Building Fund of the cathedral, on condition that the chancel and choir should be erected at once—or within a period of eighteen months. The outlook at the time was so bright that the Cathedral Chapter accepted this offer, and building, contrary to the Bishop's first design, was at once proceeded with.

At this time the diocese, as well as the city, was in a fairly prosperous condition. The roll of the clergy (in 1886) amounted to one hundred and forty-seven, the largest, the Bishop stated, of any colonial diocese except Calcutta and Madras, and the funds were holding their own. A handsome see house was also erected on the St. Alban's Cathedral property—a portion of which was deeded to the Synod for the purpose—and the Bishop, with his family, snugly ensconced in it before the close of the year. A branch of the Woman's Auxiliary to the Domestic and Foreign Missionary Society was in working operation in the diocese. The "W. A." had been formed the previous year (1885) in Ottawa, and has since proved itself a most useful and powerful organization. Bishop Sweatman has always taken the greatest interest in the work of the Domestic and Foreign Missionary Society. Before his episcopate, the diocese had done nothing for foreign missions, and on this point he spoke very earnestly in his first charge to the Synod. Through the Domestic and Foreign Missionary Society, however, the diocese was now beginning to contribute fairly well to the worthy objects represented by its name.

In 1887 the Woman's Auxiliary began to work for diocesan objects as well as for outside missions. In 1888 the Bishop stated that there were in the diocese two hundred and seven churches, against the one hundred and sixty-three when he became bishop in 1879; but he regretted to state that the parsonages were few. In that year the contributions to the diocesan missions reached a sum larger than they had ever attained before, viz., a little over fifteen thousand dollars. It is no child's play to do the work of a large diocese like Toronto. Every year the Bishop reported large numbers of people confirmed and long distances travelled. In 1888 alone the distance travelled was 4,346 miles. In that year, by the generous liberality of Church friends in Toronto, the Bishop attended the Lambeth Conference, where, from all parts of the world, one hundred and forty-five prelates of the Anglican communion were assembled together.

The Diocesan Mission Fund, in 1889, did not keep up its good record, but began to show a falling off, which somewhat alarmed the Bishop. The chancel of St. Albans had been roofed in. It was built of red Credit Valley stone and Ohio freestone; but as yet the inside was not finished, though services had been held for two years in the basement. The chapter began to feel the want of funds. In this year the diocese celebrat-

The Choir and Chancel, St. Alban's Cathedral, Toronto.

ed its jubilee, fifty years having passed since Bishop Strachan was consecrated. It was marked by a fitting celebration in Toronto, and the Bishop distinguished the event by forming a " Dean and Chapter " for the new cathedral. A large number of canons were appointed, a few of whom, however, declined to accept the honour. The Bishop himself became the dean. Since the death of Dean Grasett, no Dean of Toronto had been appointed. The Rector of St. James', Rev. Canon DuMoulin, by the new statutes became *ex officio* sub-Dean, and St. James' was to be allowed to be called, as of old, " St. James' Cathedral."

The Diocese of Toronto, for many years, had been

singularly wanting in legacies of any kind; but in 1889 Mr. Talbot, a farmer, left $4,000 to Trinity College, and about $12,000 to the Diocesan Mission Fund, the latter to be known as the Talbot bequest.

The old building of Wycliffe College was abandoned in 1891 for a new and spacious edifice on Hoskin Avenue, where under its first Principal, the Rev. Canon Sheraton, D.D., LL.D., it continues its work.

Trinity University, in the meantime, had grown under Provost Body to much larger proportions than those of its earlier days. A supplemental endowment fund was formed, and the building on two separate occasions was extensively enlarged. Provost Body resigned in 1894, and was succeeded in 1895 by Rev. Edward A. Welch, M.A., sometime domestic chaplain to the late Bishop Lightfoot.

In 1891 Bishop Sweatman was obliged to face an alarming falling off in the Diocesan Mission Fund. "The old days of mission fund debt," he remarked, "have returned," and, as for St. Alban's, the chancel internally was completed and occupied for divine service; but the debt incurred by it proved a burden well nigh too heavy to bear. The Bishop, however, has done his best for it, and when Toronto recovers from its financial trouble His Lordship will no doubt be able to overcome present difficulties, as he did those of a graver nature in the beginning of his career.

31. Right Reverend William Ridley, D.D., First Bishop of Caledonia (British Columbia).

"OLD Caledonia, stern and wild," has, in some respects, its counterpart in the bold, rugged region of northern British Columbia, called by the early Scotch settlers " New Caledonia," as the region south of it, more English in tone, was called New Westminster. Here lived wild savages of the forest; here at times trooped hordes of adventurers in search of gold; and here, too, came the missionary of God to teach men of all kinds His ways upon earth, His saving health among all nations.

About the year 1856, Captain Prevost, a naval officer stationed on the Pacific coast, called the attention of the C.M.S. to the forlorn spiritual condition of the Indians of the country, with the result that a young schoolmaster was sent from England to do this work. Fiercer or more degraded savages than the Indians of British Columbia, especially in the north, on the mainland and on the islands, could scarcely be found, yet Mr. Duncan was able to gain upon them to a wonderful extent, and win them to better ways.

At a place on the sea coast called Metlakatla, the scene of an Indian village, Mr. Duncan established a colony of Indians, taught them industries as well as religion, and succeeded in forming a contented, thriving, and happy community, all of Indians. From four

THE RT. REV. WILLIAM RIDLEY, D.D.
First Bishop of Caledonia (B.C.)
Born, 1836. Consecrated, 1879.

hundred to six hundred attended divine service every Sunday, and were governed by Christian laws.

The story of this mission, as told, for instance, in "Stranger Than Fiction," a little book published by the S.P.C.K., reveals one of the most charming results of missionary work to be found anywhere; but, alas! for things earthly—it was marred by the unhappy peculiarities of Mr. Duncan, who began to teach his Indians things contrary to the doctrines of the Church of England, especially as regards the Holy Communion, which he declined to have administered.

About this time Bishop Hills visited England, and succeeded in having two new dioceses formed for British Columbia. He kept for himself the Island of Vancouver, and divided the mainland into two parts: the northern part, under the C.M.S., to be called Caledonia, and the southern, under the S.P.G., New Westminster. The clergyman chosen for this post by the C.M.S. was Rev. William Ridley, at the time Vicar of Huddersfield.

Mr. Ridley was born at Brixham, Devon, on July 22nd, 1836. He was ordained in 1866, and in that year was sent by the C.M.S. as a missionary to Afghanistan. In 1868 he was appointed principal of the college in Peshawur. Invalided home, he served as chaplain at Dresden, in Saxony, in 1870-71. Mr. Ridley would have liked to return to Peshawur, but could not obtain a certificate of health. He therefore accepted the vicarage of Shelley, near Huddersfield. After resigning this, and attempting again to go to India, but being prevented by a return of ill-health, Mr. Ridley was instituted to the vicarage of St. Paul's,

Huddersfield, in Yorkshire, where his health again gave way. When asked, in 1879, by Dr. Tait, Archbishop of Canterbury, to be Bishop of Caledonia, he at first declined owing to frail health; but when assured by medical men that the move to a climate like that of British Columbia might be beneficial to him, he consented to go. The consecration took place on the 25th of July, 1879, in St. Paul's Cathedral.

Bishop Ridley left England in the autumn (1879), and reached Victoria, *via* New York and San Francisco, on the 14th of October. Here he met Mr. Duncan and Admiral Prevost, both of whom accompanied him to Metlakatla.

He at once established a mission at Hazleton, on the Skeena river, commencing with a day school, in which he went through all the drudgery of teaching young savages to read and write. He had an attendance of about two hundred. Some opposition was offered to his work by the medicine men, who began to fear for their own art. A band of these painted wretches tried to stop his work by dancing round the entrance to his school; but, with true British pluck, the Bishop seized one of them, and, before he could recover self-possession, had him at the river's brink, with an assurance that next time he should interrupt his work he "would assist him further down." This resolute action had the desired effect. The medicine men walked off and troubled him no more.

Here the Bishop and his brave wife (the first English woman who had penetrated so far) carried on this work until undoubted results were seen, not only upon the Indians, but upon the rough miners and traders of the region. In the spring of the year 1880, the Bishop visited other parts of his diocese in an open boat.

Before leaving England the Bishop pleaded for a steam launch. This afterwards came to him through the kindness of his friends, and he greatly enjoyed moving about from place to place in his enormous diocese in the vessel (the *Evangeline*), whose chief officer, helmsman, and sometimes engineer, he was called upon to be. Besides Metlakatla, there were three other stations where missionaries were placed. These were: (1) Nass River, with Kincolith and Aiyansh, under Rev. Mr. McCullagh. (2) Queen Charlotte Islands, where Rev. W. H. (afterwards Archdeacon) Collison, and afterwards Rev. C. Harrison, did a remarkable work. Rev. J. H. Keen was stationed at Wassett. (3) Kwagutl Mission, on the northern part of Vancouver Island, three hundred miles from Metlakatla, and belonging geographically to the Diocese of Columbia. The work here was carried on by Rev. A. J. Hall, who reduced the Kwagutl language to writing.

The troubles at Metlakatla were a great grief to the Bishop. He was obliged to go to England to confer with the C.M.S. regarding them. That a man who did the grand and heroic work that Mr. Duncan did should spoil it all by refusing to recognize the official acts of the ordained ministers of the Church to which he professed to belong was inexplicable. But Bishop Ridley waited patiently for better things. Factions arose, Mr. Duncan's Indians causing great disturbances among those who adhered to the Church.

The public peace was disturbed, and life and property were unsafe. The Bishop was obliged to appeal to the Government for protection, and a gunboat was sent to watch over the interests of those who were oppressed and threatened. Finally, in 1881, Mr. Duncan withdrew to American territory in Alaska, a large number of Indians going with him. Thus Metlakatla as a mission station was but a wreck of its former flourishing condition, but what remained was loyal and true to the Bishop and clergy of the Church. In 1884 Bishop Ridley confirmed seventeen of these loyal Indians (Tsimsheans), and administered to them and others the Holy Communion. Metlakatla thus became a true Church of England mission.

About this time the Bishop translated the Gospels of St. Matthew, St. Mark, and St. John into the Tsimshean language. In his earlier days he had been a good Arabic scholar, but whether this helped him much in Tsimshean does not appear. Since then the Bishop has devoted a good deal of attention to translational work in the diocese, and besides the Prayer Book as far the Psalms he has nearly finished the New Testament. Five languages in the diocese have been reduced to writing—the Tsimshean and another, by the Bishop; Nishga, by Rev. Mr. McCullagh; Aaida, by Rev. C. Harrison; and Kwagutl, by Rev. Mr. Hall. Mrs. Ridley, in the matter of translation, has been a great help. She is a good Persian scholar, and in earlier days was the first English woman to organize Zenana work in the Punjab, and prepared some Persian translations of English books for that work. In Germany, in 1870-71, she ministered to the sick and wounded soldiers, and was presented with the bronze cross and an autograph letter from the king. In the wilds of British Columbia she has assisted in reducing the Tsimshean language to system, and has translated into it all the hymns that are used in that tongue.

The medical men who advised Mr. Ridley to accept the bishopric were right. The health of the Bishop, in the main, has been remarkably good. At times he has suffered from rheumatism, and in 1891 was obliged to lie by for a couple of years, yet he has been, as a rule, strong and well, and has done a surprising amount of literary work, teaching, and travelling.

The church (or cathedral) at Metlakatla is the largest in British Columbia, and could be easily arranged to seat eleven hundred persons on the ground floor. There are fourteen other churches in the diocese, all of wood, and some of them quite handsome structures. There are eleven clergymen, one medical missionary with a student as assistant, and three hospital nurses (the hospital is a diocesan establishment); three white laymen, one of whom is an honorary worker; seven native catechists, and several voluntary preachers.

Thus equipped, a good work is being done. The year 1895 witnessed greater progress than any previous year, and the prayer of the faithful is that such progress may long continue. Bishop Ridley has recently returned to his diocese after a brief sojourn in his native land, and is prosecuting the work there with all his old-time energy and zeal.

32. Right Rev. Acton Wyndeyer Sillitoe, D.D., First Bishop of New Westminster, B.C.

ACTON WYNDEYER SILLITOE was born in Australia in the year 1841. Though thus born in the colonies he was brought up and educated in England, first at King's College School, and afterwards at Pembroke College, Cambridge. Here he graduated in 1862.

He was made a deacon in 1869 by Bishop Selwyn, of Lichfield, and advanced to the priesthood in the following year. After serving as curate at Brierly Hill, Wolverhampton, and Ellenbrook, he accepted, in 1876, a chaplaincy at Geneva. A year afterwards he became chaplain at Darmstadt, and to the Princess Alice. Here, in 1879, he received a call from the S.P.G. to be Bishop of New Westminster, British Columbia.

New Westminster was then but a small village. The boundaries of the diocese were to be from the forty-fifth parallel of latitude northward to the fifty-fourth, and from the Rocky Mountains on the west to the Pacific Ocean on the east. It covered an area of 160,000 square miles.

Mr. Sillitoe was consecrated at Croydon by Archbishop Tait, of Canterbury, assisted by Bishop Hills, of Columbia, and others, on All Saints' Day, 1879. He reached New Westminster on the 18th of June, 1880.

THE RT. REV. ACTON W. SILLITOE, D.D.
First Bishop of New Westminster (B.C.)
Born, 1841. Consecrated, 1879. Died, 1894.

All the clerical staff of New Westminster, two in number, met His Lordship, and welcomed him to his new diocese. His first act was joining in a service of thanksgiving in the church which was to be his cathedral. This is described as a creditable stone structure with nave, chancel, north aisle, and south transept, disfigured somewhat by a large square wooden tower built to receive a peal of bells, presented by the Baroness Burdett-Coutts. The rector was the Venerable Archdeacon Woods, Archdeacon of Columbia.

Addressing himself at once to his work, the new Bishop visited some of his mission stations, such as Sapperton, Trenant, the North Arm of the Fraser River, Burrard Inlet, Yale, and Kamloops. This latter place was noted for its cost of living. A set of horse shoes cost $6, and the day's wage of a tradesman was $5. Had it not been for the liberality of the people, missionaries could not have lived there.

The Rev. A. Shildrick was in charge of Kamloops, a district which he described as the paradise of British Columbia. At Yale, he found a population of about 2,000—fifteen hundred of whom were Chinese. In the numerous Chinese throughout the diocese Bishop Sillitoe always took a deep interest, and wherever he went he imparted to others the warm glow of his own missionary spirit. He was wont always to encourage the congregations in his diocese to give to foreign missions, notwithstanding the sore needs lying at their own doors. It is stated that the liberality of the Church people in the Diocese of New Westminster is of more than an ordinary kind. The percentage of their offerings is over two dollars a head.

The size of the diocese is so great, and the geographical obstacles, mountains, and rapid rivers so numerous, that missionary work is no easy task. The present staff consists of twenty clergy and a few lay readers. The diocese is divided into eleven parishes and seven huge missionary districts. New districts have rapidly opened, such as the Kootenay country, which, with Nelson as its centre, is attracting a large mining population.

Besides the white population, there are about forty thousand Indians and Chinese. The latter are almost wholly heathen, but of the Indians fourteen hundred are Christians, and the percentage of communicants among them, nearly fifty per cent., speaks well for their sincerity.

Year after year Bishop Sillitoe worked incessantly at his post. There were in his diocese but two places of any importance in the civil world. These were the city of Vancouver, with a Church population of 2,070, and New Westminster, with about 1,000; but as these two places are very close to one another, it must eventually be that one or other of them must decrease to the enlargement of the stronger. Vancouver is destined apparently to retain the chief position. It grew into three parishes, viz., St. James', Christ Church, and St. Paul's.

In the winter of 1893 Bishop Sillitoe was in Eastern Canada, trying to collect money for his work. On his return in March he was prostrated with a severe attack of pneumonia, which greatly weakened him. He struggled on, however, with his work, and was present at the first General Synod of the Church of England in the Dominion of Canada, which was held in Toronto in September (1893). Having returned to New Westminster, he was stricken in November with influenza. This left him still weaker, but he struggled on through the winter, taking many services and going long distances. Towards the end of May he was prostrated again with illness at Yale, from which place, after a time, he was removed to his own see house at New Westminster, where, to the great grief of the whole community, he breathed his last on the 9th of June, 1894, at the comparatively early age of fifty-three.

Bishop Sillitoe was a High Churchman, but was always fair to every one. The clergy of his diocese, whatever their Church views, vied with one another in bearing testimony to the beauty and sterling qualities of his character. The Rev. L. N. Tucker, Rector of Christ Church, Vancouver, voiced the opinion of all when he said : " No one, I am sure, could know Bishop Sillitoe intimately without being charmed by his genial and friendly manner, and without being impressed by his zeal, earnestness, and manliness. Such qualities—the gifts of the Eternal Spirit—are not likely soon to die or to be forgotten. Through them, though dead, he yet speaketh, and will speak for many years to come to all who knew him."

33. THE RIGHT REVEREND HOLLINGWORTH TULLY KINGDON, D.D., SECOND BISHOP OF FREDERICTON.

HOLLINGWORTH TULLY KINGDON graduated from Trinity College, Cambridge, in 1858, taking his M.A. in 1861. He was admitted to the diaconate in 1859 by Right Rev. Samuel Wilberforce, Bishop of Oxford, and was ordained priest in 1860 by Right Rev. W. K. Hamilton, Bishop of Sarum (Salisbury). He served as Curate of St. Andrew's, Well Street (London); as Vice-Principal of the Theological College, Sarum ; and as Vicar of Good Easter, Essex. In this position he was when, in 1881, he was invited by the Bishop and Synod of Fredericton, New Brunswick, to undertake the duties of Coadjutor Bishop of that diocese, with the right of succession.

Dr. Kingdon (for his university had conferred upon him the degree of D.D.) came to this country for consecration. The ceremony took place in the Cathedral, Fredericton, on Sunday, the 10th of July, 1881. The Metropolitan (Bishop Medley), assisted by the Bishop of Quebec (Dr. Williams) and the Bishop of Nova Scotia (Dr. Binney), officiated.

As a ripe scholar and systematic worker, Bishop Kingdon proved a valuable assistant to Bishop Medley in his old age.

THE RT. REV. HOLLINGWORTH TULLY KINGDON, D.D.
Second Bishop of Fredericton, N.B.
Consecrated, 1881.

The good old Bishop was called to his rest on September 9th, 1892, and Right Rev. Dr. Kingdon at once succeeded him as Bishop of Fredericton. His Lordship presided as such for the first time over the Synod on Wednesday, July 5th, on which occasion he delivered an appropriate and able address.

On the advice of his physician, Bishop Kingdon in this year (1893) paid a visit to England, but returned in time to be present at the General Synod held in Toronto on the 13th of September.

It may be said of Bishop Kingdon that, though small of stature, he is quick and resolute of will. He is evidently a good financier, and is of a legal turn of mind. His charges to the Synod are full of wise suggestions and exhortations regarding the business part of diocesan affairs; but he also watches carefully the spiritual progress of his diocese.

Last year (1895), on the 11th of June, the jubilee of the diocese was held—the fiftieth anniversary of the enthronization of the first bishop, John Medley. The speeches and papers delivered on this occasion were published afterwards in pamphlet form.

Owing to the liberality of the late Mrs. Gordon, a sum of money was left for the endowment of the cathedral. This enabled the Bishop to add to the Chapter by appointing Rev. Dr. Partridge, of Halifax, Dean, and the Rev. Thomas Neales, Archdeacon of Fredericton. These, with Archdeacon Brigstocke, of St. John, and Canons De Veber, Ketchum, Forsyth, and Roberts, form the Chapter. Matins and Evensong are now said daily in the cathedral, at which Bishop Kingdon and all devout Churchmen greatly rejoice.

34. THE RIGHT REV. EDWARD SULLIVAN, S.T.D., D.C.L., SECOND BISHOP OF ALGOMA.

THE name of Edward Sullivan has already been mentioned in these pages.* He was born on August 18th, 1832, in Lurgan, Ireland, and was educated first at Bandon and Clomel, and subsequently at Trinity College, Dublin, where he graduated in 1857, being third of the "Respondents" for that year.

He came to Canada, and was ordained by Right Rev. Dr. Cronyn, Bishop of Huron, in 1858 and 1859. He began his ministerial work as curate to the Venerable Archdeacon Brough, Rector of St. George's, London Township, where he remained for three years.

Mr. Sullivan's fame soon went abroad as a preacher. Without manuscript or notes, with but a Bible in his hand—in quiet but impressive style—with a manly voice pleasantly tinged with the intonation peculiar to his native land, he attracted attention everywhere; and when Mr. Bond, Rector of St. George's Church, Montreal, wanted an assistant who would be "popular in the pulpit," Mr. Sullivan was chosen. Here he remained, a power for good, especially among the young men in Montreal, until 1868, when, at the age of thirty-six, he was called to be Rector of Trinity Church, Chicago. Here he laboured as a prominent

* See under Right Rev. Dr. Bond, Bishop of Montreal.

THE RT. REV. EDWARD SULLIVAN, D.D., D.C.L.
Second Bishop of Algoma.
Born, 1832.   Consecrated, 1882.

figure in Church work in the United States for ten years, during which time he was more than once within a few votes of being elevated to the episcopate. While here the degree of S.T.D. (Doctor of Sacred Theology) was conferred upon him. In 1878 he returned to Montreal as Rector of St. George's Church. At the episcopal election in Toronto in 1879, Dr. Sullivan was the chosen candidate of the majority of the laity.

On the death of Dr. Fauquier, first Bishop of Algoma, a special meeting of the Provincial Synod was held on April 27th, 1882, to elect a successor in his office. The Bishops (in the Upper House), somewhat to the surprise of all, sent down a motion advising the postponement of an election on the grounds, chiefly, that no satisfactory arrangement had been made regarding the episcopal income. The Lower House then speedily remedied this by arranging that the different dioceses should contribute a regular amount annually, so as to make the income of the Bishop $4,000 a year. In the stirring debate which took place upon the message of the Upper House Dr. Sullivan took a prominent part, and when the Bishops at last acceded to the evident wish of the Lower House they sent down his name as their choice for Bishop of Algoma, to be approved by the Lower House. He was elected unanimously by the laity (thirty-eight votes), and by fifty-two out of the sixty-six clergy present.

The consecration took place on the 29th of June, in St. George's Church, Montreal, by the Bishop of Ontario (Dr. Lewis), assisted by Bishop Williams, of Quebec, and Bishop Bond, of Montreal. By the close of the first year Bishop Sullivan was able to state that he had travelled by land and water in the interests of his diocese upwards of eleven thousand miles.

Dr. Sullivan had been Bishop of Algoma about a year when he was elected by a large majority of votes, both clerical and lay, bishop of his own original Diocese of Huron. He was in England at the time of the election (October 17th, 1883), and declined by telegraph the tempting offer in the words: "Most grateful to Synod, but duty to Algoma compels me to decline." These heroic words did much to help the struggling diocese which Bishop Sullivan could not be induced to desert. The amount of money raised by the Bishop for the permanent endowment of Church work must ever remain a marked feature of his episcopate. He used the great powers of speech, with which God had endowed him, to obtain from the wealthy gifts and offerings that would be of avail in Algoma after he himself should be taken away.

He found himself bishop of a widely scattered diocese, much of its territory being rocky and barren, and in charge of but sixteen missionaries, most of them living in complete isolation from one another, each one pursuing his lonely way with but the dimmest ray of hope for the future. These men had a friend in Bishop Sullivan. His eloquent pleadings were exerted on their behalf. There was no Widows and Orphans' Fund, no Superannuation Fund, no "Clergy Trust Fund" (or Sustentation Fund)—nothing, indeed, to give the hard-working clergy the smallest hopes for the future, either as to their families or themselves. Besides this, but few of the clergy had houses to live in. All these privileges existed in all the other dioceses of Eastern Canada, and some of them in every diocese in the Dominion. Algoma alone stood out in the cold.

In addition to these disabilities that were fastened upon the clergy, the diocese itself possessed no permanency as regards provision for the support of the Bishop. In other words, there was no Episcopal Endowment Fund. At the Bishop's consecration an anonymous gift of one thousand dollars was made for this purpose. Here, then, was work to be done, that the diocese, first of all, might rest upon some solid foundation.

Every three years, at the meeting of the Provincial Synod in Montreal, the Bishop presented his report, and the progress in these funds which he was able to announce each time indicates that the energies of the Bishop had not been employed in vain. The following table will show the progress of these funds as reported each three years, and also the increase in the number of the clergy:

	No. of Clergy.	Widows and Orphans' Fund.	Superannuation Fund.	Episcopal Endowment Fund.
1883	16	$1,066 20		$2,510 63
1886	24	5,934 79		29,137 20
1889	27	12,599 72		30,000 00
1892	27	15,623 13	$273 18	45,774 60
1895	30	17,526 46	1,049 36	55,216 12

Besides the above funds, a Church and Parsonage Fund was formed which has reached $1,573, and a Reserve Fund for the support of the clergy—to be used only in emergency—of $10,000. This fund was commenced in 1886, owing to a legacy of $4,000 left for the purpose by the late James Kyffin, Esq., of York village, Haldimand, Diocese of Niagara. In addition to this the Bishop collected, in the early part of his episcopate, nearly nine thousand dollars for a steam yacht which he purchased and named *The Evangeline*. He found her of great value in the prosecution of his work among the numerous islands and coast settlements of the diocese.

The large increase in the Widows and Orphans' Fund in 1889 is due chiefly to the exertion of the ladies of Canada in their " Jubilee Memorial "—a movement inaugurated in the Diocese of Huron by Mrs. Boomer, herself a widow, and in commemoration of the long and prosperous reign of the widowed Queen of the British Empire. With this exception, the large amount of money now in the possession of the Diocese of Algoma is due to the exertions of Bishop Sullivan. The money was raised chiefly in the Old Country, and through the liberality of the great missionary societies.

The isolation of the missionaries has been overcome to some extent by the formation of a Triennial Council, by which, every three years, the clergy assemble together and look one another in the face. Some dignity has also been given to the diocese and to the hard-working clergy themselves by the appointment of five rural deans, and recently of an archdeacon, and by procuring the representation of the diocese in the Provincial Synod.

The diocese was first represented in the Provincial Synod in 1893, when Rural Dean (now Archdeacon) Llwyd and Rural Dean Vesey were present as delegates. Two laymen also were appointed, but did not attend.

Great additions and improvements in the church buildings have taken place under Bishop Sullivan's rule. Twenty-six new churches were erected by 1893, and ten were rebuilt. These sixty-eight churches are all free, and are out of debt. Happy, indeed, the diocese that knows no pew rents or church debts! Some of these churches, it is true, are but plain wooden structures, but there are not a few handsome stone edifices, such as St. Mary's Church, Aspdin, built by Rev. W. Crompton, who for several years gave up his whole time to building churches in Muskoka.

The good and successful work of Bishop Sullivan was suddenly interrupted in the autumn of 1893, as he was preparing to attend the Provincial Synod, by a serious attack of nervous prostration. He was ordered away immediately for a prolonged rest. The different dioceses contributed a handsome sum of money (about $2,000) for this purpose, and the Bishop went to Mentoné, in the south of France.

On his return in the spring of 1894 he resumed his work, but his strength was not by any means restored. He spent the winter again in the south of France, but, returning in the spring, he was still unable to cope with his work. The Provincial Synod of 1895 arranged that the Bishop was to spend another winter in Mentoné, with the hopes that his health might be restored, and if not, that he might retire on a pension which would secure him an income of $2,500 for life. The Bishop returned at the end of May (1896), much better in health, and addressed himself at once to the improvement of his mission fund, which, owing to his enforced absences, had fallen seriously into debt.

35. THE RIGHT REVEREND MAURICE SCOLLARD BALDWIN, D.D., THIRD BISHOP OF HURON.

ON the 17th of October, 1883, the Synod of the Diocese of Huron assembled in London to elect a bishop in succession to Right Rev Dr. Hellmuth, resigned. The result of the first ballot was the election of Right Rev. Edward Sullivan, D.D., Bishop of Algoma, who at the time was in England. Bishop Sullivan having declined, three more ballots were taken on the following day, October 18th. On the fourth ballot the Very Rev. M. S. Baldwin, Dean of Montreal, was elected by fifty-seven clerical votes (fifty-five necessary) and ninety-one lay votes (fifty-seven necessary).

Maurice Scollard Baldwin is a Canadian, and was born in Toronto in the year 1836. He is the son of the late John Spread Baldwin. His mother's maiden name was Anne Shaw, daughter of Major-General Shaw. The Hon. Robert Baldwin was his first cousin. The future Bishop received his early education in Upper Canada College, and subsequently graduated from Trinity University, Toronto, taking the degrees of B.A. and M.A. He was admitted to Holy Orders in 1860 and 1861 by Right Rev. Dr. Cronyn, first Bishop of Huron.

After serving as curate in St. Thomas—then but a small country town—he was appointed incumbent of

THE RT. REV. MAURICE S. BALDWIN, D.D.
Third Bishop of Huron.
Born, 1836.   Consecrated, 1883

Port Dover. Mr. Baldwin, at the very beginning of his ministry, showed a talent for preaching and public speaking far above the average. Possessed of fervid piety and a ready utterance, his sermons and addresses always held unabated attention; and Montreal—greedy of good preachers!—soon laid its hand upon the promising young Canadian. In 1868 he was appointed Rector of St. Luke's Church of that city; but in a short time (1870) was appointed junior assistant to Christ Church Cathedral, with the title of Canon. Here he soon attracted marked attention by his carefully prepared discourses, spoken without notes and in that clear, emphatic enunciation which has always been one of his leading characteristics.

He married, in his early clerical life, Miss Ermatinger, of St. Thomas, who, however, was left with him but a short time. In 1870 he married Sarah Jessie, youngest daughter of John J. Day, Esq., Q.C., of Montreal, a lady who has always been a valuable help in her husband's many duties.

Canon Baldwin was " evangelical " in his views as a Churchman; but it never seemed as if his motive for being so was simply to help a party, but merely because he felt that that was the right way to reach the heart of fallen man and help him on his way to God. In 1872, on the death of Dean Bethune, Canon Baldwin was selected by the congregation of the cathedral as their rector, and was appointed thereto by the Bishop (Dr. Oxenden). Archdeacon Bond, Rector of St. George's Church, was at the same time appointed Dean of Montreal; but when Dean Bond was elevated to the episcopate (1879) he bestowed the position of Dean upon Canon Baldwin. Shortly afterwards Trinity College, Toronto, his *alma mater*, admitted him *jure dignitatis* to the degree of D.D.

While in this honourable position, Dean Baldwin, as already described, was elected Bishop of Huron. He was consecrated in Christ Church Cathedral, Montreal, on St. Andrew's Day (November 30th), 1883, by Right Rev. Dr. Lewis, Bishop of Ontario, assisted by Bishop Williams, of Quebec, and Bishop Bond, of Montreal.

At his first Synod, which met in London on the 17th of June, 1884, Bishop Baldwin delivered an eloquent charge. He spoke earnestly of the kind of ministry needed at the present day—a believing ministry, and one baptized with the Holy Ghost and with fire—a ministry full also of missionary activity. On the subject of missions the Bishop speaks with all his heart. The Domestic and Foreign Missionary Society was formed in the year of his own consecration (1883)— it is but a few months older than himself as a bishop— and steadily ever since he has attended nearly all its meetings; he has written many of its most eloquent and powerful appeals, and has always been ready to use the noble gift of speech with which God has endowed him on behalf of the Society at its public meetings.

On the assembling of his second Synod, in June, 1885, the Bishop was able to say that he had visited, with a few inconsiderable exceptions, all the various missions of his extensive diocese. Regarding this visitation, he said :

"After visiting this noble diocese, and seeing the splendid farms and commodious houses to be met with in every county, and after carefully visiting all the cities, county towns, and thriving villages which stud the land, I am confident that wealth, and to spare, exists among us for every possible want of the Church. The great desideratum is to reach and utilize this wealth for the glory of God and the advancement of His name."

Bishop Baldwin's earnest appeals on behalf of Christian liberality told for good upon the funds of the diocese. In 1888 the Mission Fund debt had been reduced to five hundred dollars, and seven new churches were built and opened during the year. The Bishop in that year attended the Lambeth Conference.

The scheme for a new and grand cathedral, inaugurated by Bishop Hellmuth, having practically failed, the building known as the Chapter House was disused, and Bishop Baldwin restored St. Paul's to its original position as the cathedral of the diocese, appointing at the same time the Rev. Canon Innes Dean of Huron.

In 1880 the number of clergymen in Huron Diocese was 103. In 1892 this number had increased to 139. The churches also had increased during the same time from 203 to 246. But the Bishop felt that his diocese was undermanned. "What we need," he said, in 1892, "is a new class of young, unmarried men, who, for the love they bear to Christ, and for the glory of His great name, will be willing to go out as deacons, at least for a few years, without any stipulated salary, and depending only on that great God, who knoweth our wants, for their daily sustenance and support."

In 1893, Bishop Baldwin, who had returned from a trip through Egypt and the Holy Land and elsewhere, gave his Synod a graphic description of things he saw. The relics of the ancient past, the ruins of imperial Rome, and the traces of early Christian struggles, set the Bishop's heart aglow with the truth and force of the Holy Scriptures and the great religion which has ever been their faithful guardian.

Notwithstanding the size, wealth, and favoured situation of Huron Diocese, Bishop Baldwin was obliged to state last year (1895) that it was burdened altogether with a debt of about $17,000. This is due, no doubt, to the extraordinary financial depression which, for the last few years, has visited not only Canada, but almost every quarter of the globe. This, however, has not altered the attitude of the diocese towards outside missionary work. Huron is the only diocese (except the missionary Diocese of Algoma, which, according to its ability, does the same) that sends the money collected for domestic and foreign missions absolutely unappropriated to the Domestic and Foreign Missionary Society.

Huron College has also undergone some difficulties. Rev. Principal Miller resigned recently, but Rev. B. Watkins, from Lennoxville, has been appointed in his place, with the title of Provost of the Western University, which is now being revived.

Bishop Baldwin, in his charge of 1895, gave a masterly defence of the Athanasian Creed, and this is in keeping with the evident aim of his life, viz., to champion throughout the Divine origin and strength of the Christian religion, so that it may be established everywhere as the great power of God.

THE HON. AND RT. REV. ALBERT J. R. ANSON, D.D.
First Bishop of Qu'Appelle (Assiniboia).

Born, 1840.   Consecrated, 1884.   Resigned, 1892.

36. Hon. and Right Rev. Adelbert John Robert Anson, First Bishop of Qu'Appelle.

THE HON. A. J. R. ANSON is the brother of the late, and uncle of the present, Earl of Lichfield. He was born in 1840, and was educated at Eton and at Christ Church, Oxford, where he graduated in 1862, taking his Master's degree in 1867. After a short visit to Egypt and the Holy Land, he studied for Holy Orders in the Theological College at Lichfield, of which Canon Curties was the principal. He was ordained in 1864 and 1865 by Bishop Lonsdale, of Lichfield, and he was first curate at St. John's, Wolverhampton, then in sole charge of St. Leonard's, Bilston. In 1868 he was Vicar of St. Michael's, Handsworth, and in 1870 was presented with the vicarage of Sedgley, where he was appointed Rural Dean of Himley. In 1875 he accepted the rectory of Woolwich, one of the poorest and most difficult fields of work in the neighbourhood of London. Peculiarly zealous in his work, it was said of him that he loved the poorest and grimiest places the best. He won his people over by degrees, wherever he went, to the free-church system, and rejoiced in abolishing pew rents.

While at Wolverhampton an inward call came to Mr. Anson to offer himself for mission work abroad. God had blessed him with some means of his own, and this he wished to use, along with his strength and energy, for the expansion of the Church he loved. He had read of the spiritual destitution in Northwest Canada, and in the autumn of 1883 paid it a visit. He had an interview with Bishop Machray, who gave him a roving commission as his commissary to organize missions and superintend Church work in the District of Assiniboia, which, in August, 1883, had been set apart legally as a diocese by the Provincial Synod of Rupert's Land.

This immense district promised to be a good field for Church work. The Canadian Pacific Railway passed through it from east to west, and about midway between the north and south. Already here and there a few villages were springing up along it, and rapidly-constructed houses were clustering round the stations. Regina, the capital of the province, and headquarters of the Provincial Government and Mounted Police, was the only place where there was a resident clergyman. There were two other clergymen in Assiniboia, travelling missionaries—one (S.P.G.) to visit the railway stations, as best he could, along the line of the C.P.R.; and another (C.M.S.) ministering to Indians at Touchwood Hills.

On Mr. Anson's return to England he organized an association of influential people who, by prayer and work, might help forward the mission which he had resolved to undertake, and succeeded himself in collecting £2,500 and receiving promises of £400 a year for five years in addition. For himself he required no salary; but as it was the rule that no bishop could be consecrated unless suitable provision were made for his support, Mr. Anson stated that this step should be taken with the understanding that the episcopal income should be used by him towards the support of his clergy. The English societies voted large sums of money to aid the new mission.

Thus the projected diocese had good promise. The Archbishop of Canterbury (Dr. Benson) urged Mr. Anson to accept the bishopric ; but while he was debating the question he was offered the bishopric of Central Africa, in succession to Bishop Steer, and for a while wavered between the two. He finally chose to abide by his first intention, and was consecrated Bishop of the new Diocese of Assiniboia on the 24th of June, 1884, by Archbishop Benson, assisted by the Bishop of London (Dr. Jackson) and the Bishop of Rochester (Dr. Thorold), and others. He knelt for consecration side by side with James Hannington, who soon afterwards fell a martyr to the work in East Equatorial Africa.

The Bishop took with him a staff of eight priests, one deacon, and six lay readers. He resided at first at Regina, but in 1885 he selected Qu'Appelle Station as a more advantageous centre of Church work. The population of the diocese was found to be 16,500 white people and about 5,500 Indians, or halfbreeds. The Indians were divided among six reserves. Of the 16,500 white people about 5,700 were members of the Church.

In 1886 we find that the staff of workers was : priests 11, deacons 3, and lay readers 3. The headquarters of the missionaries were as follows (each representing a wide area and having from three to eleven out-stations attached to them) : Moosomin,

Moose Mountain, Kinbral, Grenfell, Qu'Appelle Station, Qu'Appelle Fort, Touchwood Hills, Regina, Moosejaw, and Medicine Hat.

This was a well-planned mission, and an extensive work was commenced and carried on from the beginning. The Bishop was unmarried—a strong, powerful Englishman, capable of enduring hardness and discomfort, both of which were not hard to find in Assiniboia. His clergy were enthusiastic, and willing to spend and be spent for the cause of their Lord. They were as a rule " High Churchmen," and carried on their work in that way. The Bishop lost no time in setting up at his headquarters an establishment which should be the means of supplying the diocese with men. He erected a college there at a cost of $2,800, contributed mainly by two persons only, to be known as St. John's Theological and Agricultural College. Attached to it was a farm of 640 acres. Here young men intending to settle in the country were to be instructed in farm work ; those desiring Holy Orders were to be trained for that purpose by a " brotherhood " of workers, giving their work gratuitously for the purpose. Another building was erected for the purpose of educating boys, as a feeder to the larger institution. These buildings, with the Bishop's residence, formed a prominent mark of a well-organized and efficient mission.

But this mission had evidently been planned from the very beginning upon the supposition that a large influx of population would take place in the new province. Such had been the representations in England, and such, no doubt, had been the hopes of those interested in the scheme of Northwest emigration. It must, therefore, have had a chilling effect upon the Bishop and the clergy when, as years went by, the hopes so strongly entertained were but meagrely realized. Assiniboia did not seem to promise much to the farmer. The long winters, followed sometimes by a summer frost which destroyed the very grain in the fields, put a serious check upon the rapid advancement of the country. Some of the clergy, discouraged and disappointed, withdrew to other and more promising fields; and Bishop Anson, with all the powerful aid he had from England, began to find it difficult to keep the stations he had opened supplied with men. Yet this did not deter him from causing new ground from time to time to be opened. The farm, however, was not encouraging, nor was the boys' school, the attendance at which was never as large as the Bishop had fondly hoped it would be. For a man who likes to see progress marked on everything he might touch, this must have been discouraging.

Still the Bishop persevered. Churches were built at all the chief stations and at many of the outposts. At Qu'Appelle Station, St. Peter's Church, built by the Bishop, served as the cathedral of the diocese.

Bishop Anson, from the first, organized a Synod which met regularly each year, beginning with 1884. The Bishop's addresses on these occasions were able productions, and often dealt with burning questions of the day. Bishop Anson spoke continually of what he regarded as the absurdity of calling the Church in this country the Church of England—as if it were possible that the Church of England could be in Canada! The Bishop also greatly opposed the Church in Canada

sending its missionary money away from the country—
to help support, for instance, the strong societies in
England. In fact, Bishop Anson, though an Englishman, made himself thoroughly Canadian, and evidently
longed to see a national Church built up for the
Dominion—of course in strict communion with the
mother Church, but quite independent of her.

That the Church did not grow in better proportion
compared with other religious bodies was a great grief
to the Bishop. The census of 1891 revealed this fact.
The total population of Canada proved to be 4,829,411,
of whom 1,990,465 were Romanists, 847,469 Methodists,
755,199 Presbyterians, and 644,106 Church of England.
In the Diocese of Qu'Appelle itself the Church had
lost the first place since 1885, the Presbyterians being
about 570 ahead. This, the Bishop thought, was
largely due to the large Scotch immigration which had
marked Assiniboia.

In that year, 1892, the Bishop stated that the Rev.
Shafto Agassiz had left the diocese for British Columbia,
and that he was the last left of those who had come
out with him in 1884. In eight years, then, the original
staff of missionaries had all disappeared. Others, of
course, had taken their places, but they themselves had
gone. And, somewhat to the surprise of all, the Bishop
announced that he, too, had resigned, and meant to
retire to his native land to seek some quiet place for
prayer and meditation, coupled perhaps with some light
employment, for the rest of his days. He told his
Synod that he had accomplished the work that he came
out to Canada to do, viz., to establish the diocese and
then hand it over to younger and stronger hands. It

was now established, and had an endowment of about
$50,000. There was considerable debt upon the
buildings at Qu'Appelle—and the work connected with
them had not been very encouraging. Much of the
Bishop's own money had been put into them—a large
portion of which he cheerfully bequeathed to the
diocese; the rest he hoped would some day be repaid to
him. But good work had been done elsewhere throughout the diocese. Twenty-three churches had been
built (and two more were in course of erection), and
nine parsonage houses, all almost entirely free from
debt. The number of clergy had increased from three
to sixteen.

Bishop Anson returned to England in 1892, to the
regret of all who knew him. He had made many warm
friends in Canada who will never forget him. In the
quiet little city of Lichfield, close to the beautiful
cathedral with which from boyhood he has been
familiar, not far from his old home, the seat of the Earl
of Lichfield, his nephew, Bishop Anson lives, in
spiritual charge of St. John's Hospital—a small charity
that has existed there for many years. He is still
unmarried and alone. His work is in a very small
compass—a great contrast to the huge diocese upon
which, while he was in it, Bishop Anson bestowed all
the energy and force that God had given him, even to
his own personal detriment and loss.

37. THE RIGHT REVEREND RICHARD YOUNG, D.D., SECOND BISHOP OF ATHABASCA.

BISHOP YOUNG was born on Sept. 7th, 1843, at South Park, South Lincolnshire, Eng. He was made a deacon by the Right Rev. Dr. Philpott, Bishop of Worcester, in 1868, and was priested the following year at Coventry by Right Rev. Geo. Augustus Selwyn, Bishop of Lichfield. Shortly afterwards he was appointed organizing secretary for the Church Missionary Society in Yorkshire, where he distinguished himself as an advocate of the cause of missions. During this period he married a lady well adapted to share the missionary work that her husband was called upon to do. This missionary work soon took definite shape. He was sent to Northwest Canada, and was appointed to the mission of St. Andrew's, about twelve miles from Winnipeg, where, assisted by his wife, he proved a great blessing. His people were chiefly retired employees of the Hudson's Bay Company, or their descendants.

But Mr. Young, besides these parochial duties, had other and more extensive work to do as assistant secretary of the C.M.S. Rupert's Land Mission. In this capacity he had much to do in the way of organizing and readjusting the different mission stations scattered throughout a very wide district.

In answer to an appeal from Bishop Bompas for

THE RT. REV. RICHARD YOUNG, D.D.
Second Bishop of Athabasca.
Born, 1843.   Consecrated, 1884.

help, the C.M.S. requested Mr. Young to visit the various stations throughout Athabasca and report upon them. This involved a long and trying journey by almost every method of travel under the sun He set out in the spring of 1884, first by (C.P.R.) rail to Calgary, close to the Rocky Mountains, then by stage *via* Edmonton, northward to Athabasca Landing, on the Athabasca river ; then by H. B. Co.'s boat seventy miles up the river to Peace River Landing, where he found himself on the southern borders of the civil District of Athabasca. The Peace river was reached on the 1st of July, where the future Bishop's eyes were gladdened by the sight of a magnificent stream five hundred yards wide, studded with pine-covered islands, and enclosed in banks so high as to resemble a canyon.

Dunvegan, "up the valley," was reached on July 5th. Here there was a missionary to the Beaver Indians, Rev. J. Gough Brick, afterwards moved to Smoky River. In the neighbourhood of this place there are said to be fertile prairies " ready to receive a colonial population to whom the soil and the favourable character of the climate offer strong inducements." So says an official paper published by the Bishop of Athabasca. From here Mr. Young turned northward, floating down the river on a raft. From the mouth of the Smoky river he, with Mr. (afterwards Rev.) D. Kirkby, embarked in a canoe for Fort Vermilion. This was a lonely trip of six or seven days, for five of which not a human being was seen. At Vermilion was the Rev. A. C. Garrioch, who was at work building the substantial church since known as St. Luke's ; and also Mr. C. J. Lawrence, in charge of an Industrial

School for Indian children, instituted by Bishop Bompas. The Indians here are chiefly Crees. From this place, after a week's stay, Mr. Young embarked in an Indian canoe with a Cree guide and reached Fort Chipewyan, on Lake Athabasca, on the 30th of July. Here was a mission in charge of Archdeacon Reeve, who had been there since 1879, and could speak the languages of the Slave and Chipewyan Indians. After a journey up the Slave river in the H. B. Co.'s steamer, Mr. Young left Chipewyan for home on the 27th of August, and was consecrated Bishop of Athabasca in Winnipeg on the 18th of October (1884), by the Most Rev. Dr. Machray, Bishop of Rupert's Land, assisted by Right Rev. Dr. McLean, of Saskatchewan, and Hon. and Right Rev. Dr. Anson, of Qu'Appelle.

By this subdivision of territory Bishop Bompas, who had been known as Bishop of Athabasca, became Bishop of Mackenzie River.

The following year (1885) the Bishop spent in England, working for the society and for his diocese. Leaving his family in England he proceeded to Athabasca, taking with him the Rev. M. and Mrs. Scott, both of whom had been his helpers in former days in St. Andrew's. He wintered at Vermilion, helping the poor people through a visitation of measles, and learning the while the Cree language. In the summer of 1887 Bishop Young visited Winnipeg to attend the Provincial Synod, where, to his great joy, he met Mrs. Young and the children, from whom he had been so long parted. They left for their lonely distant home in August (1887), followed by the prayers of many friends. To give an idea of the isolation to which they had gone, these friends could not hope to hear of their safe arrival till the next March, when one of the two mails of the year would arrive by dog-train.

In this lonely place, Fort Vermilion, Bishop Young organized a Synod of his diocese, which met there for the first time on the 6th of July, 1888. The clergy present were Archdeacon Reeve (of Chipewyan), Rev. A. C. Garrioch (who had removed to Dunvegan), Rev. M. Scott (Vermilion), and Rev. G. Holmes, of St. Peter's, Lesser Slave Lake. Four lay delegates were also present. This was not a large synod, nor were the chances of its increase very great, for it was decided that a quorum should consist of three clergy and two lay delegates; yet it was a bright spot in the lives of these isolated people to meet together occasionally and talk and pray over their work.

At the second Synod, which was held at Lesser Slave Lake at the close of September, 1891, some changes had taken place in the clerical staff. Archdeacon Reeve had been called to the Bishopric of Mackenzie River—Bishop Bompas having gone further north to the new Diocese of Selkirk; Rev. J. Gough Brick had opened a promising mission at Christ Church, Smoky River, to be supported by friends in Eastern Canada. Mr. Brick had worked up a large subscription list, in support of his mission, by visiting Toronto, Montreal, and other chief places of Canada, not only for missionary work, but for threshing-machine, farm implements, live stock, and other facilities for teaching his people how to farm in an improved manner. Rev. H. Robinson also had been appointed missionary at White Fish Lake. Bishop Young, in the absence of Archdeacon Reeve, was obliged to take charge of Fort Chipewyan himself for about two years. At this Synod the southern boundary of the diocese was altered so as to include Athabasca Landing, which will probably be the inlet into the country, both to the east and west. The Bishop has since taken up his residence there.

In 1893 Bishop Young visited Toronto and attended the General Synod, which was held in September of that year. As there were no means of returning to his diocese till the following spring, the Bishop and Mrs. Young spent the winter in Toronto. Here they were joined by some of their children who had been for several years in England for their education. The joy of this family reunion may be imagined; but even it was not without its cloud. One of their sons, a young man, was laid to rest in St. James' cemetery.

The Bishop with his family left for his diocese in the spring of 1894, where he has been ever since, busily engaged upon his long and trying journeys. Mr. Brick, the hero of the Smoky River mission, has been obliged to retire from it in broken health; and since then his wife has died. The cold climate and summer frosts interfered with his farming scheme; and, somewhat discouraged, he handed over the work to younger hands. The clerical staff of Athabasca, as given in the last Canadian Almanac, is as follows: Rev. G. Holmes (Lesser Slave Lake), Rev. J. R. Lucas (Chipewyan), Rev. H. Robinson (Smoky River), Rev. M. Scott and Rev. A. J. Warwick (Vermilion), Rev. C. R. Weaver (Wabiskaw), and Rev. G. W. White (White Fish Lake), all of whom minister chiefly to Indians.

THE RT. REV. CHARLES HAMILTON, D.D., D.C.L.
Second Bishop of Niagara, and First Bishop of Ottawa.
Born, 1834.   Consecrated, 1885.   Translated, 1896.

38. THE RIGHT REV. CHARLES HAMILTON, D.D., D.C.L., SECOND BISHOP OF NIAGARA, AND FIRST BISHOP OF OTTAWA.

CHARLES HAMILTON is one of the few native Canadians who have attained to the episcopate. He was born in Hawkesbury, on the Ottawa river, in the year 1834. He is the brother of the late Hon. John Hamilton, and of Robert Hamilton, Esq., of Quebec. He was sent to Oxford, where, at University College, he took the degree of B.A. in 1856, and afterwards that of M.A. in 1859. He was admitted to the diaconate by Bishop G. J. Mountain, and was ordained priest by the same prelate in 1858. After serving for a short time as curate of the Quebec Cathedral, he was appointed, in 1858, incumbent of St. Peter's Church, Quebec. He was among those elected in 1861 to represent his diocese in the first Provincial Synod, and in 1864 was appointed Rector of St. Matthew's Church, Quebec, where he manifested a great deal of zeal and devotion for the cause of God and His Church. Possessed in his own right of ample private means, he made a liberal use of them for good and holy purposes. He not only advocated the giving of at least one-tenth of one's income for the support of religion, but he practised it, to the great advantage of the Church.

In 1865 Mr. Hamilton was elected Clerical Secretary of the Provincial Synod, a post which he filled most acceptably till the year 1882, when he was called upon to preside over the Lower House of that honourable body as prolocutor. He showed much wisdom and urbanity in his management of the Synod—a body of men not always easy to control.

On the death of Bishop Fuller the Diocese of Niagara found itself without a sufficient income to support a bishop. This had been of very little moment so long as Dr. Fuller lived, for he was a man of wealth; but on his death it became a matter of grave importance. Fortunately the Synod was able to find another man of independent means willing to accept the position, and this was the Rev. Charles Hamilton. The Synod met on January 27th, 1885, and Mr. Hamilton was elected on the eighth ballot by a clerical vote of 41 to 14 and a lay vote of 25 to 22. The laity were deterred from giving a better support to Mr. Hamilton owing to his much-feared "High Church" proclivities; but the repeated confidence of the great bulk of the clergy in him, expressed in seven different ballots, at length procured his election. On the following morning Mr. Hamilton telegraphed his acceptance. He was consecrated in the Cathedral, Fredericton, New Brunswick, by the Most Rev. John Medley, Metropolitan, assisted by Bishop Binney, of Nova Scotia; Bishop Williams, of Quebec; and Bishop Sweatman, of Toronto. The Rev. Dr. Mockridge, Clerical Secretary of the Diocese of Niagara, was present, and read the duly attested certificate of election.

At his first Synod (held on the 3rd day of June, 1885, in Hamilton) the Bishop spoke with great earnestness on the subject of missions, especially of the Domestic and Foreign Missionary Society, of which society he has been from its inception a warm supporter and friend. In 1887 he was able to state that the contributions to the Mission Fund of the diocese had increased by $684, and that new ground for Church work had been taken up. In this year, also, a noted improvement had taken place in the contributions to foreign missions, the amount being $1,103, as against $371 of the previous year. Somewhat over $400 more than the previous year had also been contributed for domestic missions. By the year 1889 four new missions had been opened in the diocese, but a deficit of about two thousand dollars had occurred in the Mission Fund.

The Bishop met the difficulty of the weak episcopal endowment (which was only about $40,000) by forming a new Endowment Fund, not to be used till enough had been secured to make the total endowment at least $75,000. To this he contributed $1,200 himself, and other subscriptions were given amounting to $7,500. The Bishop also secured conditional promises from England. In 1891 the fund had reached $12,300.

On the death of Bishop Williams, of Quebec, in 1892, a large number of the Quebec clergy and laity made a long and strenuous endeavour to elect Bishop Hamilton, but a sufficient vote was not obtained.

In 1893 the Bishop proposed that an effort should be made to procure a see house for the diocese. In 1894 fair progress had been made in the new Episcopal Fund; but it was stated that, in order to secure the English grants, $5,200 would have to be raised before December, 1895. The Bishop professed himself willing to give one-tenth of this, provided the whole amount could be raised, which, accordingly, was done.

The Bishop, in May, 1895, had completed ten years of his work in Niagara. He had visited it faithfully year by year, and knew his clergy and many of the laity of his diocese well. He had helped some of them by his kindly advice and ever-open purse out of many a difficulty. His house had been open to them whenever they should choose to visit him, and a cheerful welcome accorded by himself and Mrs. Hamilton. Several new churches had been built and fresh missions opened. Some heated debates had taken place in the Synod over vexed party questions; but these had ceased and the days of peace had come. The funds of the diocese were fast creeping up to points of comparative safety—and a period of prosperity had been reached. But before another year had gone by the diocese was disturbed by the sudden call given to Bishop Hamilton by the newly formed Diocese of Ottawa to be its bishop.

Under the heading of Archbishop Lewis we have already given an account of the formation of an Episcopal Endowment Fund for the proposed new Diocese of Ottawa. The fund was completed, and the new Synod called together on the 18th of March, 1896, in the city of Ottawa, to elect a bishop. On the first ballot there were 13 clerical votes for Bishop Hamilton out of 53, and 11 for Rev. A. Phillips, of Hawkesbury. The other 29 votes scattered among eight different persons. The lay suffrages, representing 49 parishes, showed an extraordinary scattering of votes. The Very Rev. Dean Carmichael, of Montreal, received 11 votes out of 49, and the Bishop of Niagara 8. The remaining 30 votes were scattered among 16 different "candidates." In the second ballot Bishop Hamilton received 22 clerical and 15 lay votes, and on the third ballot he was elected by 33 clerical and 25 lay votes—25 lay votes and 27 clerical being necessary for a choice.

His Lordship at the time was in the Diocese of Algoma, taking duty for Bishop Sullivan. The telegram announcing his election followed him through an abundance of snow before he could be found. He accepted the position by telegram, subject to the reception of his resignation of his present diocese by the House of Bishops, as required by canon of the Provincial Synod. The House of Bishops accepted His Lordship's resignation at their meeting in Montreal on the 17th of April, and Bishop Hamilton a few days afterwards was installed in his new cathedral, Christ Church, Ottawa. He met with a magnificent reception in Ottawa on the 30th of April, when many of the élite of the capital vied with one another to welcome what Ottawa had been wanting for many years—a bishop of its own.

Thus did Ottawa rejoice and the Diocese of Niagara was distressed. The Episcopal Endowment Fund of Ottawa being small, yielding an income of only about $2,000 a year, Bishop Hamilton will be of the greatest possible use there—with his private means, always generously used, and with his ripe experience. Wherever he goes he carries with him his cheerful and courteous bearing, which wins the hearts of men. He has gone back close to the place of his birth, and his voice, which was first heard on the banks of the Ottawa, will now be lifted up in the same region on behalf of the great cause which he for so many years has made his own.

39. THE RIGHT REV. WILLIAM CYPRIAN PINKHAM, D.D., D.C.L., SECOND BISHOP OF SASKATCHEWAN, AND BISHOP OF CALGARY.

WILLIAM CYPRIAN PINKHAM was born in St. John's, Newfoundland, in the year 1844—in the same year that Edward Feild was consecrated Bishop of that colony. He was educated at the Church Academy, St. John's, and after teaching for a short time in one of the public schools proceeded to England in 1865, and studied at St. Augustine's, Canterbury. In 1868 the S.P.G. appointed Mr. Pinkham Curate of St. James' Parish, Rupert's Land.

On arriving in Canada he found that the Bishop of Rupert's Land (Dr. Machray) was in London, Ont., to which place he at once proceeded, and was admitted by Bishop Machray to the diaconate. By the end of 1868 he found himself Curate of St. James', under Archdeacon McLean, and was admitted to the priesthood in 1869. He became Rector of St. James', Dr. McLean being made Bishop of Saskatchewan in 1874.

In 1874 Mr. Pinkham was appointed a delegate to the Provincial Synod of Rupert's Land, and retained that position till elevated to the Upper House.

When the first Education Act was passed, in 1871, Mr. Pinkham was appointed a member of the Council of Education, and in 1872 Superintendent of Educa-

THE RT. REV. WILLIAM CYPRIAN PINKHAM, D.D.
Second Bishop of Saskatchewan.
Born, 1844.   Consecrated, 1887.

tion.' In 1879 the Archbishop of Canterbury (Dr. Tait) bestowed upon him the degree of Bachelor of Divinity, "on account of his services to the Church, and especially in the cause of education."

In 1881 he was sent to Eastern Canada to study the Normal and High School system, the result of which was that, by his advice and direction, the present splendid school system of Manitoba was set up. In that year also he was appointed Secretary of the Synod of Rupert's Land, and in 1882 was made an Archdeacon, in which capacity he did good service in organizing missions throughout the diocese, and in pleading its cause in the older parts of Canada and in England.

Archdeacon Pinkham, having thus become a prominent figure in the Church of the Northwest, was looked upon as a coming bishop, which forecast was fulfilled on the lamented death of the heroic John McLean, first Bishop of Saskatchewan, in 1887. The choice of his successor rested in the hands of the Archbishop of Canterbury (Dr. Benson), who, on the recommendations made to him, appointed the Archdeacon. He was consecrated in Holy Trinity Church, Winnipeg, on Sunday, August 7th, 1887, by the Most Rev. the Metropolitan (Dr. Machray), assisted by Bishop Horden, of Moosonee, Bishop Young, of Athabasca, and Bishop Anson, of Qu'Appelle. Bishop Thorold, of Rochester (England), was also present. Bishop Whipple, of Minnesota, and Bishop Walker, of North Dakota, represented the United States; and Bishop Baldwin, of Huron, older Canada.

The Provincial Synod met in Winnipeg on the following Wednesday, and passed a resolution dividing the Diocese of Saskatchewan into two parts—the civil District of Saskatchewan to form one, and the civil District of Alberta, to the northwest, extending to the Rocky Mountains, to form the other, the latter to be known as the Diocese of Calgary—Calgary, though but a mere village, being its chief town. The funds raised by Bishop McLean, viz., $73,146 (Episcopal), and about $11,000 (College), also about $5,000 for Clergy Endowment Fund, were to be left for Saskatchewan, and a new episcopal endowment was to be formed for Calgary. Bishop Pinkham was to be bishop of both dioceses until such endowment should be raised, when he was to have his choice as to which diocese should be his. In the meantime he preferred to live at Calgary, and Prince Albert ever since has awaited what it once had—a resident bishop.

Bishop Pinkham has a wide field. The area of Calgary alone (*i.e.*, the District of Alberta) is 100,292 square miles, or nearly twice the size of England!

In 1888 the Bishop went to England, attended the Lambeth Conference, held interviews with the different societies regarding the funds necessary for his work, and collected by subscriptions, for a see house at Calgary £395, for school funds £152, and for the General Mission Fund of both dioceses £369.

On the 21st of February, 1889, he met his Synod of Calgary. The veteran Metropolitan (Dr. Machray) was present and preached the sermon. On August 28th of the same year he presided for the first time over the Synod of Saskatchewan at Prince Albert. The Church population of the diocese was about 3,500.

In that summer (1889) the Bishop had travelled nearly five thousand miles, more than half of which was by open boat. In 1891, however, he was able to speak of the railway which had been built to Prince Albert, and which greatly facilitated travel. The clergy of Saskatchewan by that year had increased from thirteen to sixteen.

The Bishop went to England in 1892, and spent several months trying to raise funds for the Calgary Episcopal Endowment, with the result that about $12,400 was raised and placed at interest by the S.P.G. in trust for the diocese—to be kept till it should reach $50,000, when grants amounting to over $10,000 additional may be claimed from the societies. A see house had not yet been procured, and the Bishop rather complained at being obliged to pay house rent and taxes amounting to about $700 a year. The clerical staff, however, had increased from ten to fifteen In Saskatchewan the clergy list had risen to twenty, and the Bishop looked forward to a steady increase in these numbers, but earnestly hoped that the time might soon come when each diocese would have its own bishop.

The Bishop receives large sums of money from England, from the Canadian Government, the Domestic and Foreign Missionary Society of Canada, especially through the Woman's Auxiliary, but not enough to enable him to overtake his work. This work is almost entirely missionary. Very little support comes from within. The Bishop is obliged to look outside for it, and therefore is continually anxious about funds. But he is still in the prime of life, strong, vigorous, and hopeful; and, with God's help, will no doubt see the realization of the great objects that he has in view.

40. THE RIGHT REV. FREDERICK COURTNEY, D.D.,
FIFTH BISHOP OF NOVA SCOTIA.

THE Synod of Nova Scotia assembled in Halifax on Wednesday, July 6th, 1887, to elect a bishop in succession to the Right Rev. Dr. Binney. Means were taken to make the stipend of the incoming bishop $6,000 a year. The custom in Nova Scotia is to nominate a person or persons for the bishopric. In this case the Rev. J. C. Edgehill, D.D., Chaplain-General of H. M. Forces, and the Right Rev. Edward Sullivan, D.D., Bishop of Algoma, were nominated. The first ballot resulted in the election of Dr. Edgehill by 70 clerical votes (necessary 46) and 56 lay (necessary 53), Bishop Sullivan receiving 20 and 48. Dr. Edgehill was in Germany at the time and could not decide. He asked for a week to consider. The Synod therefore adjourned till August 10th. Dr. Edgehill having declined the bishopric, Archdeacon Gilpin (of Halifax, N.S.) and Bishop Sullivan were nominated. Four ballots were taken without a result, the clergy voting largely for Archdeacon Gilpin and the laity for Bishop Sullivan. On the following day these two names were withdrawn, and Right Rev. Dr. Perry, Bishop of Iowa, in the United States, was nominated and elected on the first ballot almost unanimously. No answer from Bishop Perry being received up to Friday evening, August 12th, the Synod adjourned to the 9th of

THE RT. REV. FREDERICK COURTNEY, D.D., S.T.D.
Fifth Bishop of Nova Scotia.
Born, 1837.   Consecrated, 1888.

November, only to hear that Bishop Perry had declined, thinking it best for all that he should remain in his own native land. The Synod, having left the matter in the hands of the Archbishop of Canterbury and other English prelates, could not proceed to an election, and therefore adjourned to the 1st of February, 1888. The Archbishop of Canterbury failed to find any one willing to accept the position, owing to the uncertainty of election, which by the constitution of the Synod of Nova Scotia had to be held. When, accordingly, the Synod met in February voting had to be resumed. The Rev. Dr. Courtney, Rector of St. Paul's Church, Boston, U.S.A., was nominated and elected, three only of each order voting " No." Dr. Courtney accepted, and thus a long and anxious struggle was ended.

The Rev. Frederick Courtney, S.T.D., though a resident of the United States, was a British subject. He was born in England in the year 1837, and having graduated at London University was duly ordained and held an English living. Receiving a call to be assistant minister of St. Thomas' Church, New York, he came to this side of the Atlantic and tried a residence under the stars and stripes. It was soon found that the sturdy Englishman was no ordinary man. Tall and commanding in appearance, of a well-cut intellectual countenance, with speaking powers far above the average, he soon became known among the vestrymen of the United States, who were on the lookout for able men to fill their pulpits. St. James' Church, Chicago, was the first to claim him as rector, and there, in the largest church of the great city, he soon became known as a man of eloquence and power. He removed from Chicago to Boston, where he was when elected Bishop of Nova Scotia.

Dr. Courtney was consecrated in St. Luke's Cathedral, Halifax, on St. Mark's Day, the 25th of April, 1888, by the Metropolitan (Bishop Medley), Bishop Lewis, and Bishop Williams. It was a great, solemn and stately function. A deputation from the United States, headed by the great Phillips Brooks, then Rector of Trinity Church, Boston, was present.

The Bishop met his first Synod in Halifax on June 29th, 1888, and delivered a very able address bearing upon many important subjects of the day. He then went to England and attended the Lambeth Conference. The Synod of Nova Scotia Diocese assembles only every second year. Consequently the Bishop's address, covering as it does a period of two years, is unusually full of material. Bishop Courtney's addresses are carefully prepared, and deal with all important matters, diocesan or otherwise, with much exactitude and force. In 1890 he dwelt forcibly upon Christian union and other matters that sprang from the Lambeth Conference. He also dwelt earnestly upon the necessity of establishing a Church school for girls in Nova Scotia, the result of which was that a very superior school was established at Windsor in January, 1891.

The Bishop was attacked by a very heavy illness in November, 1890, which nearly proved fatal. When able he went to his native land for an extensive visit, from which he returned with his health restored.

At the Synod of 1892 Bishop Courtney made a strong appeal on behalf of King's College, Windsor, which was not attracting students in anything like the number that such an institution should. The Collegiate School and the school for girls were doing well, but the college needed more friends and more support from those who were such. In 1893 a very successful missionary conference was held in Yarmouth. Interest in missions has always been one of Bishop Courtney's leading characteristics. He has been known to hold the attention of a congregation easily for over an hour in advocating missions, and the Secretary of the Domestic and Foreign Missionary Society can testify to the Bishop's ever cheerful readiness to advocate the claims of the society at its public meetings. His Lordship is an earnest advocate of tithe-giving. " However large may be a man's individual gifts, if they do not *exceed* the tenth of his income he is not generous, and if they do not come up to that he simply robs God." So he told his Synod in 1894, and on this principle, from his own continued liberality, he certainly seems to act. His whole address to the Synod of 1894 was considered so weighty and excellent that it was printed in pamphlet form.

Bishop Courtney has long desired a division of his large diocese, and, in his address referred to, he offered to give up a thousand dollars a year of his income towards the support of a bishop, provided $20,000 be raised within five years. Nova Scotia, the first colonial see, has had no subdivision since New Brunswick was formed into a separate diocese fifty-one years ago ! It remains to be seen whether the clergy and laity of the ancient see will take advantage of the liberal offer made by him who so worthily fills the position of its fifth bishop.

41. THE RIGHT REVEREND WILLIAM DAY REEVE,
SECOND BISHOP OF MACKENZIE RIVER.

WILLIAM DAY REEVE was born in 1844, at Harmton, a small village of Lincolnshire, England, where also he received his early education. After two years' practical experience of farm work, followed by a business training, he conceived a great desire to be a missionary, and offered himself to the C.M.S. This institution put him in training at its own college at Islington, and while in the junior theological year he was chosen on the recommendation of Rev. W. W. (afterwards Archdeacon) Kirkby to go to Northwest America. The young missionary had only about a month in which to procure a year's supplies, get married, and obtain the necessary outfit for himself and his bride. In April, 1869, the wedding took place, and four days later the young couple set sail for New York. From St. Cloud, Minnesota (the farthest point to which they could go by rail), they reached Winnipeg after twenty days' wearisome travel over six hundred miles of prairie. On June 6th (1869) Mr. Reeve was admitted to the diaconate by the Metropolitan (Bishop Machray) at St. John's Cathedral, Winnipeg. Shortly afterwards he and his wife started for Fort Simpson in one of the Hudson Bay Company's boats. The route was by way of Lake Winnipeg, up the lower part of Saskat-

THE RT. REV. WILLIAM DAY REEVE, D.D.
Second Bishop of Mackenzie River.
Born, 1844.   Consecrated, 1891.

chewan river, then northward to Athabasca, a long toilsome journey of three months, marked by all sorts of weather, and the attacks of myriads of mosquitoes and sandflies. The Mackenzie River and Selkirk districts then had only two missionaries: Rev. W. C. Bompas, who had no certain dwelling place, but wandered from fort to fort, from tribe to tribe, by boat, canoe, and dog-sleigh; and Rev. R. Macdonald, who lived at Fort Yukon, fifteen hundred miles northwest of Fort Simpson.

These young wanderers at last reached their new home, and were warmly welcomed by the few people there. It was a dreary home. Letters came but twice a year, in August and March; supplies of tea, flour, clothing, and groceries came only once a year, and sometimes failed altogether. Vegetables could only be grown at times—when the "summer" would remain long enough to admit of it. Other food, however, such as moose, reindeer, rabbits, and fish, was abundant. A new life had to be begun, and a new language learned.

In 1874 Mr. Bompas was made Bishop, and his first episcopal act was to ordain Mr. Reeve to the priesthood. He also appointed him his chaplain and registrar. In 1875 he went to Fort Rae, a lonely spot about two hundred miles east of Fort Simpson, and situated on a northern arm of Great Slave lake. Here he and his wife started a boarding school for Indian children in a little rough-and-ready building fourteen feet square. Returning to Fort Simpson in 1877, they experienced great suffering for want of food. The gaunt form of starvation was before them for many months, but, by God's mercy, they subsisted till fresh supplies arrived. In 1879 Mr. Reeve moved to Fort Chipewyan, on Lake Athabasca, situated about four hundred miles south, and a little east of Fort Simpson, and in the following year he took his wife and children to England, and carried through the press " Bishop Bompas' Translation of the Gospels in Tenni or Slavi for Mackenzie River Indians."

Here occurred one of those trying separations characteristic of work in the Northwest. Mr. and Mrs. Reeve had to leave their children, except the youngest (a baby), in England for education. They returned to Chipewyan in 1881, and resumed their work of teaching, ministering, and nursing the Indians of the district. In 1883 Mr. Reeve was made Archdeacon of Chipewyan, and in the next year found himself separated from his old companions of Mackenzie River by the formation of the new Diocese of Athabasca, under Bishop Young, Fort Chipewyan falling within its bounds.

In 1889 the Archdeacon went to England, and again saw through the press some missionary translational work of Bishop Bompas and Archdeacon McDonald. It was about this time that the subdivision of the Diocese of Mackenzie River began to be earnestly pressed. There were Indians and traders at the old mission station of Fort Yukon, in the Selkirk region, that required the immediate oversight of a bishop. As far back as 1885 Bishop Bompas had pressed it upon Archdeacon Reeve that he should allow himself to be made a Bishop in furtherance of this much-desired object. It was not till 1891 that the Archdeacon consented, and, when he did, the brave old soldier of the frozen north betook himself to the bleak regions of the Yukon, and left his younger brother to superintend the less lonely territory of the Mackenzie district.

On his way from England to the Northwest the Archdeacon spent a short time in Toronto, Montreal, and other parts of older Canada, collecting subscriptions to aid him in his work. In October, 1891, he addressed the missionary meeting of the Domestic and Foreign Missionary Society, and many were moved to tears at the tales of privation and hardship that he told connected with the missionary work in the frozen north.

Archdeacon Reeve was consecrated in Winnipeg, in the Church of the Holy Trinity, on Advent Sunday, November 29th, 1891, by the Metropolitan (Dr. Machray), assisted by Bishop Anson, of Qu'Appelle, and Bishop Pinkham, of Saskatchewan.

He started work at the old mission station of Fort Simpson, on the Mackenzie river, with a clerical staff of seven.

The stations in the two extremes of the diocese are more than eleven hundred miles apart, and the nearest are nearly two hundred miles from one another.

Bishop Reeve visited older Canada again in 1892. The Rev. I. O. Stringer and Rev. T. J. Marsh, who are Canadians and ex-students of Wycliffe College, Toronto, accompanied His Lordship on his return to his work. They are supported by the friends of Wycliffe College. Mr. Stringer has established a mission on Herschel Island, the most remote inhabited spot in the Dominion. To this place a Mr. Whittaker went to help him last year (1895). The whalers there have subscribed $500 towards the expenses of the mission, the first time on record of contributions for missions given on the Arctic Ocean. Miss Marsh has also gone to the work, and is helping her brother at the Hay River mission. Dr. Reazin, too, a young medical missionary, has gone from Toronto to help Mr. Marsh. Thus an important Canadian mission is being established in Mackenzie River.

Bishop Reeve is indefatigable in ministering to those isolated missions, cheering every one with his manly and hopeful words, and with his reassuring presence.

His episcopal residence at Fort Simpson—simply a plain wooden structure—was recently destroyed by fire. It was a great disaster to the Bishop. The house and the whole of the contents were destroyed, as were also all the supplies. The Bishop and Mrs. Reeve escaped with difficulty, and took refuge in the Hudson's Bay fort.

Contributions are being sent from all parts of Canada, and in time, no doubt, the loss will be repaired and the Bishop's good work allowed to go on as usual.

THE RT. REV. ANDREW HUNTER DUNN, D.D.
Fifth Bishop of Quebec.

Born, 1839.   Consecrated, 1892.

42. THE RIGHT REV. ANDREW HUNTER DUNN, D.D., FIFTH BISHOP OF QUEBEC.

AFTER a long struggle, the Synod of Quebec, assembled on the 21st of June, 1892, elected the Rev. A. H. Dunn, of England, Bishop. A large number of the Synod desired a Canadian, but they were divided in opinion between Bishop Hamilton, of Niagara, and Canon Thorneloe, of Sherbrooke, Diocese of Quebec.

Mr. Dunn was born in 1839, at Saffron Walden, in Essex. On leaving school he spent nearly two years in Germany, and subsequently entered Corpus Christi College, Cambridge, where he obtained two scholarships, and eventually graduated as twenty-ninth wrangler in January, 1863. Admitted to the diaconate in 1864, he was appointed to the curacy of St. Mark's, Notting Hill. He was priested on Trinity Sunday, 1865. In 1871 he was appointed to South Acton, a rapidly increasing mission district of London. Here for twenty-one years Mr. Dunn laboured incessantly to meet the wants of a great working-class population, and was the means of erecting two handsome permanent churches, one large temporary church, and six mission churches, besides schools and parsonage. Mr. Dunn became so deeply interested in this work that the important living of Great Yarmouth, when offered to him, could not tempt him from it. His parishioners then presented him with a handsome testimonial amounting to hundreds of pounds.

Mr. Dunn arrived in Canada in time to be present at the Provincial Synod which met in Montreal on September 14th.

He was consecrated in Christ Church Cathedral, Montreal, on Sunday, Sept. 18th, 1892, by the Right Rev. Dr. Lewis, Bishop of Ontario.

Bishop Dunn soon found himself busy in his extensive diocese. In point of territory it is as large as it was in the days of Bishop G. J. Mountain. The dioceses in the east subdivide very slowly.

The Bishop presents his work to the Synod in the form of a diary, telling them exactly what he has done each day. And the record shows an unusually busy life. In journeys often, in speeches, lectures, sermons, confirmations—in matters diocesan and matters provincial and general, he is ever on the alert ; a busy, active Bishop, and cheerful all the while.

Now and then His Lordship and Mrs. Dunn "take a run to England," but it is only for a short period, and generally the Bishop manages to gather a little money for some of his outlying missions. His address to Synod last year showed that in the number of the clergy, and in churches built and consecrated, the work in the diocese, notwithstanding many drawbacks, is progressing.

THE RT. REV. W. J. BURN, D.D.
Second Bishop of Qu'Appelle.
Born, 1851. Consecrated, 1893. Died, 1896.

43. THE RIGHT REV. WILLIAM JOHN BURN, M.A., D.C.L., SECOND BISHOP OF QU'APPELLE.

WILLIAM JOHN BURN was born in 1851, at South Moor, Sunderland, County of Durham, England, and was educated at Richmond Grammar School, Yorkshire, and St. John's College, Cambridge, of which college he was a scholar. He graduated with first-class mathematical honours. After ordination, in 1874, Mr. Burn remained at Cambridge for a short time as mathematical tutor, and in 1876 was appointed first incumbent of St. Peter's, Jarrow-on-Tyne, where he did a remarkable work, chiefly among artisans, in a parish of eight thousand people, for over ten years, when his health gave way and he was obliged to resign. He spent his winters abroad, and returned a few months at a time to help Canon Body in mission work and retreats.

In 1890 Mr. Burn married Maud Mary, daughter of the Rev. S. Banks, Rector of Cottenham, Cambridge, and was appointed by the Crown to the vicarage of Coniscliffe, near Darlington, where he was when the Archbishop of Canterbury (Dr. Benson) offered him the Bishopric of Qu'Appelle. He was consecrated in Westminster Abbey on the 25th of March, 1893, by the Archbishop of Canterbury, assisted by the Bishop of London (Dr. Temple) and Hon. and Right Rev. Dr. Anson, late Bishop of Qu'Appelle.

The Synod of Qu'Appelle met on July 5th, 1893, under the presidency of Rev. J. P. Sargent, commissary. Bishop Burn was present in Toronto at the General Synod (September, 1893), and on the 30th of May, 1894, presided over his Synod in Qu'Appelle. His charge was concise and business-like. The diocese, financially, was not in a good condition. The property at Qu'Appelle, including the college and see house, was burdened with debt, and had to be relinquished. The Bishop removed to Indian Head, where Lord Brassey, who is an extensive landowner in Qu'Appelle, built a residence for him. He also built a church and a home for girls, which is presided over by Mrs. Burn.

Bishop Burn delighted in spiritual work. He wished his Synod to assemble biennially, in order that he might meet the clergy in alternate years for devotional purposes. His experience and ability in holding missions and retreats would have been of great use in work of this kind; but, alas, for things earthly! While this book was passing through the press Bishop Burn was called away. He died suddenly of heart failure on June 16th, 1896, shortly after presiding over his Synod.

As to his diocese he said that the life there is one continual struggle; climate severe, places scattered, isolation very trying; it is the heroism of loneliness; excluded from outside daily sympathy; out of touch with the minds and hearts of the children of the forest; scarcely any increase in population. Yet there are men ready to occupy many places of this kind if the money were but forthcoming.

THE RT. REV. WILLIAM WILCOX PERRIN, D.D.
Second Bishop of Columbia.
Born, 1848.   Consecrated, 1893.

44. THE RIGHT REV. WILLIAM WILCOX PERRIN, M.A., D.C.L., SECOND BISHOP OF COLUMBIA.

THE Synod of the Diocese of Columbia met on the 22nd of November, 1892, to elect a successor to Bishop Hills. There were twenty-one clergymen present, and thirty-six laymen. The votes during the several ballots that were taken were pretty evenly divided among Archdeacon Scriven, who presided over the Synod, Dean Carmichael, of Montreal, and Rev. Canon Padget, of England ; and "for reference to the Archbishop of Canterbury." On the fifth ballot the reference to the Archbishop was carried by 21 clerical and 24 lay votes.

His Grace shortly afterwards appointed the Rev. William Wilcox Perrin. Mr. Perrin was born at Westhery-on-Tryon, Gloucestershire, England, on August 11th, 1848, and was educated at King's College, London. He graduated from Trinity College, Oxford, in 1870, and was admitted a deacon in 1871, and ordained priest in 1872 by the Bishop of Winchester (Dr. S. Wilberforce). His ministerial life in England was all spent in Southampton, first as Curate of St. Mary's, and next as Vicar of St. Luke's, both of which were parishes of over ten thousand inhabitants, and had a large staff of clergy.

On being called to the Bishopric of Columbia Mr. Perrin received the degree of D.D. from Oxford.

He was consecrated side by side with Mr. Burn, Bishop-designate of Qu'Appelle, on March 25th, 1893, Mr. Burn being consecrated first.

Bishop Perrin arrived in his diocese on the 18th of May, 1893, and was enthroned at a public service on June 29th, the day of his first Synod. His Lordship's address on the occasion was brief, yet hopeful as to the future. In the autumn (1893) the Bishop attended the first General Synod, held in Toronto, and spoke enthusiastically about the new and much enlarged world to which he had been called as a worker in the Church.

The episcopal endowment yields an income of $3,500. The see house is called "Bishopsclose." The Bishop is unmarried. His sister keeps house for him. The Archdeaconry Fund yields $1,800 a year, and the Endowment of Christ Church Cathedral $1,600.*

All the other clergy depend upon voluntary support. They receive no grants from the S.P.G., but about a thousand a year is obtained from friends in England. The clerical staff of the diocese is at present twenty.

In 1895 Bishop Perrin, who had been prostrated by a severe and painful illness, went to England, but returned recently to his diocese with his health restored.

* The cut of the Cathedral which appears on page 172 is from a photograph kindly supplied by R. Maynard, photographer, Victoria, B.C.

THE RT. REV. JERVOIS A. NEWNHAM, D.D.

Second Bishop of Moosonee.

Born, 1854.   Consecrated, 1893.

45. THE RIGHT REV. JERVOIS ARTHUR NEWNHAM, D.D., SECOND BISHOP OF MOOSONEE.

JERVOIS A. NEWNHAM was born at Combe Down vicarage, Bath, England, in 1854. His father at the time was Vicar of Corsham, Wilts. He came to Montreal in 1873, and graduated from McGill College in 1878. He then passed through the Montreal Diocesan Theological College, and was ordained deacon in 1878 by Bishop Oxenden, and priest in 1880 by Bishop Bond. After serving for a couple of years as missionary at Onslow, Diocese of Montreal, he was made Curate of Christ Church Cathedral, Montreal, in 1882. In 1886 he was appointed Rector of St. Matthias' Church, Montreal. In 1891, as we have seen under the life of Bishop Horden, Mr. Newnham went out to Moosonee with a view to succeeding to the bishopric there. He threw himself at once vigorously into missionary work. Within four months he was able to conduct divine service and preach in the Cree language. He returned to Montreal in 1892, and married Miss Lettie Henderson, daughter of Rev. Canon Henderson, Principal of the Diocesan College, Montreal. He made the greater part of the long journey down by canoe, paddled by Indians. He received about this time the degree of D.D. from St. John's College, Winnipeg.

Bishop Horden, as we have seen, died in January,

1893, and Dr. Newnham was at once nominated by the C.M.S. as his successor. He was consecrated Bishop of Moosonee on August 6th, 1893, in Holy Trinity Church, Winnipeg, by the Metropolitan of Rupert's Land (Dr. Machray), assisted by Bishop Young, of Athabasca, Bishop Pinkham, of Saskatchewan, and Bishop Burn, of Qu'Appelle.

The new Bishop was unable to attend the General Synod in Toronto, for had he done so he would not have been able to reach his distant diocese till the following year.

The Bishop from time to time has published, in different periodicals, vivid descriptions of his life and work. The breaking up of the ice at Moose Fort in May, 1893, and again in 1894, gave him great anxiety and sleepless days and nights. The increasing waters and crashing ice carry everything away. The see house itself is always in danger, and the Bishop wants a new one on higher ground—not a palace, but "a good strong log or frame house."

In 1895 Bishop Newnham paid a visit to his old home in Montreal, and spent some time trying to collect money for his work. On his return to his diocese he engaged at once in active work, and has already taken many wearisome and trying journeys.

THE RT. REV. JOHN DART, D.D.
Second Bishop of New Westminster, B.C.
Born, 1837.   Consecrated, 1895.

46. The Right Rev. John Dart, D.D., Second Bishop of New Westminster.

JOHN DART was born in Devonshire, England, in 1837. He was educated at St. Mary's Hall, Oxford, and went to India, where he became warden of St. Thomas' College, Ceylon. He was ordained deacon in 1860 and priest in 1861 by the Right Rev. J. Chapman, first Bishop of Colombo, and was examining chaplain to Bishop Piers Claughton, second bishop of that diocese. Mr. Dart procured the affiliation of the college with the University of Calcutta.

Returning to England he graduated in his University, B.A. in 1867 and M.A. in 1871, and was appointed principal of the Training College, York, and afterwards vice-principal and science lecturer in St. Peter's College, Peterborough.

Subsequently he came to Canada, and was appointed, in 1878, President of King's University, Windsor, Nova Scotia, and Canon of St. Luke's Cathedral, Halifax. King's conferred upon him the degree of D.C.L. in 1877. In 1885 Dr. Dart returned to England.

On the death of Bishop Sillitoe, the Synod of New Westminster elected as bishop the Rev. W. Hibbert Binney, of England, son of the late Bishop of Nova Scotia; but on his declining the position the appointment was placed in the hands of the Bishops of Caledonia (Dr. Ridley) and Columbia (Dr. Perrin), who, with the Bishops of London (Dr. Temple), Norwich (Dr. Sheepshanks), and St. Alban's (Dr. Festing), selected Canon Dart. He was consecrated in St. Paul's on June 29th, 1895, by Archbishop Tait, of Canterbury, and other English bishops. The University of Oxford, in the same year, conferred upon Bishop Dart the degree of D.D. He and Mrs. Dart, with their four sons, arrived at New Westminster in August, 1895.

The Cathedral, New Westminster, B.C.

THE RT. REV. JOHN PHILIP DuMOULIN, M.A., D.C.L.
Third Bishop of Niagara.
Born, 1836. Consecrated, 1896.

47. THE RIGHT REVEREND JOHN PHILIP DUMOULIN, M.A., D.C.L., THIRD BISHOP OF NIAGARA.

THE Synod of Niagara met in Hamilton on the 12th of May, 1896, to elect a bishop in succession to Bishop Hamilton, translated to Ottawa. From the first the choice of the great bulk of the clergy was for Rev. Canon DuMoulin, Rector of St. James' Cathedral, Toronto; but the laity supported, by a small majority, first the Rev. Rural Dean Armitage, of St. Catharines, and then the Very Rev. Dean Carmichael, of Montreal. Six ballots were taken without result; but, on the morning of the 13th, the next (or seventh) ballot elected Canon DuMoulin, only four clergymen and six parishes voting against him.

John Philip DuMoulin was born in Dublin in the year 1836, and was educated there. For a time he was a student of Trinity College, Dublin, but did not proceed to a degree. He was one of the celebrated three brought out from Ireland by Bishop Cronyn, of Huron—Sullivan, Carmichael, DuMoulin. Ordained by Bishop Cronyn in 1862 and 1863, he served as curate to Archdeacon Brough, Rector of St. John's, London Township. He married Frances, the Archdeacon's fifth daughter, in 1863.

After serving a short time as curate at Galt he was called to Montreal, where he became successively curate of Trinity Church, and assistant minister of St.

James'. In 1871 he was appointed Rector of St. Thomas' Church, Hamilton. In 1872 he was elected Bishop of Algoma, but declined.* He returned to Montreal in 1875, as Rector of St. Martin's Church, from which he was called, in 1882, to be Rector of St. James' Cathedral, Toronto, an endowed living of five thousand dollars a year and rectory. Here he greatly strengthened his preaching until he made the pulpit of St. James' a power, not only in Toronto, but in the whole Province. His noon Lenten sermons every day throughout Lent (except on Saturdays) were a masterly effort. Each day the large cathedral was thronged with eager listeners.

The consecration took place in St. James' on the 24th of June, 1896. Archbishop Lewis officiated, Bishop Sweatman (of Toronto) and Bishop Sullivan (of Algoma) assisting. It was a magnificent ceremony. Dean Carmichael preached the sermon. Thus the "three," now elderly men, met again from distant places—filling high positions in the Church of God. Dean Carmichael's reference to his "brother, friend, companion, of more than thirty years of strangely united life," was most touching.

This brings our book to an end. While it was going through the press one bishop, alas!—Bishop Burn, of Qu'Appelle—was called to his last rest, and another was elected and consecrated. So the work goes on. May it all be for the glory of God and the welfare of His Holy Church!

* See page 268.

www.ingramcontent.com/pod-product-compliance
Lightning Source LLC
Chambersburg PA
CBHW022101300426
44117CB00007B/538